An Illustrated History of Fashion

500 Years of Fashion Illustration

© Alice Mackrell 1997
First published 1997

Printed in Hong Kong
for the publishers
B.T. Batsford Ltd
583 Fulham Road
London SW6 5BY

http://www.batsford.com

ISBN 0 7134 6776 2

A CIP catalogue record for this book is available from the
British Library.

French translations are by the author.

Front cover illustration: Fashion plate by Georges
Barbier from *Le Journal des dames et des modes*, 1913
(private collection)
Back cover illustration: Coloured etching from *Journal für
Fabrik, Manufaktur, Handlung und Mode*, 1793 *(Victoria and
Albert Museum, London)*

An Illustrated History of Fashion

500 Years of Fashion Illustration

Alice Mackrell

B.T. Batsford Ltd . London

Contents

4: The Growth of Fashion Illustration in the Nineteenth Century

5: Fashion Illustration in the Twentieth Century

To Charles

Acknowledgements

Ever since I wrote my M.A. thesis on French fashion plates during the *Directoire* and my Ph.D. thesis on dress in *le style troubadour* 1774-1814, at the Courtauld Institute of Art, London, I have had in mind a book on the theme of costume and its visual sources. Louis XIV said that 'costume is the mirror of history'. Costume and its illustration reflect a good deal about the styles and political, economic and social attitudes of an epoch. Drawings, woodcuts, etchings, engravings, costume books, fashion plates, paintings, sculpture, portraiture, caricatures, photographs, films and advertisements show how people looked in their clothes and how clothes affected their behaviour and deportment. They also show how garments related to accessories and express the fashionable ideal of a period. It is through visual documents that the mood and atmosphere of an era can be gleaned. Essential components to which the visual evidence must be linked are original surviving fashionable garments, whereby the look of a costume, its cut, shape, proportion, fabric design, colour and decoration can be appreciated in three dimensions. Like the images that illustrate the endlessly changing variety of fashionable apparel, the specimens themselves are wonderful examples of aesthetic expression.

In preparing this book, I have been helped very generously by many people to whom I would like to offer my thanks: Ann A. Abid and Andrea S. Moore, Cleveland Museum of Art; E. Bauchard, French and Company, Inc., New York; Jacklyn Burns, J. Paul Getty Museum, Malibu, California; Gwenyth Campling, Royal Collection Enterprises, Windsor Castle; Margaret Cooley, National Gallery of Art, Washington D.C.; Mary Corliss, Museum of Modern Art, New York; James Costel, Christie's, New York; John Delaney, Imperial War Museum, London; Kate Fielden, Bowood House, Calne, Wiltshire; Rosalind Freeman, National Museum of Wales, Cardiff; Philippe Garner, Sotheby's, London; C.M. Gee, Keats House, Hampstead, London; Mari Griffith, National Gallery, London; Stephanie Harovas, Sotheby's, New York; Robert C. Kaufmann, Metropolitan Museum of Art, New York; David L. Kencik, San Diego Museum of Art; Bunty King and Stephen Duffy, Wallace Collection, London; Mara Lindsey and Sarah Bober, Kimbell Art Museum, Forth Worth, Texas; William Mackrell; Harry Matthews; Lorraine Mead, The Condé Nast Publications, Inc., New York; Richard Mortimer, Westminster Abbey, London; Louise Newman, Christie's, London; the late Madeleine Nicolas, Musée de la Mode et du Costume, Paris; Nancy Osborn, Victoria and Albert Museum, London; Karen L. Otis, Museum of Fine Arts, Boston; Sue Parkes, Birmingham Museums and Art Gallery; Mary Phillips, Aquascutum, London; Georgina Pope, Christie's, London; Lieschen A. Potuznik, Art Institute of Chicago; Richard Reynolds and Martina Stansbie, B.T. Batsford Ltd.; Penelope Ruddock and Rhian Tritton, Fashion Research Centre and Museum of Costume, Bath; the late Otto Thieme and Jay Pattison, Cincinnati Art Museum; Heather Tilbury, Susan Ash and Jo Rothwell, Heather Tilbury Associates, London; Robert Harcourt Williams, Hatfield House; and to the staffs of the Bibliothèque de l'Opéra, Paris; Bibliothèque Doucet, Paris; Bibliothèque Forney, Paris; Bibliothèque Nationale de France, Paris; British Library, London; Musée Bonnat, Bayonne; Christie's Images, London; Courtauld Institute of Art, London; London Library; Musée des Beaux-Arts, Nantes; Musée du Louvre, Paris; National Museums and Galleries on Merseyside; National Portrait Gallery, London; Philadelphia Museum of Art; Réunion des musées nationaux, Paris; Tate Gallery, London; Victoria and Albert Museum, London; Yale University Art Gallery, New Haven.

Dr Alice Mackrell
Hampstead, London

Portrait miniature of Marguerite Gérard, painted by François Dumont, 1793.
Seated at her easel, the artist is in the height of fashion, even if impractically dressed for painting. She wears a white satin skirt, a yellow silk tunic with a delicately embroidered motif of leaves, which is held in place by a very wide blue sash, achieving the fashionable high waistline, a white muslin bandeau trimmed with blue ribbons in her unpowdered hair arranged in curls à l'antique, a purple sleeveless overdress arranged to fall like a shawl, and blue shoes with white ties. This is a superb example of the rendering of fabrics, and shows the continued popularity of silk and satin during the French Revolution. *(Reproduced by permission of the Trustees of The Wallace Collection)*

1: Portraits of Fashion and Developments in Fashion Illustration to 1600

Early Manifestations of Fashion

Up until the mid-fourteenth century the main visual sources of the Middle Ages – paintings, manuscripts, sculpture, funerary effigies, brasses and incised slabs – depict a uniformity in male and female dress. The main garments were a long tunic or *cote*; a long supertunic or *surcote*; and a long cloak or *mantel* which was held in place by a cord. The whole set was known as a *robe*.

However, an advance in tailoring techniques in the fourteenth century and the use of buttons, first introduced into the West via the Arabs and Moors in the thirteenth century, firmly established a distinctive costume for men. The long, loose-fitting *cote* was replaced with a short, tight-fitting version cut close to the hips. This new style had to be cut and fit in sections and could be fastened at the front with buttons. Exposing the leg called for tight, well-supported hose which was fastened to the tunic by points or laces, the whole ensemble showing off the shape of the body. The female version of the *cote* remained long, with a train that lengthened the overall line, and with lacing that showed off the contours of the bust and hips. In addition, the new *surcote ouverte*, or open-sided gown, dramatically cut away to the hips, enhanced the graceful outline of the body from shoulder to hips. These slender, close-fitting outfits echoed the long, elegant lines of Gothic art and architecture.

The parting of vestimentary ways, short costume for men and long costume for women, is an important milestone in the long development toward modern fashion, with short garments for men being the most significant innovation in men's fashions that western Europe had yet experienced. The foundation of guilds signified that the making of clothes was now a craft requiring skilful artisans. Short garments for men did not, however, put a complete end to long costume, witnessed by the voluminous garment with long hanging sleeves called the *houppelande*, popular from c.1360, but even this succumbed to a short form.

It is impossible to pinpoint the exact provenance of short costume for men. What is certain is that these new manifestations in fashion ran parallel with Humanism, literally, a devotion to human interests, the concern with the individual man being a main preoccupation, and the Renaissance, which awakened the same attitudes. Threads running parallel in art and costume are perhaps illustrated best in Italy. The idealization of beauty and the perfection of the human form preoccupied artists as diverse as Giotto, Pisanello, Raphael and Bronzino. Fashionable men and women reflected these themes in their appearance, wearing dress that was elegant, harmonious and distinctive. The idea of the fashion designer can also be said to have originated in Italy.[1] Antonio Pisanello, Antonio Pollaiuolo and Jacopo Bellini all designed costumes and fabrics. Pisanello is the example *par excellence* of the artist as Renaissance man, for he worked in several media: painting, drawing, portrait

(Top) Drawing of a knight and a lady by Villard de Honnecourt, c. 1235.
Both the knight and the lady wear long *cotes*, the knight with fine *solers* (slippers), the lady with a sleeveless wide-cut *surcote*. Both wear a cloak called a *manteau à parer* or *manteau noble*. His soft curls and fringe are in the fashionable hairstyle for men. The lady has covered her hair with a *coif*. (Bibliothèque Nationale de France, Paris)

(Left) 'A Weeper from the tomb of Edward III', attributed to John Orchard, c. 1377-86.
The short, tight tunic with large buttons and the jewelled belt emphasize the shape of the body. (By courtesy of the Dean and Chapter of Westminster)

(Right) 'The Sun', painted by an Anonymous English illuminator. From *Liber Cosmographiae* by John Foxton, 1408.
This *houppelande* demonstrates just how short men's garments had become. The gown has voluminous, closed, bag-type hanging sleeves, a high-buttoned collar, floral embroidery throughout, trimmings at the neck and cuffs, and possibly a white fur lining. Other highlights are the close-fitting white hose with long-pointed toes. (The Master and Fellows of Trinity College, Cambridge)

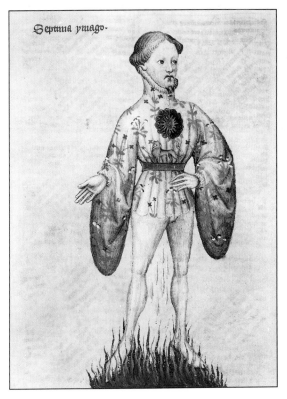

exceptional knowledge of the three-dimensional nature of costume and an imaginative rendering of the tactile qualities of fabrics and their ornamentation, especially of embroidery and fur. Pisanello's costume pieces show that, during the Renaissance, clothing was capricious rather than functional, diversified and related to place and occasion.

It was during the Renaissance that an interest developed in the dress of other nations. Foreign dress was often described in the work of chroniclers and diarists. At this time, change in fashion was largely due to curiosity about the styles of various countries made accessible through the greater mobility of people around the globe. Fortunately, there were a group of artists who were avid to know about fashions and customs and in their peregrinations recorded their impressions by making woodcuts.

The woodcut is thought to have been used in textile printing in the Middle East as far back as the fifth century and became a very popular technique during the fifteenth century. The design is executed on a smooth block of wood, the parts that are to appear white in the print are cut away with the aid of knives and gouges, leaving the design standing in relief. This is covered with printing ink and pressed against a sheet of paper.

In Renaissance Germany, the idea of the fashion portrait was beginning to evolve. As early as 1460, Jorg von Ehingen, a knight errant, adorned his memoirs with woodcut portraits of the kings and princes under whom he had served. Bernhard von Breydenbach made woodcuts of the costumes of various countries and peoples including Saracens, Jews, Greeks and Turks in his travel book *Peregrinations interram sanctum* published in Mainz in 1486. But the main channel through which forms of fashion were recorded and disseminated in the

medals, dress and textiles. His long career was spent at some of the most impressive courts of Italy, notably the Gonzaga in Mantua, the Este in Ferrara and with King Alfonso of Naples, where he would have been expected not only to design sets, banners, triumphal arches and other decorations but also costumes. His studies show an

A Bridal Pair, painted by an Anonymous South German Master, Upper Rhine Region, c. 1470.
The natural silhouette of these figures is exemplified through their garments. The young man wears a close-fitting, short tunic, tight hose, *poulaines* (pointed shoes) and a *jembelet* or jewelled garter on his left leg. The young lady wears a jewelled circlet around the top of her long, loose hair which matches her necklace and bracelet. Her plain gown fits smoothly over her bodice and waist. Her left sleeve is in a different colour and material from the rest of her gown. Their fashions are derived from the styles of northern Italy. (*The Cleveland Museum of Art, Delia E. Holden Fund and L.E. Holden Fund, 32.179*)

Portrait of Eleonora di Toledo, Grand Duchess of Tuscany, from the studio of Agnolo Bronzino, c. 1550.
Bronzino's portrait is significant for it illustrates the exaggeration and artificiality of fashion in mid-sixteenth-century Europe: the large-scale, bold, decorative pattern, the distortion of the shoulders by the shoulder wings which are slashed to show puffs of the chemise, the gold braid partlet nettings spiked with pearls on both sides of the square neckline, the slashed sleeves with firm braid-edged panes again showing puffs of the chemise pulled through and caught with jewels. The line of the dress is confined by jewels and braid, with the bodice extremely elongated and constructed over the rigidities of a corset framework. Also rendered unnatural is the hair, rigidified by the gold caul studded with pearls. (*Reproduced by permission of the Trustees of the Wallace Collection, London*)

late fifteenth century was the work of Albrecht Dürer. He was a master of the woodcut and also achieved a subtle mastery of line engraving, the process of making prints in which the design is cut straight into the surface of a copper plate. Dürer also experimented with the new technique of etching. Although line engraving flourished in the sixteenth century in Europe generally, it had already been pioneered quite separately in Germany by artists such as Martin Schongauer who died in 1491. Through the woodcut and the engraving, the costumes observed by Dürer became known all over Europe. Dürer visited Venice in 1594 and again in 1595 and recorded the fashionable dress of Venetian women. His portrait of 'A Venetian Noblewoman' shows the fashionable lady in an extremely high-waisted dress. Venetian love of complicated fabric design is evident as is a preoccupation with sleeves. In this case they are *finestrella* sleeves, divided into two halves and connected by straps, which permit the sleeves of the chemise underneath to be pulled through. It is an early example of slashing.

Perhaps the most salient aspect of Dürer's work for fashion and its illustration is his rendering of both the front and the back view of the fashionable lady's dress. During the twentieth century the back view of a fashion designer's costume has often been perceived by fashion photographers as the side which reveals the harmony of a designer's creation. Dürer made a speciality of recording both views, a tradition that would be followed by Hollar, Watteau, Tissot and Renoir.

James Laver has commented that the movement towards modifications of national characteristics in costume begins in the first half of the fifteenth century.[2] The main influences came from the Italian states and the courts of France and Burgundy. Many of the Italian states were noted not only for their creative activity but also for their development of silk weaving and the lush and luxurious patterns of their silks. Venice's pivotal location, poised between East and West, gave it an international market. The Venetian noblewoman depicted by Dürer wears one of the beautifully patterned Venetian silks and its sinuous floral motif, soft texture and smooth sheen serves to stress the lines of the female body.

In France and Burgundy the factors were different. These areas were closely formed court societies. The Dukes of Burgundy were politically ambitious and needed an opulent costume to match their political power. Men took shortness and tightness to an extreme by having the chest and shoulders of their doublets padded, the sleeves full and with gathers and the waistline low with a cinched effect. The extraordinary hairstyles and peaked hats added to the vestimentary capriciousness of the male courtiers. Bruges, Ghent and Ypres were rich towns with their own cloth and silk industries and Antwerp staged an annual fair on an international scale for the textile industry. Due to trade connections, Burgundian fashions spread to England.

The quest for physical beauty and elegance, reflected through dress, continued throughout the sixteenth century. Italy again provided the impetus for it was there that a philosophy of fashion and its ancillary subject, deportment, was discussed and analysed. In 1528 Baldesar Castiglione wrote a treatise entitled *Il Libro de Cortegiano* (*The Book of the Courtier*) which was translated into many European languages. Set in 1507 at the court of Urbino, the book describes, through imaginary discussions among members of the court, the qualities that constitute the perfect courtier. Castiglione writes that he often is asked for sartorial advice.

> For in this matter we see endless variations: some dress after the Spanish style, others like the Spanish and others again like the Germans; and there are those who dress in the manner of Turks.[3]

The essential quality of Castiglione's courtier, which had significant repercussions for the phenomenon known as the English gentleman, was *sprezzatura*, 'best perhaps rendered as careful and graceful off-handedness'.[4] Even near the end of the sixteenth century Fabritio Caroso, in his *Il Ballarino* (Venice, 1581), advised men, with accompanying illustrations, on how to dance, how to wear a cloak, and how to don and doff their hats. Women were given instructions on the management of the trains of their gowns and the most charming way to sit when wearing a farthingale. Fashion had turned deportment into an art in itself.

Portrait of Robert Dudley, Earl of Leicester, K.G., painted by Steven van der Meulen, c. 1560-65.
Fashionable men's dress under Elizabeth I shows much Spanish influence. The collar has reached its maximum height. *Pickadils* (the edgings) at the top of the standing collar of the doublet support a pleated, starched ruff and also appear at armseye, cuffs, and bottom of the doublet. The doublet is fastened by a row of buttons ending in a slight, peascod-belly shape and is pinked with small punctures combined with slashes. A medallion of the Order of the Garter hangs from a precious-jewelled chain. The narrow belt follows exactly the waistline of the doublet. The carrying of a sword was associated with courtly rank. The Earl's wide, curving moustache and his beard with the jaw shaved above the line of the moustache are very English. (*Reproduced by permission of the Trustees of The Wallace Collection, London*)

Sixteenth-Century Costume Books

The sixteenth century was a great age of discovery and exploration which increased the desire for knowledge of the costume and customs of other nations. In addition it was the era when two ideas merged perfectly, 'curiosity with elegance'[5], with tremendous results for fashion. Colonization resulted in increased trade for western Europeans. Their new affluence furthered the concept of individual appearance and personal enrichment where rank and status would be denoted by the quality and richness of clothes and accessories, in particular, jewellery.

The second half of the sixteenth century heralded a new visual source of documentation: printed costume books. The invention of movable printing types by Johannes Gutenberg in Mainz in 1454 meant that books could be printed cheaply, and many costume books were published in several editions and translations. Their numbers grew as printing spread to the great book publishing centres of Paris, Venice, Antwerp and Frankfurt. Costume books illustrated the current fashion in the major cities of Europe, and some depicted past fashions. A section of each book also concentrated on the costumes and way of life of the countries being discovered and explored. J.L. Nevinson, in his authoritative article 'The Origin and Early History of the Fashion Plate', states that 'it is in this connection that the word "fashion" was first used in its modern sense.' He defines fashion 'as a general style of dress appropriate for a particular person to wear at a certain time of day, on a special occasion or for a specific purpose', and states that the main functions of fashionable dress 'are to draw attention to the wearer, to define his social position, and to show who he is and what he is doing.'[6] It is with the publication of this large spate of books containing costume plates that the antecedents for the fashion plate of the eighteenth century can be found. The indispensable source for the definitions of the costume plate and the fashion plate is Vyvyan Holland's *Hand-Coloured Fashion Plates 1770 to 1899*.[7] The costume plate was an illustration which showed fashionable ways of dressing. It also recorded fashions of the past. Regional and national dress and theatrical costume also fall within the parameters of the costume plate. The fashion plate, on the other hand, not only recorded contemporary dress but also forecasted what the fashionable style would be like in the near future. Costume books are classified under the generic name of *Trachtenbücher*, derived from the German word 'Tracht', meaning 'dress', 'fashion'.

The Italian engraver Enea Vico compiled a series of large, clear single engravings of figures in national dress entitled *Habitus Nostrae Aetatis*, dated 1556. They were printed in Venice in 1558 under the title *Diversarum Gentium Aetatis Habitus*. One of Vico's costume plates is of a woman wearing an ample cloak or 'falie'. She is presumably a citizen of Flanders and is assigned the Latin name 'Flandrensis'. Mrs Ghering-van Ierlant, in the catalogue of the exhibition *Mode in Prent, 1550-1914* held at the Nederlands Kostum-Museum in the Hague (1988-9), has doggedly pursued her appearances for the rest of the sixteenth century. Such conscientious and precise methodology underlines how costume plates were copied or re-worked and re-used by contemporary artists. Vico's 'Flandrensis' makes an appearance in François Desprez's costume book *Recueil de la diversité des habits qui sont de présent usage*. The *Recueil* was first published in Paris in 1562 with a second edition in 1564 and a third in 1567. It contains 121 woodcuts set in attractive artistic borders. The format is small scale, each page being only 5 ⅞ x 3 ⅞ inches. Apart from its borrowing from Vico, it remains a good general study on the diversities of dress, its originality lying in its comparative studies.

Another costume book heavily indebted to Vico is Ferdinando Bertelli's *Omnium Fere Gentium Nostrae Aetatis Habitus*, published in Venice in 1563, followed by a second edition in 1569. The book is quarto in size and the costume engravings are set in plain borders. Practically all the plates can be traced back to Vico, the only distinction being that Bertelli usually sets the engravings in reverse. Two other members of the ubiquitous Bertelli family added greater originality to their books. Donato Bertelli's *Le Vere Imagini et Descritioni delle più nobili città del mondo*, dated 1569, and Pietro Bertelli's *Diversarum Nationum Habitus*, dated 1589, added pull-up flaps to some of their plates thereby putting Venetian ladies in rather risqué poses! Although Donato's work is a travel book, he included all the plates from Ferdinando's *Omnium Fere Gentium Nostrae Aetatis Habitus*.

One of the most artistically conceived of the sixteenth-century costume books was written and illustrated by Nicholas de Nicolay: *Les Quatres premiers livres des navigations et pérégrinations Orientales*, published in Lyon in 1567. The engravings are much larger in size than those in the other books discussed, measuring 10 ¾ x 6 ⅞ inches. They are exquisitely rendered in subtle hues of grey and black. The use of cast shadow, which gives the figures a very life-like appearance, was unique among contemporary costume books. Nicolay concentrated on Turkey, Greece, the islands of the Mediterranean and North Africa. The insightful comments Nicolay makes in his introduction on the way he compiled his book leaves no doubt about the authenticity of the costumes portrayed and discussed. He travelled for some fifteen years in the company of Signor d'Aramonte, Ambassador of the King of France, to 'le grand Turc'. The importance of Nicolay's study in the annals of sixteenth-century costume books is underscored by its being printed in the most editions: three in France,

two each in Italy and Germany, and one each in Antwerp and London. Nicolay's illustrations are considered the most influential introduction to Turkish dress and were copied until at least the first quarter of the eighteenth century.

The most versatile and productive artist of the period was Jost Amman. Although Swiss, he lived and worked in Nuremberg. He was a painter, printmaker and writer. In contemporary books he is referred to as a *Kunstreisser*, an artistic draughtsman. His mastery of copperplate engraving and, especially, of woodcut was an important contribution to fashion history in itself, for his drawing of clothing is always precise, clear and elegant. Amman's output was truly remarkable: a tournament book

(*Thurnier Buch*, 1566); a book on occupations and professions (*Eygentliche Beshreybung*, 1568); a book on military costume (*Fronspergers Kriegsbuch*, 1577) and an art and instruction book for young beginners (*Kunst and Lehrbüchlein*, 1578). He designed playing cards, a very valuable yet little-known and rarely-used source for costume. Called the 'Little Master' by contemporaries, Amman compiled two costume books: the *Habitus Praecipuorum Populorum . . . Trachtenbüch*, a folio volume of woodcuts published in Nuremberg in 1577, and the *Gynaecorum Sine Theatrum Mulierum*, a quarto volume of woodcuts published in Frankfurt in 1586, the German edition entitled *Frauenzimmer Trachtenbüch*. Both costume books show regional costumes of all classes, the emphasis being on the German city states. With such a prodigious

'Cortigiana Veneta', ('Venetian Courtesan'), engraved by Pietro Bertelli. From his *Diversarum Nationum Habitus*, 3rd ed., 1591. The dress is made of a sumptuously-patterned brocade indigenous to Venice and depicts the diversity of Venetian fashions. Attached to the back of the bodice is an open, fan-shaped ruff while the *décolletage* of the square-cut neckline is bordered with a lace-edged chemise. Masculine features can be observed: the body of her gown curves into the distinctive peascod-belly shape and has decorative shoulder wings. The view of her on the left shows not only her *chopines* (stilts) and decorated stockings but also her masculine-style breeches, an undergarment characteristic of her profession. Typically Venetian is her horned and curled hairstyle. (*Victoria and Albert Museum, London*)

Dame Persienne   Fille Persienne   Fille Persienne
Erbar Fraw in Persia   Jungfraw in Persia   Jungfraw in Persia

an *oeuvre* it must be asked how accurate are the costume plates. On his home ground, the dress distinctions of the various German city states are original and reliable, and his sources detailed. Both Mrs Ghering van-Ierlant in her catalogue and Jo Anne Olian in her article on costume books cite his printing one of his plates twice in the *Frauenzimmer Trachtenbüch*: the first time as 'Eine Frau aus England' and the same print a second time as 'Eine fürneme Frau von Rom'. Both of Amman's costume books also show a predilection for Vico's engravings.

The relative unimportance of English dress is underlined by the fact that Enea Vico did not illustrate any examples and Desprez included only one plate in his *Recueil*. The first costume books to pay any attention to English dress were compiled by Abraham de Bruyn. His *Diversarum Gentium Armatura Equestris*, a quarto volume containing 52 engravings, was published in Cologne in 1577. De Bruyn's *Omnium Poene Europae, Asiae, Aphricae Atque Americae* was published in Antwerp in 1581. This latter volume had a quite different format from the other costume books, showing around five figures in costumes in a horizontal arrangement across the page. Sometimes the horizontal groups were arranged in tiers.

Fashion influences were shifting. In 1525 Spain had won the Battle of Pavia and so became the most important economic and political power in Europe. The stiff silhouette of Spanish costume pervaded the dress of western Europe including that of the Italian states who had dictated fashion for so long. The *cuerpo baxo*, a quilted, boned under-bodice, lined with canvas and trimmed with wire, inflicted a taut, geometrical shape from shoulders to waist.

Persian Women, engraved by Jean-Jacques Boissard. From his *Habitus Variarum Orbis Gentium*, 1581.
In sixteenth-century western Europe there was a vogue for Oriental dress, the source being illustrations from costume books. Particularly popular among fashionable women were the cut and silhouette of full-length robes and ornate headdresses from Persia. *(British Library, London)*

In England, the visit of King Philip II of Spain in 1554 to marry Queen Mary ensured the predominance of Spanish fashions for many years, despite the war between the two countries in the 1580s. The severe lines of the Spanish style manifested themselves in Elizabethan female dress in such details as the tight, elongated bodice, the stiffened two-piece under-bodice, and the bell-shape skirt, its shape formed by the stiffened understructure called the farthingale, a series of hoops of cane or, later, of whalebone. This widening of the skirt was counterbalanced by a new accessory worn around the neck called the ruff which became a characteristic feature of Elizabethan costume. A particularly distinctive Spanish garment featured by de Bruyn was the *ropa*. This was the fashionable Spanish outer garment opening all the way down the front with padded rolls at the top of the sleeves. However, the very voluminousness of the Elizabethan gown gave it a much more relaxed look with far less of the character of Spanish austerity.

De Bruyn shows that Englishmen also followed the rigorous Spanish fashions. Essential items were the shirt, doublet, ruff, cloak, hat, gloves and leather boots. Doublets were very tight in the torso, coming to a sharp point at the waist called a peascod-belly. The corset-like effect was provided by stiffenings and padded linings, while the male ruff evolved from the frills of the shirt collar.

One of the rarest costume books from this period is Jean-Jacques Boissard's *Habitus Variarum Orbis Gentium* published in Malines (Mechlin) in 1581. A new standard of illustration was reached with Boissard's 67 costume designs, all executed in exquisite pen and grey and brown wash. The costume illustrated is mainly cosmopolitan and urban, and represents the countries which Boissard visited. The name of each costume is given in French, Latin and German. The delicacy of the technique, the elegance of the figures – largely of noblemen and noblewomen arranged in groups of three or four per drawing – their individualization and movement, giving the impression of being drawn from life, and the sumptuousness of the costume with its lavish detail all ally Boissard's work to the fashion plate.

The best-known and most eminent of the genre, indeed the costume book that perhaps epitomizes sixteenth-century Renaissance man's quest for an encyclopaedic knowledge of dress, is Cesare Vecellio's *De gli Habiti antichi et moderni di diverse Parti del Mondo*. It is the most universal gathering together of the costumes of various nations and is the first to publish the clothing of previous periods, mainly in the sections on Venice and Rome, chiefly based on the study of works of art preserved in churches and public buildings. Published in Venice in 1590, it contains 420 woodcuts, drawn by Vecellio and

cut in wood by the Nuremberg artist Christoph Krieger, referred to in the book as 'Cristoforo Guerra'. The plates are accompanied by descriptions of the costumes written in Latin. Vecellio divided his work into two parts: Book I has 361 illustrations of costumes of Europe, including Turkey, and Book II is a compilation of 59 plates of Asian and African clothing. A second, enlarged edition entitled *Habiti antichi et moderni di tutto il Mondo* has a total of 507 woodcuts, including a survey of the dress of the New World, with the descriptions written in both Latin and Italian. This edition was published in Venice in 1598. Both costume books are octavo in size and each costume plate is framed in a decorative border.

Like those before him, Vecellio, a cousin and assistant of the great Venetian painter, Titian, laid stress on the costumes of his own country and region. He was born about 1521 in Pieve di Cadore, just outside Venice, and died in Venice in 1601. It is therefore his section on Venetian dress, customs and manners that is the most interesting and reliable. The addition of plates of architectural views and daily life on the canals of the city provides a fascinating historical and social record of sixteenth-century Venice.

Vecellio writes very vividly, for example, on the process of hair-bleaching and the clothing worn by Venetian ladies for the occasion.

> In Venice, on the roofs of the houses, they use structures of wooden squares in the form of loggias called balconies, in which all or most of the women of Venice assiduously bleach their hair with various kinds of waters or potions made for this purpose, and this they do in the fullness of the sun. They are seated with a small sponge attached to the end of a stick and thus they wet their hair. They wear clothing of silk or light material called a *schiavonetto*, and on their heads a hat of fine straw called a *solana*, to protect them from the sun, and a mirror in one hand.[8]

One of the great strengths of Vecellio is that he records textiles that were made and sold by merchant drapers who plied their trade, for instance, at the Italian courts, and who, therefore, would have been *au courant* with current tastes. He singles out and salutes individual drapers such as Master Bartolomeo Bontempede whose establishment was located at the sign of the Chalice in Venice. As J.L. Nevinson rightly points out, when we find an indoor dress of Venice in 1590 depicted and described in detail and are told at whose shop its materials may be found surely we are not very far from the idea of a fashion plate.[9]

A great deal of discretion must be applied when using parts of Vecellio. Jo Anne Olian has cogently stated that possibly only the Venetian and historical costumes are original.[10] Looming large among the artists whom Vecellio copied is Enea Vico. A close examination of Vecellio's tomes also show borrowings from Jost Amman for Germany and central Europe, Jean-Jacques Boissard for Lombardy, Tuscany, Turkey and the Orient, and Bartolomeo Grassi for Flanders and England. His second edition with the section on the garb of the New World is heavily indebted to the engravings of Theodor de Bry after John White's watercolours of Virginia for Thomas Harriot's *Briefe and True Report of the New Found Land of Virginia*, printed in Frankfurt in 1590.

Vecellio considerably smartened up his second edition. He shortened his captions and his introduction and dropped much anecdotal information on how he came to compile his work, including the costumes he saw and the letters and drawings of his cicerones in various cities of Italy. The *Habiti antichi et moderni di tutto il Mondo* has historically always been held in high regard. The most flattering tribute paid to Vecellio occurred in Venice in 1664 when his magnum opus was reprinted. He was erroneously named as the brother of Titian with some of the visual work attributed to Titian himself. For the next two centuries the view prevailed that the *Habiti* was the work of Titian.[11]

The sixteenth century was the golden age of the *Trachtenbücher*. Costume books did continue to be published, indeed, there was a veritable inundation of them in the nineteenth century. More immediately, however, at the end of the sixteenth century they were beginning to lose their novelty and exoticism and some became mere pastiches. Their great value is as source books and works of reference, particularly for artists and playwrights. Sir Philip Sidney may well have been familiar with both Boissard's and Nicolay's books when describing dress in *Arcadia*. Inigo Jones, when designing masque costumes from 1605 to 1640, referred to the works of Boissard, de Bruyn and Vecellio.[12] Historically, Vecellio may be singled out for his comprehensiveness, having been utilized by innumerable producers of plays and masques as well as by classical actresses, most notably Ellen Terry, who found his studies invaluable.

Portrait Miniature of a Gentleman, painted by Nicholas Hilliard, c. 1588
This young English courtier wears a huge finely pleated cartwheel ruff that envelops his neck. Negligently thrown over his shoulder is a short cloak which has fur revers and is fur-lined. His doublet has a pronounced peascod-belly shape. It is made of a contrasting black-and-white material which has been serrated and made into interlocking panels and trimmed with large decorative buttons. The sleeves are heavily padded giving a very bulbous shape. This is offset by brief trunk hose and white stockings. A narrow belt and white shoes with long pointed toes and pinked uppers complete the outfit of this etoliated gentleman. *(Victoria and Albert Museum, London)*

Portrait of a Lady, painting attributed to Marcus Gheeraerts the Younger, c. 1590-1600
Over her conically-tiered headdress, made up in ruched gauze and adorned with pansies, the unknown English lady wears her hair long and loose. The surface of her robe has a whirling design of embroidered flowers, fruits and birds, and the hem is edged with lace. Her gauzy-silvery overgown is scattered with spangles. Striking accessories are a thin, black-cord necklace to which rings are attached and pearls, the jewel most associated with the Elizabethan age. *(Reproduced by Gracious Permission of Her Majesty the Queen)*

Miniature Painting and Embroidery in Elizabethan England

In the late Middle Ages England was not, as we have seen, of particular importance in the development of fashionable dress. During the late Elizabethan period, however, the great visual glory of England was miniature painting, especially that of Nicholas Hilliard and Isaac Oliver. Their small, jewel-like portraits executed in body colour on vellum, just like medieval manuscript illuminations, provide exact and detailed information on fashions. While dress still remained under Spanish influence in its structure – female and male garments being subjected to exaggeration and an artificial appearance – differences appear. Colours are brighter and luxurious materials have their surfaces broken up by decorative patterns. The whole embellishment conveys a romantic, Arcadian feeling.

An art form complementary to miniature painting was embroidery. Since the Middle Ages England had excelled in ornament with needlework. During the Elizabethan period domestic embroidery flourished. The main subject matter of the professional and amateur embroiderer was flowers, a distinctively English motif. The source of these flowers were numerous contemporary herbals and specialized books printed especially for embroidery such as *La Clef des champs* by Jacques Le Moyne de Morgues, published in London in 1586. Creative ability in embroidery was very much a part of young women's education and the invention of steel needles and the importation of a variety of coloured silks gave them a new stimulus. Their techniques became more varied, such as the use of metallic silk threads for the striking flowers depicted on both men's and women's garments and accessories. A small number of specimens survive, mostly of embroidered linen in the form of jackets (also called waistcoats), shirts, chemises, coifs, hoods, nightcaps, gloves and purses.

London was a centre for dress production and, by the end of the sixteenth century, milliners began to sell ready-made embroidered nightcaps, waistcoats, shirts, coifs and gloves. As the quest for decoration and embellishment heightened in the seventeenth century, there was an ever-increasing development of the fashion trade and of shopping opportunities for fashionable society.

The Search for New Fashions

Although Hispanic fashions were still pre-eminent at the end of the sixteenth century fashionable men and women were on the look-out for new styles. The miniature painting and embroidery of the late Elizabethan period are testaments to the delight in bright colours and pattern surfaces which infused the constricting modes.

In the 1580s a very popular and fashionable garment for men was the mandilion, a short, loose jacket with hanging sleeves. Only the top buttons were fastened and it was worn sideways. Contemporaries referred to the mandilion as being worn 'Colley-Westonward', meaning awry.

The preponderance of lace collars was another fashionable detail. Many fine pattern books for lace were published in the sixteenth century. The most celebrated German example of the genre, as well as the first by a woman, is *Nüw Modelbuch*. The authoress, who on the title page and in the Preface only gives her initials, R.M., wrote that the art of pillow-lace had been introduced into her country 25 years previously in 1536 by merchants from Venice, thus providing an approximate date, c.1561, for her pattern book. Consisting of 164 woodcuts of lace patterns, the book's originality lay in its use of white on black and in the insightful comments, for example, on the cheapness of making and cleaning lace as opposed to clothes adorned with gold and silk.

For the most part, pattern books for lace were published in Venice. A magnificent collection of lace patterns can be found in Vecellio's *Corona delle nobili et virtuoso donne* published in 1591. In the sixteenth century, England was noted for fine embroidered laces such as filet, drawnwork and cutwork. As an alternative to the ruff, men wore the falling band, a turned-down collar made of, or edged with, an embroidered lace. Women wore the *rebato*, a high lace collar pinned to the bodice and wired so that it stood up and fanned out around the back of the neck and head.

Portrait of Queen Elizabeth I, The Rainbow Portrait, painted by Marcus Gheeraerts the Younger, c. 1600.
The Queen's attire presages many of the fashions of the seventeenth century. Her over-garment is draped over one shoulder. The bodice of her gown of linen is ornamentally embroidered in multi-coloured sprigs and the lace edging, though made of *reticella* or Roman lace, anticipates the large scallops of seventeenth-century lace. The gold-wired veil behind the Queen's two ruffs trails off in the horizontal manner of the seventeenth century. Her hairstyle of trailing locks to one side was very fashionable in the seventeenth century. (By courtesy of the Marquess of Salisbury)

NON SINE SOLE
IRIS.

In France, where needlepoint was influenced by Venice, ladies wore the *rebato* as early as 1553 when Catherine de' Médicis introduced it to France from Italy on her marriage to Henri II. During the reign of Henri III (1574-89) these collars became very large, forming a fan-shape that framed the head. At the end of the sixteenth century they fanned out even more and much later were called Médicis collars because they had been worn by Marie de' Médicis, the wife of Henri IV.

The Orient was a source of continued fascination and influence. Oriental fabrics were valued highly for their decorative repertoire and technical skill. The undulating patterns of flowers and foliage seen on western European textiles, particularly those of Venice, had an Oriental provenance. In France, at the fashion-conscious court of Henri III dazzling dresses *à la turque* in bold colours and sprinkled with precious stones were worn at royal *fêtes* and masques.

Costume books, particularly the works of Boissard and Nicolay, extended the boundaries of western fashion. The image of the 'Virgo Persica' or 'Persian Maiden' in Boissard's costume book was the source for the *Portrait of a Lady* located at Hampton Court Palace. Dated c. 1590-1600 and attributed to Marcus Gheeraerts the Younger, the portrait shows the romantic, flowing, loose cut of the exotic Persian robe, probably worn by the lady to a masque and perhaps also for her private delectation as relief from the stiff Spanish silhouette. Another interesting aspect of the portrait is the lady's long, loose hair and the conically-shaped headdress which was also copied from Boissard. Even Queen Elizabeth herself succumbed to the allure of these fantastic headdresses. The elaborate, highly decorated, curvilinear example in her *Rainbow Portrait* closely follows that of Boissard's 'Sponsa Thessalonicensis', a bride of Salonica. More of these bizarre designs were elucidated in his *Mascarades* of 1597.

The search for new fashions came from many quarters including a most unlikely one, children's garments. Children were dressed as miniature adults, yet, at the end of the sixteenth century, there was a trend toward greater ease and freedom of movement of their dress. Reformers in England in the 1570s and 1580s were already recommending that clothing for children be warm and light for reasons of health and physical well-being.[13] Details of fashion were chided. Many fashionable late-Elizabethan parents complied, permitting their children to forego some of their own elaborate and exaggerated dress. Portraits of girls often show them looking happy and relaxed in their long gowns without the rigid stomacher, the farthingale and the ostentatious headwear of their mothers. Boys are frequently portrayed wearing a wide, loose collar and a doublet and breeches free of padding, the pared-down effect achieving a trim outline of the figure. These softer, simpler styles of dress for boys and girls were models for the future.

By the end of the sixteenth century there was a distinctive air of changeability in fashion. Prevailing modes were not only flamboyant and distorted but also easy and comfortable, imaginative and inventive. This art of nuance presaged the development of new types of fashions in the next century.

Portrait Miniature of a Little Girl, painted by Isaac Oliver, 1590. Little girls wore the dress of their mothers but the absence of a stomacher and farthingale shows how less formal fashion could be. Her layered ruff, too, is far smaller and in a simpler style than that worn by adults. Her waistline is at its natural level emphasized by the strips of black velvet down the front of the black satin bodice. (*Victoria and Albert Museum, London*)

2: Fashion Engraving, Portrait Painting and Fashion Journalism in the Seventeenth Century

Fashion in Transition

Louis XIV said that 'costume is the mirror of history'.[1] This statement of *Le Roi Soleil* reflects his absolute monarchy whereby dress in the seventeenth century was manipulated to secure France's role as fashion leader of the world. John Evelyn, a collector of drawings and an informative writer on the fashions of his time, astutely remarked in *Tyrannus, or The Mode*, 1661, 'It is plainly in their interest and they gain by it. Believe it, La Mode de France is one of the best returns they make, and feeds as many bellies as it clothes backs.'[2] Dress at the court of Louis XIV was more than a matter of frivolity. It was government policy.

While there was already a trend toward greater ease in dress at the end of the sixteenth century, Spanish influence still predominated in Europe as the seventeenth century unfolded, with exaggerated and constricting fashions being worn. In England, the accession of James I in 1603 saw no dramatic changes in fashion, certainly as far as women were concerned. Male fashions followed Spanish styles but there were certain modifications. Men were more inclined to be adventurous than women. James encouraged extravagant tastes among his favourite

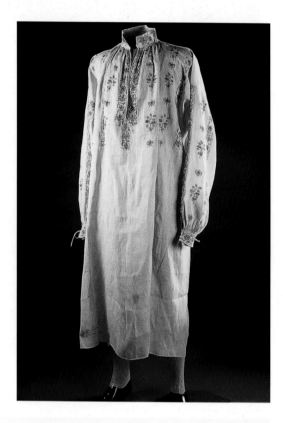

English man's white linen shirt embroidered in black silk thread, 1600-10.
A fine example of precise and exquisite blackwork used both fashionably, as a form of decoration, and practically, as a means of strengthening the garment. The most visible parts of the shirt are those which are subject to the hardest wear, at the neck, wrists, and centre-front. They are covered with a delightful pattern of coiling stems, roses, oak leaves, insects and birds. Blackwork embroidery, thought to be Arabic in origin, spread from Spain to England before the beginning of the sixteenth century, and was particularly fashionable from the 1530s to the 1630s. (*Museum of Costume, Bath*)

Portrait of Sir Walter Scott with his son Walter, painted by an Anonymous Artist, 1602.
Sir Walter is in the height of formality with a ruff that reaches right up to his ears, a white satin doublet, and brown velvet jerkin. The jerkin, heavily encrusted with pearls and silver, has a short skirt consisting of a number of overlapping tabs. His trunk hose is paned and edged with silver and his pale buff canions (short breeches) are fastened with tight white silk garters. Young Walter wears a less formal style with his falling band, a turned-down collar edged with lace, and his blue suit trimmed with small stripes of silver comprising a doublet with narrow sleeves and shoulder wings and close-fitting Venetians. He wears plain blue stockings. Both wear novel square-toed shoes with uppers ending in a small tongue over which the straps from the heel are tied in a bow, and round-brimmed hats. Sir Walter's hat is decorated with a jewelled feather held in place by a pearl brooch. His brushed-up moustache is worn with a pickdevant beard. (*National Portrait Gallery, London*)

1602

S.ʳ Walter Ralegh Knight Lord Warden of
the Stanneries   of the
& of the Isle of Iarsey & her M. Lieute
nant generall of the Counties of Devonshyre & Cornwall.

male courtiers and his court was renowned for its effeminate and dissolute character, lavishly exhibited through dress.

The fashionable Jacobean gallant opted for an elongated line above the waist, a silhouette maintained by means of heavy fabrics and linings rather than padding and bombast. Doublets still came to a point or arch at the waist but were shorter and not so pronounced, leading to the disappearance of the peascod belly. The doublets were close-fitting with the sleeves narrow and tight, puffed and padded and the shoulder wings smaller. These modifications contributed to a less distorted outline of the upper torso. By 1610 the ruff had been replaced by a standing collar decorated with lace, drawn threadwork or cutwork. Voluminousness was reserved for the trunk hose. While becoming longer, it continued to be wide at the top and now became very bulky above the knees, an effect achieved through pleating from the waistline. To accommodate the broad line of the trunk hose, the waistline rose slightly, serving to emphasize the leaner line of the upper torso. Jacobean courtiers decorated their costumes and the early years of the reign of James I saw an acceleration in trade, most notably in luxury goods such as imported rich silks, lace, and embroideries.

There is a dearth of complete, genuine outfits and it is only from portraits that the appearance of the Jacobean men of fashion can be appreciated. The miniature portraits of Isaac Oliver, in particular his study of Richard Sackville, 3rd Earl of Dorset, superbly illustrate English male fashions. The clothes worn by the Earl of Dorset were no invention on the part of the artist as an inventory of the Earl's wardrobe documents the items of dress in the portrait.[3]

The formal ending of sumptuary legislation in England in 1604 was a sign that society and dress were in a state of transition. The expansion of the money market and corresponding growth in capitalism meant that the wealthy merchant class could marry above their station and wear the luxurious fashions of the nobility.

With the growth of Puritanism it was inevitable that male fashions during the reign of James I be attacked and that the sartorial thoughts and demeanour of Henri IV and the French court be the corrective yardstick. In contrast to his predecessor, Henri III, Henri IV was a man of humble tastes with an almost missionary spirit of sobriety and decorum. In addition to his own example, Henri IV issued sumptuary legislation with a view to curbing the importation of gold and silver tissues of foreign manufacture. Henri IV's quest for moderation in dress was buttressed by the aftermath of the Wars of Religion. The turmoil had led to a devaluation of currency which left the French nobility poverty-stricken and unable to afford costly fashions.

In France the Spanish influence was still conspicuous but it was moderated by a relaxation of rigidity in favour of the natural outline of the body. Peascod-belly doublets were rejected for those which were close-fitting and longer, and for fuller trunk hose, their shape maintained by the fabrics and interlinings. Ruffs grew smaller and were superseded by falling bands or turned-down collars. Short cloaks were softly draped and sometimes a satin scarf was worn diagonally across the chest. Fashion in France was the fashion of the court. The *bourgeoisie* wore plain clothing made of wool. The garments of French courtiers were still made of silk but with noticeably fewer trimmings, especially of gold and silver, than during the reign of Henri III. And, compared to their English counterparts who took a particular delight in the decoration of silk and velvet by lavish embroidery, the dress of the courtiers of Henri IV appeared almost austerely simple.

In England, Queen Anne of Denmark, the consort of James I, had an obsessive enthusiasm for sumptuous finery. While the basic components of women's dress remained the same as in the late Elizabethan period, Queen Anne had, if anything, an even greater love of magnificent apparel – and of the huge French farthingale which set it off to advantage – than Queen Elizabeth I herself. Some changes to the modes of the late sixteenth century did take place. The French, wheel-shaped, slightly tilted farthingale became more exaggerated due to the very elongated front of the stiffened bodice. An alternative to the French farthingale was the roll farthingale or bum roll (*cul postiche, hausse-cul*). Padded with cotton or horsehair, it was tied around the waist

under the skirt to distend the garment at the hips. Introduced in the second half of the sixteenth century when it was not considered fashionable, it was now an alternative for women of quality. However, women in Spain, Italy, the Spanish Netherlands and Habsburg Austria adhered to the bell-shaped Spanish farthingale, and in the matter of the neckline, the Spanish style continued to stress total coverage of the boned bodice. The rigid, covered Spanish bodice made jewellery an important feature of fashion. Christie's New York sale of Objects of Vertu in October 1993 included a Spanish colonial gold chain from the wreck of the *Nuestra Senora de Esperanza*, which sank in 1658 in the 'Mystery Bay', Gulf of New Mexico. Although Spanish men wore gold chains due to restrictions limiting their ornamentation to hat badges and chains, the delicacy of this rare surviving specimen suggests it was intended to be worn by a woman. In the auction catalogue several portraits were shown for comparison, including Velázquez's *Infanta Margarita of Spain* dating from 1659 showing her wearing one very similar to the specimen being sold.

But in England low necklines were the norm. Queen Anne was unduly proud of her bosom and wore extremely low-cut bodices. Pictures of her invariably highlight her vanity. *Décolletage* was the subject of much outrage on the part of fashion moralists like Thomas Tuke and of mirth on the part of dramatists such as Ben Jonson.

Lady Anne Clifford in her *Diary* alluded to an informal fashion, the waistcoat or jacket, also called a doublet. Lady Clifford wore it with her nightgown but it could also be worn simply with a petticoat, as the skirt was then called. The waistcoat was an alternative style of bodice. While close-fitting, it was unstructured, unlike the stiff, long, pointed bodice, and not busked. The garment was essentially straight cut but with gussets at the hips to provide flare and fullness, curved fronts, and under-arm seams. The neck had no collar, and the long sleeves ended with turned-up cuffs to which were added cuffs made of lace, linen or lawn. Fastenings down the front could be ribbon ties, buttons or hooks and eyes. Popular until the 1630s, the peculiarly English version was made of linen and was heavily embroidered with motifs of interlacing patterns of coiling stems, flowers, leaves, fruits, insects and birds.

In 1994, Christie's South Kensington offered for sale one of the rarest elaborately embroidered linen doublets,

dated 1610-20, to come on the open auction market together with precise documentation in the form of a portrait, dated c. 1615 (attributed to Paul van Somer) of the original owner, Margaret Layton, wearing it. Christie's negotiated the private sale of the doublet and portrait to the Victoria and Albert Museum, London. The portrait shows that the doublet has never been altered and as such is one of the most important specimens of seventeenth-century English embroidery known to have survived. Margaret Layton wears her doublet with a falling white lace ruff, white lace cuffs, black loose open gown and gauzy red and gold apron. On her head she wears a cornet edged with white lace and topped with a red plume, earrings and an earstring in her left ear. It is the sort of ensemble worn by a prosperous merchant's daughter in early seventeenth-century London. No comparable surviving specimen appearing also in a contemporary portrait is known to exist, making doublet and portrait veritable icons of fashion and fashion illustration.

France had not acquired an informal style of fashionable dress to the extent that England had so successfully. With her son Louis XIII only nine years old at the time of the assassination of Henri IV in 1610, Marie de' Médicis was crowned Queen Regent, her Regency lasting until 1617. While holding to the strictures of court dress she was nevertheless a woman of considerable taste in clothes. Her name will always be synonymous with the elegant, high-standing, fan-shaped, pleated lace collars which played a special role in the historical revival called *le style troubadour*.[4] Marie de' Médicis contributed many other details of extreme beauty and delicacy to French dress confirming that the revolution in women's costume was coming from France. Portraits of her, for example those by Rubens, show that she liked a more flattened farthingale, a high waistline, a quilted bodice, the low neck adorned with a gauze flouncing, white *fichu* or falling collar in cutwork, the patterns in the shape of leaves or flames, and *manches balloonnées*, sleeves which were puffed and paned. A more fitted, broader silhouette bereft of surface ornamentation was the new mode. These changes in women's dress in France were brought to the Caroline court by Marie de' Médicis's youngest daughter, Henrietta Maria, when she became Queen of England in 1625.

English woman's doublet of linen embroidered in coloured silks and metal threads, 1610-20.
Distinctive to Elizabethan and Jacobean England were linen doublets or jackets beautifully embroidered in brightly coloured silks and metal threads on themes reflecting the English love of flowers, gardens and the countryside. *(Museum of Costume, Bath)*

Fashion Follows Power

Spain's influence on fashion started to decline from the 1620s in direct relationship to the ascendancy of France. The destruction of a significant proportion of Spain's commercial potential was self-inflicted. When King Philip III issued his pragmatic against brocades in 1600 and banished the Moors from Spain in 1609, he set the country's textile industry on a ruinous path. The weaving industry, run largely by Moorish craftsmen, fell into disarray and Spain depended increasingly on the importation of luxurious textiles. The Spanish and French were already at war when France formally entered the Thirty Years War (1618-48) in 1635. The French defeat of the Spanish at Rocroi in 1643 marked the end of a string of brilliant victories and the start of France's military supremacy in Europe. The plumeting of Spain's military prowess was quickly followed by the loss of political clout.

Dress was emblematic of the power struggle. Realizing that Spain's superiority, including her fashions, was already on the wane, King Philip IV issued his *Capitulos de Reformacion* in 1623, banning French dress and introducing a compulsory suit to be worn at court. An historical revival, consisting of a sixteenth-century style black doublet and breeches, the suit was meant to convey a symbolic image of Spain's golden past. It was official court dress until 1700 when French fashions were adopted as a result of King Louis XIV of France proclaiming the Bourbon dynasty, naming his grandson, Philip V, King of Spain.

From the mid-seventeenth century, the accolade of most powerful country in Europe was transferred to France. Fashion accompanied France's quest for power at every stage. The royal authority of Louis XIII and Louis XIV was indebted to a group of officials who engineered France's economic recovery. Finances were established, agriculture and transport improved, and luxury industries, especially textiles, under Louis XIV's celebrated minister, Colbert, encouraged. The magnificence of French modes would be the means of visually demonstrating France's supremacy and growing dominance over her neighbours.

Early Baroque Fashions

Fashion from about 1625 to 1715 reflected the creative elements of the Baroque movement. At the end of the sixteenth century the disunity caused by the Reformation had not been rectified. Baroque originated in Italy about 1600 by dint of the Church's endeavours to renew and reaffirm Catholicism through the use of art as propaganda. People would be won back to Catholicism through flamboyant painting, sculpture and architecture that appealed directly to their senses and emotions. This corresponding renewal of Catholicism and revival of the arts became known as the Counter-Reformation. Directly linked to the Catholicism of the Counter-Reformation, the Baroque movement spread from Italy, varying according to the spiritual climate of the country concerned: more pronounced in Catholic Austria, Spain, southern Germany and France, less so in Protestant England, Holland and Scandinavia. In France, the acute minister Colbert saw that the religious aspects of the Baroque style could enhance an autocratic regime through glorification of the monarch.

The essential characteristics of the phase known as the Early Baroque (c. 1625-60) were sweeping movement, light and colour, escape from restraint, extravagance and theatricality. In France fashionable dress reflected these new artistic motifs with great verve and virtuosity.

The Fashion Engravings of Jacques Callot and Abraham Bosse

The Early Baroque styles required lighter textiles that flowed effortlessly, reflecting the contours of the body. Satin and velvet were still the two main fashionable fabrics, a new softness in the weave producing a natural texture. Rich, crisp silks were manufactured at Lyon, where a silk industry was rapidly developing.

Fashionable women abandoned the farthingale and the skirt of the gown now billowed by means of the support of an attractive and elaborate petticoat. An important fashion garment in itself, the petticoat or *friponne* was strikingly revealed as the skirt of the gown was stylishly draped or looped up with ties or pins.

For fashionable men a swashbuckling image, associated in France with *The Three Musketeers* and in England with the Cavaliers, was the ideal. The three principal items of dress remained the doublet, breeches and cloak. The doublet was unstiffened with short skirts or *basques* and a slightly high waistline. The sleeves were slashed with panes to show the colour of the lining and also the expanse of white shirt beneath. Decorative points or *aiguillettes* were attached to the waist to which were fastened the breeches. Breeches were long, loose and unpadded and trimmed with braid or ribbons on the outside seam, matching the doublet.

A real innovation was the fashion for soft leather boots worn indoors and outdoors. Some boots were very high and tight-fitting with high heels and squared toes. They had turned down tops and were worn with stockings or, very inventively, with boot hose trimmed with lace which came over and echoed the tops of the boots. Perhaps the most characteristic were the short 'funnel' boots with widely flared turnover tops, worn with boot hose that was often decorated with lace to match the falling collar.

Jacques Callot and Abraham Bosse are the two artists most associated with the engraving of fashions during the reign of Louis XIII. Jacques Callot (1592-1635) was one of the first French artists to work exclusively as an engraver and draughtsman. His output was prodigious, with more than 1,000 etchings and 1,000 drawings extant. Callot was celebrated for his realistic style. He studied engraving in Rome from about 1608 to 1611. From there he went on to Florence in 1612 where he enjoyed the patronage of the Grand Duke Cosimo II. With great flourish Callot recorded the contemporary life of Florence, in particular fairs and festivals and outdoor theatrical performances. He also perceptively observed courtiers, soldiers and, most poignantly, characters he saw at the *commedia dell'arte* such as beggars and

hunchbacks. He returned to Nancy, his birthplace, in 1621, where he spent most of his career although he also worked in Paris and the Low Countries. Callot's most interesting illustration of fashion is his collection of etchings entitled *La Noblesse de Lorraine* (1624), a series of twelve plates depicting the fashionable dress of the *dames* and *seigneurs* of his native city.

This was a time when technological improvements were taking place in the intaglio methods of engraving. The main intaglio process that Callot advanced was etching. It is a method of engraving where the copper plate is coated with a wax and resin mixture, called the ground. The etcher then draws with an etching needle on the ground, exposing the copper wherever he wants a line to

La Galerie du Palais, engraved by Abraham Bosse, c. 1640. This was the fashionable shopping venue of the period. Gloves, fans, ribbons, lace collars and cuffs are all lavishly displayed. (*The Metropolitan Museum of Art, New York, Rogers Fund*)

print. The copper plate is then immersed in acid which eats away at the exposed parts. The etcher can achieve subtle variations of tonal line by 'stopping out' part of the design with varnish while another part is bitten into more deeply. Callot's unique contribution was the invention of a new hard covering for the copper plate, replacing the wax with a kind of varnish used in lute-making. This enabled him to draw much finer lines, attaining scrupulous accuracy in his costume designs.

Abraham Bosse (1602-76) was engraver at the French court. He taught at the Académie Royale in Paris from its foundation in 1648 until 1661, and wrote a treatise on engraving. This background, together with being the son of a master tailor, makes his huge *oeuvre*, more than 1,500 prints, a particularly rich and authoritative documentary source of fashions during the age of Louis XIII. Such was his interest in portraying fashion for its own sake that even the figures in his religious and allegorical works are clothed in contemporary dress!

The elegant, carefree worldliness of aristocratic French male dress is delightfully rendered by Bosse in the series *Le Jardin de la Noblesse Françoise dans lequel ce peut ceuillir leur manierre de Vettements* (1629). French noblemen loved to dress up and show off. They displayed heedless extravagance, changing their wardrobe frequently because town and country *bourgeoisie* started to ape their fashions, including their rich silk fabrics. Heretofore it was possible to identify a French person's rank in society through dress but this changed under Louis XIII. The love of finery and the need to keep constantly abreast of fashion trends on the part of the nobility was carried to such extremes that much sumptuary legislation was issued. The series, *Pièces concernant la mode et les édits (éditées par LeBlond, Mariette ou Daret)*, dated about 1634, containing ten plates, of which six were drawn and engraved by Bosse, describes the consequences of Louis XIII's sumptuary legislation.[5] Bosse's *Le Courtisan suivant le dernier édit* and *La Dame réformée* show compliance to the royal writs, the costume altogether more simple, made in plain stuffs, and bereft of ornamentation. However, the edicts were not obeyed for long and the forbidden finery reappeared. It was a matter of reputation and pride to the noblemen to keep ahead in matters sartorial. Indeed, shopping had become not only a caprice but a serious occupation. The fashionable venue for shopping in Paris was the Galerie du Palais. Here were the shops where mercers, linen-drapers and textile merchants sold their wares. Bosse's splendid engraving, *La Galerie du Palais*, dated c. 1640, precisely details all the sundry accessories indispensable to the *beau monde*, such as lace, collars, cuffs and the band-boxes to put them in, gloves, fans, caps and ribbon bows or 'galants'.

Portraiture in England at the Court of Charles I

The sheer love for portraiture of the English was even stronger in the seventeenth century than it had been in the sixteenth century. And, fortunately, for the costume historian, it was the practice for painters to inscribe their portraits with a date and even the sitter's age. Attitudes had changed: court painters were no longer mere craftsmen but persons with status and influence in society. Furthermore, the sitter was as much interested in his costume as his physiognomy. Indeed, the sitter's dress became a key to representing his character. In addition, most artists and their rich clients wanted fashions to be painted with minuteness and fidelity. Such was the sober objectivity and detailed observation in seventeenth-century English portraiture that painted costumes can very often be matched with existing specimens. The embroidered linen jacket worn by Margaret Layton for her portrait painted by Marcus Gheeraerts the Younger in 1620 has already been discussed (see p28). The lush suit worn by Henry Rich, 1st Earl of Holland, for his portrait painted in the studio of Daniel Mytens inscribed 1632-33 is very similar in style to the magnificent suit of slashed yellow satin, dated c. 1630, in the collection of the Victoria and Albert Museum.

The Anglo-Dutch portrait painter Daniel Mytens was appointed 'one of our Picture Drawers' by Charles I in 1625. He was noted for his full-length portraits which were the epitome of the restrained elegance and grandeur at the court of Charles I. What Mytens lacked was variety and vigour, characteristics amply provided by Anthony Van Dyck, the Flemish painter who supplanted him in 1632. Van Dyck remained Charles I's court painter until his death in 1641. He enjoyed enormous prestige and was awarded a knighthood. During his nine years he was preoccupied almost entirely with portraiture and it is through his work that the Caroline court has been immortalized. Indeed, Charles I deserves our gratitude. With his formation of a superb collection of paintings and his patronage of Van Dyck, one of the greatest portraitists, England and English portraiture linked up with cultural Europe. The exhibition entitled *The Swagger Portrait*, held at the Tate Gallery, London in 1992, had as its sub-title *Grand Manner Portraiture in Britain from Van Dyck to Augustus John 1630-1930*. While the Tate Gallery's exhibition rushed through three centuries of noble self-aggrandisement, it is noteworthy that the swagger portrait, that is, the portrait as a public statement demonstrating social status, began with Van Dyck. His swagger portraits were showy displays of how glamour can be given expression in brushstrokes and were insightful social documents of monarchy and aristocracy. Fashions at the court depended on the monarch and his circle. Newness and diversity were ways they could set the tone and underline their superiority. This was ever more important during the reign of Charles I when the middle classes were slavishly keen to ape the fashions at court. An avid collector of paintings and a lover of masques, Charles's love of finery and application of an artistic termperament to clothes is affirmed by his wardrobe accounts.[6] The portraits of Van Dyck depict the new, relaxed sartorial atmosphere. It is the textiles, silk, satin, taffeta and lace that Van Dyck captures with such brio and finesse. Clothes at the court of Charles I were always made in the finest materials which perhaps only the rich merchant class could aspire to imitate. Lace, for which the wardrobe accounts of Charles I show that he had a great fondness, was extremely costly. It was used to make wide collars to adorn costumes for both men and women and to trim the wrists of shirts for men and the sleeves of gowns for women.

English dress was given a fillip by the marriage of Charles I to Henrietta Maria, not a Spanish Infanta, but a French princess. The French style for men and women was easy and elegant with soft, plain satins, silks and taffetas emphasizing the natural contours of the body while the large, lace collars called attention to the face. Van Dyck painted many seductive portraits of the new Queen. *The Swagger Portrait* showed as its first exhibit a portrait *Queen Henrietta Maria with Sir Jeffrey Hudson*, dated 1633, which exudes an atmosphere of *luxe et volupté*.

Wenceslaus Hollar in England

Wenceslaus Hollar was born in Prague in 1607. As a young boy he was interested in drawing. With the onset of the Thirty Years War and its repressions, he went to Frankfurt where he trained and worked as an engraver in the workshop of Matthias Merian in 1627. Hollar had already established his reputation as an etcher of small genre scenes in Cologne and elsewhere when in 1636 he met the second Earl of Arundel. He subsequently joined the Arundel household in London where he engraved a wide range of subjects from portraits to views of London. He decided to specialize in the rendering of women's dress, the first artist specifically so to do.[7]

His first English publication was a series of 26 engravings, the *Ornatus Muliebris Anglicanus*, published in 1640. The prints are small, less than six inches high, with the scope of the work expressed in the subtitle: *the Severall Habits of English Women from the Nobilite to the Country Woman as they are in these times*. Hollar depicted garments from the whole social scale, from the noblewomen attired in the high-waisted fashions associated with Queen Henrietta Maria in the portraits of her painted by Van Dyck to a country servant out shopping, carrying her basket, the embroidered hem of her dress looped up out of the mud and showing off her pattens. The series is invaluable for two reasons: for showing that sartorial distinctions between the social classes were carefully observed and for

Portrait of Henry Rich, 1st Earl of Holland, painted in the studio of Daniel Mytens, 1632-33.
The assimilation of French elegance during the reign of Charles I is evident in this suit. The doublet is deeply paned revealing an expanse of white shirt and the colour of the doublet lining, all magnificently set off by the lawn collar edged with lace. The breeches are long and full attached by hooks and eyes instead of points. The gauntlet gloves are in the English style as are the leather boots, long, high-heeled with turned-down cuffs in a scalloped pattern echoed in the lace-edged lawn boothose over them. (*National Portrait Gallery, London*)

portraying their dress in both front and back views with equal care and precision. His next series of 36 prints, the *Theatrum Mulierum*, was published in 1643, and in 1646 was enlarged to a set of 100 prints under a new title, the *Aula Veneris*. Again, the plates are small in format, being just four inches high, but the theme is much wider in scope than the *Ornatus Mulieris Anglicanus*, containing finely delineated drawings of the costumes of women in Europe. The study is largely based on Hollar's own original material – sketches he made of real women during his peregrinations around Europe – but a few of the plates are based on the work of others. Perhaps Hollar's most celebrated series is the wholly original *The Four Seasons*. These are large engravings which exist in two forms: a set of three-quarter length figures published in 1641 and a set of full-length figures published in 1643-4. The costumes, depicted with great intricacy, are most likely based on the wardrobes of the Countess of Arundel who favoured the long-waisted, pointed bodices which at first glance might seem to prognosticate the Restoration fashions of the 1660s. Although undoubtedly fashionable, showing many of the new details of women's dress of the early 1640s, the garments are probably closer to the style of Queen Anne of Denmark rather than to the French style affected at the court of Queen Henrietta Maria from which the Countess kept aloof.[8]

Certain precautions have to be applied when using the works of Hollar. He did borrow from others, including Abraham Bosse, often reversing the figures.[9] Some costume historians issue a caveat about Hollar's short-sightedness. However, while his engravings are small-scale and his figures somewhat lifeless, he nevertheless observed the fashions of the feminine world around him with exactness and flair. This is shown in his handling of

(p34) *Portrait of Charles I*, painted by Daniel Mytens, 1631. This portrait gives an excellent view of the significant elements in men's fashions at the court of Charles I: the dominance of the lace collar, the vertical slashing of the doublet allowing the shirt to show through, the full, unstiffened breeches and the soft boots, all creating a sense of ease. The points around the waist are purely decorative. Charles I's wardrobe accounts list a whole host of accessories, including the blue ribbon sash of the Garter George. The outfit, complemented by the long, flowing hairstyle with a lovelock and the Vandyke beard, evokes the casual, restrained elegance of the early Baroque style in masculine dress. *(National Portrait Gallery, London)*

(p35) *Portrait of Queen Henrietta*, painted by Sir Anthony Van Dyck, c. 1632-35.
The evolution of a new, soft, fluid line in the cut, colour and texture of female fashion is evoked in this superb portrait. The wide, lace collar, trimmed with a jewelled brooch and simple

pearls, and the puffed sleeves finished with lace emphasize a gently rounded and expansive silhouette typical of the early Baroque. The French-born Queen arranged for the tailor Monsieur Pin to come to England to make her bodices and underskirts thus guaranteeing the vogue for French styles. *(National Portrait Gallery, London)*

Portrait of Queen Henrietta Maria with Sir Jeffrey Hudson, painted by Sir Anthony Van Dyck, 1633.
The adoption by fashionable women of elements of male attire for hunting was a favourite topic of moralists. The Queen's hunting costume mirrors masculine dress in her bodice and wide-brimmed, plumed hat. Her long, curled hair with a lovelock falling over her left shoulder also echoes masculine hairstyles. Her dwarf wears a suit, lace collar and boots in the style of a man of fashion. *(National Gallery of Art, Washington, Samuel H. Kress Collection)*

Nobilis Mulier Anglica *in altilu Facinali*

the minutiae of dress. He had a predilection for the voluminous furs of the 1640s, notably the tippet and the muff, drawing them at their most luxurious at a time when accessories were of exceptional importance for fashion.[10]

Caricature

Another form of illustration, near inseparable from portraiture itself, and where fashion is a central ingredient, is caricature. Leading Italian Baroque artists including Bernini, Guercino, Pier Francisco Mola and Carlo Maratta were brilliant caricaturists, satirizing many affectations including dress. Fashionable dress, particularly among men, was caricatured in broadsheet cartoons in London in the seventeenth century, especially

from the 1640s. One such broadsheet of 1645 printed an engraving entitled 'The Habit of an English Gentleman' which ridiculed his short, be-ribboned doublet and breeches, leather boots with wide tops and foamy lace linings, long hair and patched complexion. Anonymous French artists made drawings of French court gentlemen in 1634 and in 1646 where their costume, appearance and stance are remarkably similar to the English gentlemen.

By the time of the Restoration in England male attire was being commented upon for its pronounced effeminacy. A new term, 'fop', was given to fashionable men having a feminine appearance. The scene was set for the eighteenth century, one of the great ages of caricature, when fashionable dress and hairstyles would be evergreen topics of visual satire.

Late Baroque Fashions

The reign of Louis XIV saw Paris replace Rome as the centre of the Baroque style, a development with much importance for fashion.

Male attire depicted in fashion engravings and portraits bears witness to such flamboyant outbursts as petticoat breeches festooned with ribbons and ribbon bows. Such fantastic abandon in decoration was due to the temperament of Louis XIV who would not abide plain garments and his cousin Charles II, who, after a period of impoverished exile, entered into the spirit of sartorial intoxication in the French style on the Restoration of the Stuart court in England in 1660.

Yet beneath the whirl of fanciful decoration lay precise, geometric structure. The Dutch artist, Gerard ter Borch, noted for his small portraits of elegant society distinguished by the careful treatment of their garments, painted in the early 1660s a *Portrait of a Young Man*. An aristocratic Dutch gentleman wears petticoat breeches that are copious and be-ribboned. He is also wearing ribbons round his waist and on his shirt sleeves as well as on his hat and shoes and even around his wrist. Yet his black and white outfit – from the sugarloaf hat to the lace collar, bolero jacket, petticoat breeches, and high-heeled shoes – make a series of patterns that form an exquisite diamond-

'An English Noblewoman', engraved by Wenceslaus Hollar. From his *Theatrum Mulierum*, 1643.
The back view shows the natural waistline and double sleeves, new fashion details in the mid-1640s. The pinning-up of the skirt focuses attention on the petticoat, turning an item of

underwear into a feature of fashionable dress. Outdoor accessories are the hood, a plain linen triangular collar worn over a warm kerchief and a large fur muff. Hollar's flair for capturing the texture of fur is exemplified in this engraving. *(Private Collection)*

Gasniers Tom X
Sdvé du Roi Paris

Gentilhomme d la suite de la Maries
Comtesse de Guebriant

Fashion Engraving, Portrait Painting and Fashion Journalism
in the Seventeenth Century

both recorded it precisely in their diaries. As the son of a tailor and a man of impeccable taste in clothes, Pepys wrote most interestingly and descriptively of the new fashion prescribed by Charles II. For 8 October 1666 he noted in his *Diary*:

> The King hath yesterday in Council declared his resolution of setting a fashion of clothes which he will never alter. It will be a vest, I know not well how; but it is to teach the nobility thrift, and will do good.[11]

It is a moot point whether the new style of fashion for men should be assigned to England or to France.[12] As early as perhaps 1662, a very similar vest, the *justaucorps à brevet* ('patent *justaucorps*') had been introduced by Louis

shaped silhouette.

While the geometrical structure of interlocking triangular shapes continued in male fashionable dress throughout the early 1660s sartorial folly still ran riot with yards and yards of ribbon trimming short doublets, wide petticoat breeches, shirts, hats coming high to a point, canons and high-heeled shoes.

It is not often that an exact year can be assigned to a revolution in vesture. Samuel Pepys and John Evelyn

A French Court Gentleman, drawing by an Anonymous Artist, 1646.
Here, the fashions of the French court are wittily observed. The doublet, now a short coat insouciantly unbuttoned, reveals a frothy linen shirt. The breeches, short and tubular, with a rather apron-like effect, are absurdly bedecked with *galants* or ribbons. *(Victoria and Albert Museum, London)*

Figure à la mode, engraved by Romeyn de Hooghe, Amsterdam, c. 1670.
One of a series of twelve fashion illustrations by the Dutch engraver inspired by his time spent in Paris. Manners during

the *le grand siècle* were codified and practised. When a gentleman greeted a lady he took off his hat with a theatrical flourish. For fashionable men the focus was placed upon the legs and feet through the use of petticoat breeches, heeled shoes and ribbon ties. *(Victoria and Albert Museum, London)*

Portrait of Samuel Pepys, painted by John Hayls, 1666.
The diarist is dressed in a brown silk Indian gown with wide sleeves and no lapels and a plain full shirt and loosely knotted neckcloth. This form of fashionable undress was a garment of leisure at home and suitable for receiving visitors. *(National Portrait Gallery, London)*

XIV, albeit restricted to a very few courtiers.

What is certain is that a reform of male dress had taken place, settling into a carefully planned language of clothing. The new fashion for a three-piece suit consisted of a coat, waistcoat and knee-breeches with an emphasis on structure, fit and harmony, the ultimate consequences of which can still be seen today.

Women's dress also displayed some striking changes with reform coming from the French court. For formal and court wear in England, dresses continued to consist of a separate bodice and skirt. The close-fitting, boned bodice had once again become long-waisted, coming to a deep point in front. The neckline was low-cut and plain for it was the fashion to cover it with a collar or border made of lace or with a diaphanous scarf. The skirt was gathered at the waist into small pleats and hung in loose folds to the ground. The Museum of Costume at Bath has a rare and complete example of a dress dating from the English Restoration period.

Etiquette was much stricter at the French court. In the 1680s distinctions were made between *le habit de ville*, town dress, that is fashionable dress, the *mode*, and, court dress. The distinctive *grand habit* was an official court

Two Ladies of the Lake Family, painted by Sir Peter Lely, c. 1660. The soft, voluminous fabric, low *décolletage* with an edge of linen smock falling over the bodice of the gown, and large, full sleeves, held in place by clasps, are the distinguishing features of the pseudo-classical style. The play of light and shade upon the material enhances the feeling of 'timelessness'. *(Tate Gallery, London)*

English dress of silver tissue, 1660-70.
This dress, consisting of a separate bodice and skirt, is a rare surviving specimen of women's fashion from the Restoration period in England. Because of its exceptionally fine material, silk woven with metal thread, low-cut bodice and short sleeves, it was intended for formal or court wear. The fashionable silhouette was long and rigid, with the bodice heavily boned and stiffened, and the waist sloped to a deep point at the centre front. A white linen shift was worn beneath the dress and the *décolletage* was trimmed with a deep collar of Venetian needlepoint lace. *(Museum of Costume, Bath)*

uniform which was worn right up until the French Revolution. In the presence of royalty ladies wore a long bodice mounted on a boned foundation. It had an off-the-shoulder neckline covered with a small lace border and short sleeves trimmed with lace ruffles called *engageantes*. A long train was worn over the skirt with the skirt and trimmings being allowed to follow the fashionable line. The *grand habit* was imitated at the majority of European courts, with even the Hapsburg court in Vienna, and eventually, the Spanish court jettisoning their own court dress, the latter adopting the French style in 1700 when it got a French king.

In England and France there was also a vogue for various informal styles of fashionable dress. One type was a 'timeless' pseudo-classicism. While clearly based on the same line as formal wear, this style was far less structured and controlled, having a softer, flowing line with the neckline and the sleeves the main focus for evoking the 'antique' mood. In England this feeling in dress was evoked as early as the 1630s in the portraits of Van Dyck.

By the 1660s, the 'classical' manner became studio-portrait attire in the dextrous hands of Sir Peter Lely. He was the master *par excellence* of portraying glamour and sensuality, expressing the changed atmosphere that had taken place with the English Restoration court. Horace Walpole, writing in the eighteenth century, called this dress depicted in Lely's portraits 'a sort of fantastic night-gowns (*sic*) fastened with a single pin.'[13]

Of all the beauties at the court of Charles II the one Lely painted the most often and who had the most influence on his art was Barbara Villiers, Duchess of Cleveland. She was to Lely what Lady Emma Hamilton would be to George Romney in the eighteenth century. The catalogue of *The Swagger Portrait Exhibition* points out that what has fascinated commentators most about the work of Lely is his 'juxtaposition of glowing flesh with his superb arrangement of fabrics.'[14] His portrait of Barbara Villiers shown in the exhibition relies heavily on her charms and her marvellous gold dress. Indeed, Lely painted his sitters very directly; they and their dress having something of the registrative quality of fashion

plates. After his death in 1680 a large amount of pieces of silk and satin and even whole costumes were in his studio and were subsequently sold to other painters, although for the true continuation of this tradition of dressing we have to await the work of Sir Joshua Reynolds in the 1770s.[15]

Another informal gown was the mantua or *manteau* as it was called in France, where it was a natural development from the *robe de chambre*; it was the dominant fashionable garment until the end of the reign of Louis XIV and must have come as a welcome relief to fashionable townswomen after the severely structured clothes they had had to endure. The *manteau* also presaged the lighter styles of the eighteenth century. In England, an early form of encyclopaedia entitled *An Academy of Armory*, written by Randle Holme and published in Chester in 1688, contains some excellent descriptions of women's dress including the *mantua*, 'a kind of loose Garment without, and stiffe Bodies under them, & was a great fashion for women about the year 1676. Some called them Mantuas.'[16]

Later Fashion Engraving and the Beginning of Fashion Journalism

During the reign of Louis XIV everything concerned with art and craftsmanship was minutely organized under Colbert. The Gobelins tapestry factory, for example, was taken over by Colbert on behalf of Louis XIV in 1662. In 1663 Colbert established the Manufacture des Gobelins in Paris on behalf of the King. It produced not only tapestries but also all forms of furnishings. Charles Le Brun, 'le grand peintre du grand siècle' was appointed Director, setting a tone appropriate to the grandeur of the reign of Louis XIV. *L'Histoire du Roi*, the celebrated tapestries designed by Le Brun, are an excellent visual source for showing the contrast between the outmoded styles of the Spanish aristocracy and the new fashions of the French nobility which were to spread across Europe.

Portrait of Louise de Keroualle, Duchess of Richmond, painted by Pierre Mignard, 1682.
Mignard was portrait painter to the French court rising to the position of *premier peintre*. Louise de Keroualle, a celebrated court beauty is depicted in the much-favoured 'classical', informal style of dress. Her bodice is lightly boned but not in the structured, rigid manner of formal fashionable dress.

Formal brocaded silk with a scroll design was popular in France but it was smooth and lustrous and simple in cut. Also very French is the exquisite lace which edges the neck and sleeves of her smock. The treatment of the neckline and sleeves of the ensemble are hallmarks of the pseudo-classical style. (*National Portrait Gallery, London*)

The main drawbacks of the *poupées* were their costliness and their delicacy in travel.

The last quarter of the seventeenth century saw French fashion engraving reach its peak of achievement. This was in large measure due to the *Petite Académie*. Established in 1663, this small, erudite institution was akin to a fine arts commission, advising Colbert on artistic matters and the appropriation of imagery promoted by the government. In the 1670s the *Petite Académie* permitted the printing of large quantities of fashion engravings which were avidly collected, most notably abroad by influential people as diverse as Samuel Pepys in England and royal princes in Germany, thus becoming a successful avenue for systematically advertising French styles in foreign lands. The name of the engraver, the date, the name and address of the publisher from which they were sold, were all given. The Crown authenticated each print with its own seal of approval – *avec Privilège du Roy* – both maintaining the accuracy of the print and underlining the social hierarchy of fashion. The prints themselves are exquisitely hand-coloured and are accompanied by a brief description of the dress drawn. Given the frequency of the prints and the quality of the artists – J. D. de Saint Jean (who was made an *agréé* of the *Académie Royal de Peinture et de Sculpture* in 1687), Sébastien Le Clerc (who engraved Lebrun's famous tapestry series on *L'Histoire du Roi*), Jean Le Pautre (who was connected with *Le Nouveau mercure galant*), the great Arnoult and Bonnart families, and Antoine Trouvain, whose series entitled *Appartements royaux* offers a unique insight into the court at Versailles – it must be the case that they were not only chronicling the fashions but also allying with tailors, dressmakers, and milliners, providing a wide diversity of new styles or different forms of present fashions. The fashion engravers would also have been aided by the tight organization of dress production under Colbert. In 1655 *Les Maîtres-Marchands-Tailleurs* (the Master Merchant Tailors) combined with *Les Maîtres Pourpointers* (the Master Doublet Makers) to form *Les Maîtres-Marchands Tailleurs-Pourpointers*, their new statutes granted on May 22 1660. They received letter patent giving them alone the right to produce tailored clothes, thus effectively controlling the

The word *mode* dates from this period and Paris for the first time can be called a fashion centre in the modern sense. News of French fashions were difficult to obtain and so their dissemination became precisely organized. The first fashion couriers in the seventeenth century were the *poupées* or fashion dolls, although references to these mannequins date back to the fourteenth century when they purveyed French court fashions. Two dolls, *La Grande Pandora* in the *grande toilette* and *La Petite Pandora* in *négligée*, carefully dressed by the leading Parisian dressmakers and milliners, were sent from Paris to London every month and, later, to other European capitals. They were excellent for showing the cut and the details as well as the textiles of the two styles of dress. By creating a demand for fabrics they also accelerated the growth of France's already flourishing textile industry.

Dame en echarpe, engraved by I.B.F. Bonnart, 1685.
This lady wears a large gauze scarf, patches on the face serving as ornaments, or, more vainly, to cover blemishes, a mask which either protected the complexion or preserved the wearer's anonymity, an ample lace cape, a top petticoat and a trained overskirt looped up into intricate folds, held in place by bows. *(Private Collection)*

Dame de la Cour en jupe d'hermine, engraved by N. Bonnart, 1693.
The court lady is very opulently and warmly dressed for the winter weather. Her gored skirt is made of ermine and her cuffs and bodice are fastened by cords trimmed with decorative tassels, while her fur muff is embellished with a fringed bow. She wears an extremely high *fontange* from which very large lace streamers hang which could easily be brought around the front and knotted at her throat. *(Private Collection)*

fashion trade. Colbert also gave female workers in the trade new status in 1675 when he authorized a system for sewing-women. Young girls could study cutting and dressmaking to qualify as *couturières*, or cutters/seamstresses. They could work in four areas: the *couturière en habit* made women's clothes, the *couturière en corps*

d'enfant made children's clothes, the *couturière en linge* made linen underwear and the *couturière en garniture* made trimmings.[17] Timely advice for these admirable fashion engravers would also have come from *Le Tailleur sincère*, the earliest known French treatise on tailoring published in 1671 by le Sieur Benoist Boullay, which gave detailed text and instructions on the cut of garments. A unique distinguishing feature of fashion engravings for women's dress was the frequent inclusion of pieces of fabric exactly cut to overlay within the outline engraving of a particular section of the dress. The Pierpont Morgan Library in New York has one of the greatest collections of the engravings of these late seventeenth-century French fashion artists. Many of the plates were cut away contemporaneously and backed by actual textiles of the period, enhancing the decorative character of female fashions and giving a big stimulus to the textile trade. This corpus of engravings is indispensable for dating the fashions of the later part of the reign of Louis XIV, especially their seasonal variations, and for studying the types of fashionable fabrics worn.

Another innovatory way in which French fashions were methodically and stylishly publicized abroad was through fashion journalism. Periodicals had heretofore been a masculine bastion dealing with national events, politics and wars. In 1672 a playwright *manqué*, Jean Donneau de Visé, founded a magazine, *Le Mercure galant*, which he addressed directly to fashionable ladies by providing news of the social world of the court, royal balls and masquerades, feasts, and princely marriages, as well as reviews of plays, songs, ballads and articles on fashion.[18] Donneau de Visé was responsible for editing the magazine and for writing the articles. From 1672 to 1674

Dame de la plus haute qualité, engraved by J.D. de St Jean, 1693.

A young noblewoman ultra-fashionably dressed in her *manteau* which is made of silk and has loose-fitting elbow-length sleeves and a stomacher trimmed with *échelles*, rows of ribbon bows arranged like the rungs of a ladder. The skirt is looped back to show the contrasting lining and striped brocaded silk petticoat. Her headdress is the *fontange*, a cap with four tiers of lace which are supported by a *commode*, a wired frame. Two long lace streamers fall from the sides of her face and flow down her back. *(Private Collection)*

Homme de qualité en habit d'hiver, engraved by J.D. de St Jean, 1678.

The fashion engravings of St Jean provide valuable references about the seasonal variations in dress. The long cape is edged with rich trimmings while the *justaucorps* is garnished with large buttons down the front and is left unbuttoned to show off the fully buttoned waistcoat with cuffs that turn back over the coat. Fashion interest is focused on the accessories: the lace cravat decorated here with a wide bow, the large fur muff with ribbon bow, the fringed gloves, the hat with its brim turning up at the front and back anticipating the *tricorne* and the shoes with high heels and buckles. The Baroque's heavily-laden effect on costume needed a hairstyle to match in the form of a long, full wig. *(Private Collection)*

Fashion Engraving, Portrait Painting and Fashion Journalism
in the Seventeenth Century

six numbers in all were published. In 1677 *Le Mercure galant* obtained a *Privilège du Roy* and with a dedication to the Dauphin was re-organized under a new title, *Le Nouveau mercure galant*. From 1678 to 1685 the *Extraordinaire* or supplementary numbers were published at the end of each quarter which totalled 32 numbers in all. The magazine was now an organ of modish propaganda for the French court and royal government and flourished into the 1690s with fashionable people in Berlin, Brussels, London, Madrid, Venice and Vienna informed of the latest French fashions. Donneau de Visé provided whole series of articles in which the *Extraordinaire* numbers were accompanied by fashion engravings. The names and addresses of the shops which sold the textiles and decorative trimmings of the clothes illustrated were also supplied. One of the most delightful and informative prints appeared in the *Extraordinaire* for January 1678.[19] Entitled *Intérieur d'une boutique parisienne de mode* it was engraved by Jean Le Pautre after Jean Bérain Ier, *designateur ordinaire du Cabinet du Roy*. Thirty different items of dress and twelve examples of fabric can be identified which were numbered and described in the text of the magazine. This engraving alone merits close study for the wealth of information it contains on fashionable textiles and accessories. As editor, Donneau de Visé relied on support from the fashion trade and so he frequently name-dropped. In connection with this engraving he writes, for example, that other small-patterned materials could be had from 'chez le Sieur Baroy, au Cloître Saint Opportune', and ribbons could be obtained from 'sieur le Gras' in the Palais Royal itself. He warmly thanked M. Bérain Ier for making the drawing and M. Le Pautre for engraving it while tantalizing the ladies by saying that the two artists did not have time to do more work 'because the Spring fabrics have only just begun to appear.'[20]

Le Nouveau mercure galant was the first modern-style magazine in its fashion coverage. It gave exact descriptions of clothing appropriate for formal and informal dress including their seasonal variations noting, in particular, types of materials. New fashions for the following season or year were published or advertised. All these innovations on the part of the editor showed keen judgement and met with success, further boosting the French textile industry and the sphere of influence of French fashion. The periodical had no immediate followers, being alone in publishing and advertising new fashions and in giving fashion news in advance. The only other printed sources for providing fashion information were the annual almanacs and the individual fashion engravings of the artists. *Le Nouveau mercure galant* has a special place in the annals of fashion literature and fashion illustration for being the first, and for nearly a century, the only magazine to feature and illustrate articles on contemporary fashions.

(p48) *Homme de qualité sur le théâtre de l'Opéra*, engraved by J.D. de St Jean, 1687.
This 'man of quality' sports a new style of wig, the *perruque in-folio*, where the long curls are brought forward over the shoulder, and is counterbalanced by a large hat curved up and adorned with ostrich feathers and coloured ribbons. The same arrangement can be seen in the cravat and knot of ribbons. This engraving reflects how an exuberance and extravagance in taste could be imposed on the formalization of the *justaucorps* and waistcoat through the use of lavish amounts of metallic lace and bullion fringe, echoed even in the trimming of the gloves. *(Private Collection)*

(p49) *Homme de qualité en habit garny d'agrémens*, engraved by J.D. de St Jean, 1693.
A casual elegance distinguishes the dress of this young nobleman. The vast expanse of his impeccable white linen shirt is partially filled by his long, linen Steinkirk cravat. This cravat is thought to have taken its name from the famous battle of 1692 when French soldiers, surprised by the enemy, hurriedly put their cravats through the buttonholes in their coats to be ready to face their opponents. His *habit d'agrément* (informal suit) is worn without a waistcoat and with loose-fitting breeches. Interest in his *justaucorps* focuses on the pockets. Slit vertically until 1690, they are now horizontal with flaps added. *(Victoria and Albert Museum, London)*

Intérieur d'une boutique parisienne de mode, engraved by Jean Le Pautre after Jean Bérain Ier. From *Le Nouveau mercure galant*, *Extraordinaire de janvier* 1678.
The *boutique* contains bolts of floral fabrics which were popular for women in the 1660s and 1670s, but the fashionable lady shopping wears a petticoat made of striped material, the favourite design of the 1680s. Other female items include slippers, gloves, ruchings, ribbons, caps, bows and scarves such as the lady shopper is wearing. For the man of fashion there are boots, shoes, wigs, cravats with their strings in bows, scarves, sashes, gloves, shallow-crowned hats, and petticoat breeches with ribbons. *(B.T. Batsford Ltd Archive)*

3: The Flowering of Fashion Illustration in the Eighteenth Century

The End of the Reign of Louis XIV

At the beginning of the eighteenth century the court of Louis XIV at Versailles was firmly established as the centre for art, culture and fashion. French fashions and *le grand habit* dominated at the courts right across Europe. Spain, Austria, Prussia and Saxony, Sweden and Russia slavishly copied France. The court at Versailles, however, was no longer the scene of gaiety and pleasure. Louis XIV was now an old monarch, preoccupied with pious virtue, as was his mistress and clandestine second wife, Mme de Maintenon. Her devoutness determined the lifestyle and the wardrobe of the King and his courtiers. The closing years of the reign of Louis IV, and the end of the Late Baroque style in fashion, were characterized by rigidity and dignity. While the fabrics were lavish enough, the general appearance was one of stiffness and formality. Mme de Maintenon saw that women's fashions reflected a similar sense of restraint and grandeur.

These formal images of the court are most successfully conveyed in the portraits of Nicolas de Largillière. One of the ablest and most prolific portrait painters of the later part of the age of Louis XIV, he purveyed the last phase of the Late Baroque style, known as classic Baroque. The sitters are dressed in heavy, pompous clothes, echoed in their furniture and palatial interiors.

While the end of the seventeenth century had a relatively large number of artists producing engravings of the

Portrait of Prince James Francis Edward Stuart and his sister Louisa Maria Theresa, painted by Nicolas de Largillière, 1695. The Stuart children were in exile in France and wear the structured fashion of the French court. Princess Louisa wears a *fontage* headdress, a stiff-bodied gown with a long-trained skirt which French noble ladies wore on great royal occasions and a lace apron. The Prince wears his own hair but it is in the style of the fashionable full-bottomed *perruque en crinière*. His *justaucorps* has large sleeve cuffs and stiffened skirt. His brocaded waistcoat has sleeves with deep cuffs turned over those of the *justaucorps*. Across his *justaucorps* is the blue sash and Garter order. The Prince's lace cravat is offset by a series of bows. The suits, sword and his rigid stance reflect the formality at the French court. *(National Portrait Gallery, London)*

Portrait of Louis XIV and his Heirs, painted by Nicolas de Largillière, 1710.
The grandson of Louis XIV, Louis, duc de Bourgogne, on the right, is more fashionably up-to-date than his elders, the King and the Dauphin. His *justaucorps* with its horizontal pockets and large buttoned-back cuffs matching the waistcoat displays a new direction in its velvet fabric and relative simplicity. He is also wearing a Steinkirk cravat, low-heeled shoes, and a lower-style *perruque*. The stately governess, the duchesse de Ventadour, is dressed very soberly in her *grand habit* and *fontanges*. Louis XIV's great-grandson, the young duc de Bretagne, the future Louis XV, is still in a long dress and leading strings. The three heirs of Louis XIV portrayed here, all died before him. *(Reproduced by permission of the Trustees of the Wallace Collection, London)*

French style of dress, illustrations of fashion on paper are less fully recorded at the start of the eighteenth century. There are few costume plates as such. Fortunately for the costume historian, Bernard Picart drew and engraved a collection of 74 plates which appeared in different series but which collectively are entitled *Diverses modes dessinées d'après nature*. Published retrospectively in Amsterdam in 1728 they constitute a most valuable visual encyclopaedia of modes. After Picart's death in 1733 his widow compiled a catalogue where she listed the plates with their dates by series.[1] The vivacity of Picart's technique was sustained by precise drawing, minute attention to detail and a form of elegance that announces the spirit of early eighteenth-century France and the work of Jean-Antoine Watteau. Picart's drawings of figures in casual poses and softer styles of dress show that, far from disappearing as Louis IV and Mme de Maintenon would have wished, informality had been ushered in with the new century.

Louis XV and the Rococo

On the death of Louis XIV in 1715 his five-year-old great-grandson became Louis XV. Philippe, duc d'Orléans, the uncle of Louis XV, was appointed Regent during the minority of the young King. The period from the death of Louis IV to the death of Philippe, duc d'Orléans is known as *La Régence* (1715-23). While Louis IV had given France a most magnificent period of *gloire* in all the arts, including costume, he had also left debts totalling 2,000 million *livres* caused by his involvement in wars, building programmes and the way of life of *Le Roi Soleil* at Versailles. The nation felt a sense of gloom as a result of the war of Spanish Succession (1701-13) and the death of the King's three heirs. Yet it also felt a sense of relief. One of the first acts of the Regent was to close the *château* of Versailles and move the court back to Paris to the Palais Royal. It was a move which saved millions in the aftermath of the lifestyle of pomp and splendour at Versailles. The economy, though devastated, had a basic soundness which assisted a moderately fast recovery. The Regent also had the benefit of a system of government that had been professionally developed under Louis XIV. Philippe was a man of taste and a connoisseur which ensured a highly civilized court and patronage of the arts. The Regent's many mistresses contributed to the female dominance of the court which would accelerate under Louis XV and lead to a highly cultivated development of fashion.

The establishment of the court at the Palais Royal signalled a shift of power to a new centre, to 'society'. Not only courtiers but also bankers and businessmen connected with the court built their houses in Paris and had them decorated in the lightness and gracefulness of the new style, Rococo. *Le style Régence* marked a transition from the heaviness and weightiness of the Late Baroque to the lightness and gracefulness of the Rococo, a style which was fully established by 1730. Rococo, which derives from the French word *rocaille*, meaning rock-work, was essentially a style of interior decoration. The interiors of these town houses were most elegant, comprising asymmetrical, softly undulating and curving architectural forms and the use of ornamental motifs such as foliage and S- and C-shapes including shells, bat wings and palm branches. The attributes of delicacy, playfulness, wit and the ornamental breaking up of the surface were also admirably exemplified in furniture, porcelain, gold and silversmiths' work and in the painting, sculpture and costume of the period. A new dimension to the Rococo style, or the *style Louis Quinze*, a synonymous label, was added with the opening up of trade to the Orient. Chinese influence manifested itself in a design style known as *chinoiserie*. Fanciful Chinese landscapes peppered with colourfully-dressed mandarins, pagodas and parasols were some of the Oriental, ornamental effects that featured in the Rococo/ *style Louis Quinze*.

When the Regent moved the court from Versailles to Paris the capital became the centre of art and politics. The King and his court lost their stranglehold on the patronage of the arts. Not just the aristocracy but the rich, merchant-middle class and the financiers could become art collectors and patrons. The same artist could be employed by the King and a banker. In addition, the Paris *salons* under the aegis of women were introducing new ideas on art, behaviour and costume, for the art of fashion became a part of good manners and deportment a necessary element of polite society.

There wer few, formal, ceremonial occasions when women would have to be presented to the child-King dressed in *le grand habit*. The rigid etiquette of the court had eased, even if Madame, widow of Monsieur, brother of Louis XIV, demanded that women coming to see her wear *le grand habit*. The most typical gown was the *sacque*, a loose gown which flared out at the bottom, the back

attached to the neckband with gathers at first, then with pleats, and the front either seamed from just below the waist or open to show off the petticoat. This garment had several stages in its development, starting well before 1715, and a variety of names assigned to it. At first it was intended for *negligée*, a term used for informal attire. The early *sacque* was the *contache*, perhaps derived from the Polish word *kontusz*, a loose, cone-shaped garment with hanging or split sleeves, rather akin to the caftan, which was put on over the head. The theatre contributed an interpretation with the *andrienne*, a shapeless gown worn by the actress Mme Marie Dancourt in 1703 in Terence's *Andriana*. Madame, in a letter written in 1721, said the inventor of the *robe battante* was Mme de Montespan in order to camouflage her many pregnancies by Louis XIV[2]. *Robe battante* meant 'ringing gown' implying its bell shape. Another contemporary reference, in *Le Mercure de France* in 1729, referred to the *robe volante* as being universally worn. The name of the *robe volante* or 'flying' denoted its floating movement. Yet another version was the *robe retroussé dans les poches*, meaning 'gown turned up into the pockets', for the fullness of the back material was caught up into slits that were placed in the skirt to give access to the pockets which were placed under the *paniers*.

To fill out the early *sacque*, a gum-stiffened petticoat called a *criarde* was worn, so-called because of the noise it made. Following the *criarde* came the *paniers*, a round underskirt stretched out over metal hoops. *Paniers* was an apt name because of its basket-like shape. It was towards 1720 that the *sacque*'s pleats became more formalized, falling in a graceful but more fitted manner.

The essential lines of men's fashionable dress, comprising a coat, waistcoat and breeches, had become established at the beginning of the eighteenth century and did not alter dramatically. The emphasis was placed upon trimmings on the coat and waistcoat in the form of braid and embroidery which were applied down the centre fronts, the centre backs from the waist downwards, in and around the pockets and on the cuffs. Large floral silks were often used to make the coat and breeches but by the end of the second decade of the eighteenth century such floral designs were mostly reserved for the waistcoat. In the 1720s women's silks with small floral motifs were especially woven for men's suits and their designs did not change significantly in the first half of the eighteenth century. Clothes for men were rich and the relationship between the courtiers and the wealthy merchant-middle class and financiers who could afford them were close. Even after Louis XV returned to Versailles, the relationship between court and upper *bourgeoisie* endured.

Fashion Engraving and Portrait Painting in France and England

The artist who, in his *sanguine* drawings and in paintings such as *L'Enseigne de Gersaint* (1720) most exquisitely captured the elegant, flowing quality of the *sacque*, was Jean-Antoine Watteau, one of the key artists of the Rococo. Indeed, the *sacque* is often called the 'Watteau gown' and the distinctive pleats, *plis Watteau*. One of the triumphs of Rococo fashion illustration and a masterpiece of graphic art is Watteau's *Figures de différentes Caractères*, which was commissioned by his close friend, Jean de Jullienne. Along with three other friends of Watteau, de Jullienne received the artist's drawings

Gilles and His Family, painted by Jean-Antoine Watteau, c. 1716. Watteau was the first artist to be described as a *peintre des fêtes galantes*. The *fête galante* joined together real and dream-like motifs, the sources being the theatre, the *bal costumé*, and aristocratic amorous dalliances set in an Arcadian landscape. The influence of the *commedia dell'arte* on the *fête galante* is vividly depicted here, especially in the picturesquely-costumed central figure of Gilles (Pierrot). The melancholic lady on the left wears the most fashionable garment of Watteau's time, the *sacque*, the loose pleats falling from the shoulders in the back, and becoming lost in the folds of the gown. *(Reproduced by permission of The Trustees of The Wallace Collection, London)*

Before the great age of the fashion plate, illustrations on paper lack continuity and there is a discernible gap in the first quarter of the eighteenth century. They did not begin to flourish again until the mid-1720s. François Octavien, although not a pupil of Watteau, is considered one of his best imitators in evoking the fashions and mood of this early period. In 1725 he drew and engraved a series of five plates describing the fashions of both women and men which was published under the title *Figures Françoises Nouvellement inventées par Octavien*. Although small in format (260 x 175 mm) they are carefully observed and are especially commendable for the details of dress and their accessories. A landmark is reached in 1729 by Antoine Hérisset *le père* with his set of twelve drawings which he engraved for his *Recueil des différentes modes du temps*. The title page/frontispiece is important because Hérisset's engravings of garments and accessories could be had from him, *chez un fripier*, that is, a clothes-dealer. Copies were made of Hérisset which seem to have been sold as fashion illustrations for the *fripier*, named as Jacques Chéreau. The engravings are meticulously drawn and show front and back views as well as indicating fabrics. There are some five versions of the *Recueil* of which one is said to have been printed in Germany, making it most likely that some descriptions were prepared for the export market.[3] Hérisset was exceedingly up-to-the-minute, for instance, illustrating a group of men wearing *redingotes*. In 1728 the *Mercure de France*, the direct successor of *Le Nouveau mercure galant*, pointed out that the *redingote*, a heavy, wide-cut coat for men, was a new fashion from England.

In France, the lacunae in fashion engraving can easily be filled in by the large number of marvellous painters who rendered the fashions so fastidiously in their paintings. To Jean-Antoine Watteau can be added François de Troy, Nicolas Lancret, Jean-Baptiste Pater, Jean-Marc Nattier, François Boucher, François-Hubert Drouais and Louis Carrogis, called Louis de Carmontelle.

just before the artist died in 1721. As a *homage* to Watteau, de Jullienne decided to have the drawings engraved and published as a book. He gave the work to the publisher and engraver, Jean Audran, who commissioned eleven other artists to engrave the drawings. Amongst them was François Boucher who worked on about 150 of the 351 plates. The book was published in two volumes in 1726 and 1728 as is shown in the advertisements in *Le Mercure de France*. It had a profound effect on all later eighteenth-century artists and remains one of the most accurate records for fashion during the period.

Portrait of Madame Marsollier and Her Daughter, painted by Jean-Marc Nattier, 1749.
It was at the court of Louis XV that a fashionable ceremony was established: visiting a lady at her *toilette* where she had on display a sumptuous silver or silver-gilt toilet service in keeping with her social standing. The most lavish services had to include a large mirror, variously shaped boxes, a jewel case, a glove stand, a pin cushion and clothes brush. The boxes were used for powder, patches, feathers, creams, combs, soaps, and sponges. Nattier brilliantly evokes the new casual elegance in his subject and setting, painting a mother with her daughter in her boudoir. *(The Metropolitan Museum of Art, New York, Bequest of Florence S. Schuette, 1955)*

La Modiste (La marchande de modes. Le Matin), ascribed to François Boucher, 1746.
The *modiste* or *marchande de modes* was a veritable artist in fashion, creatively decorating dresses, petticoats and hats with all manner of trimmings – gauzes, ribbons, nets, pieces of fabric, fur. She also made some articles of dress such as the cape (*mantelet*), the pelisse (*plisse*) and the court mantilla (*mantille de cour*). Boucher's observation clearly conveys the colours and textures as well as the pleasures of fashionable, aristocratic life. *(Reproduced by permission of The Trustees of The Wallace Collection, London)*

François Boucher was the son of a designer of embroideries, who worked first as an etcher-engraver-illustrator. He engraved much of Watteau's work and mastered every branch of the arts including designs for fans, slippers, tapestries and porcelain. Boucher was the favourite artist of Louis XV's mistress, Mme de Pompadour, whom he painted several times and to whom he gave lessons. This most remarkable woman stands out as the arbiter, indeed the embodiment and sustainer, of Rococo taste, so much so that *le style Louis Quinze* is often called *le style Pompadour*. Her elegance, wit and charm not only made her the favourite mistress of

Portrait of the marquise de Pompadour, painted by François Boucher, 1759.

The marquise wears the *robe à la française*, the gown she popularized during her lifetime. The marquise's has a square neckline and a fitted bodice fastened on either side of the *échelles*. The sleeves are short and narrow, reaching to the elbows just above the lace *engageantes*. The skirt of the *robe à la française* opens out over a *jupe* lavishly garnished with flounces, ribbons, and floral-patterned blonde-silk lace. Small *paniers* support the gown at the sides under the petticoat. The marquise's *robe à la française* is the definitive fashion statement of the Rococo style of which she was patronness. François Boucher was the artist *par excellence* of the Rococo, who had a genius for interpreting its dominant fashion features: a concentration on curvilinear forms and three-dimensional trimmings and a delight in the tactile qualities of fabrics. He also shows dress as an integral part of the whole, harmonizing with the flowers, foliage, garden furniture and sculpture. *(Reproduced by permission of the Trustees of the Wallace Collection)*

Portrait of Madame Favart, painted by François-Hubert Drouais, 1757.

With the coming to maturity of Louis XV, rules governing court life and court etiquette returned. The *sacque* became more formal: fitted to the waist and with the bodice cut separately and seamed to the skirt, it was known all over Europe as the *robe à la française*. Drouais's portrait of the famous French actress sitting in a slightly-turned position allows us to see clearly the construction of the bodice, the pleats flowing from the shoulders and the three-tiered lace ruffles called *engageantes* below the self-ruffles of the sleeves of the dress. Mme Favart's powdered hair is swept and waved back away from the face in the style known as the *pompadour*. *(The Metropolitan Museum of Art, New York. Mr and Mrs Isaac Fletcher Collection)*

the King but also the real power behind the throne. She was an ardent patron of the new learning of the Enlightenment and her unique position at the court of Louis XV enabled her to support *philosophes* and encyclopaedists, most notably Voltaire and Diderot. She oversaw a cultural flowering of supreme luxury and sophistication in the arts. In fashion Mme de Pompadour brought the *robe à la française* to such a state of beauty and grace that it was worn all over Europe until well into the 1770s and was practically synonymous with French national dress. Derived from the *sacque* it was a formal gown with a *jupe* (petticoat or underskirt), fitted tight to the waist, with a stomacher pinned to the sides of the bodice decorated with rungs of ribbon bows with yet more bows adorning the sleeves and voluminous *engageantes*, lace cuffs with two or three tiered ruffles which finished the sleeves.

François-Hubert Drouais trained under Boucher. His portraits allow one to see very clearly the construction of the *robe à la française* in such magnificent portraits as those of Mme de Pompadour and the actress Mme Favart.

Louis de Carmontelle specialized in a technique called *aux trois crayons* which Watteau had made popular in the early part of the eighteenth century. Carmontelle painted charming studies of the aristocracy where the *robe à la française* can be seen to advantage. It is significant that Pierre de La Mésangère, editor of the influential and widely-circulated *Le Journal des dames et des modes*, bought 520 portraits by Carmontelle.[4]

In England there was a dearth of both fashion engraving and portrait painting in the first quarter of the eighteenth century. Horace Walpole later attributed the decline in painting to the virtual grip that Sir Geoffrey Kneller had had on portraiture, churning out mechanical poses on a mass-produced scale. As for attitudes to dress by artists, *The Spectator*, in its number for 28 July 1712, wrote

> Great Masters in Painting never care for drawing People in the Fashion; as very well knowing that the Head-dress or Periwig that now prevails and gives a Grace to their Portraiture at present, will make a very odd Figure and perhaps look monstrous, in the Eyes of Posterity. For this reason they very often represent an

illustrious Person in a *Roman* Habit, or in some other dress that never varies. [5]

In many of his portraits Sir Joshua Reynolds used 'classical' draperies to achieve this 'timeless' dress, using Lely as an inspiration. Timelessness was also a theme he lectured on in his *Discourses* delivered to students at the Royal Academy. Timelessness was also achieved through a return to themes such as the Gothic and the Oriental, the popularity of masquerades enhancing this feeling.

Portrait of the Princesse de Salm Seated with her Son, the Prince de Salm, by a Chinese Pavilion. Black lead, red chalk and watercolour drawing by Louis Carrogis, called Carmontelle, 1770.
This side view of the Princesse de Salm again shows the beauty of the *robe à la française*. Particularly exquisite are the sea of trimmings that decorate the dress from the bodice to the hem. The young prince is the zenith of noble magnificence in his ornate three-piece suit, the *habit à la française*, with the coat long and straight in cut. He wears a bag-wig where the *queue* or pigtail is enclosed in a square black silk bag drawn in at the nape of the neck with a running string which is concealed by a stiff black bow. *(Christie's Images, London)*

The miniaturist and enameller Bernard Lens dealt with the contemporary. Headdresses for women and hairstyles for men were the theme of his series of pen-and-ink drawings: *The Exact Dress of the Head, Drawn from Life at Court, Opera, Theatre, Park & c. By Bernard Lens, in the years 1725 & 1726 from the Quality & Gentry of ye British Nation.* It consists of 29 pages, the first 25 devoted to drawings of women's caps and lappets and the last four to gentlemen's wigs, with one braided, shallow three-cornered hat shown, with another such hat adorning the cartouche on the title-page. One of the disadvantages of the series is that there are no captions or descriptions.

Perhaps Lens thought the verbose title commentary enough! In total there are 87 half-length studies, each only about 5 x 3½ inches. Yet they are never monotonous for they show precise differences in the arrangement of the fashions in female headwear and male hairstyles for the years 1725 and 1726.

In the 1720s and 1730s, with the introduction of a particularly English genre, the conversation piece, groups of people rather self-consciously gathered in an indoor or outdoor setting, a good overview can be obtained of the fashions of the upper and middle classes.

During the second half of the century the Grand Tour was *de rigeur* for aristocratic Englishmen and provided an occasion for recording their dress. When culminating their tour in Rome, Pompeo Batoni was the painter they sought out. He painted them either wearing their own fashionable suits or in the Italian taste. Batoni was a talented draughtsman and a costume study in chalk of an oil painting of an Englishman dressed in fashionable attire, dated about 1751 survives. These artists are important to the history of fashion for three reasons: for filling the gap in visual sources, for having a fresh eye with which to scrutinize English dress and manners, and, through their teaching, for helping to promote native artists to carry on their work.

Hubert-François Gravelot came to London from France in 1733. The son of a Parisian tailor and a pupil of François Boucher, Gravelot was a notable designer and engraver of book illustrations. He was one of the first artists to illustrate a new literary form, the novel, examples including Samuel Richardson's *Pamela* (1742) and Henry Fielding's *Tom Jones* (1750). Gravelot became a friend of William Hogarth whose early training and work was infused with the Rococo style that the Frenchman had introduced into England. Hogarth himself visited Paris in 1743 and again in 1748. Hogarth was an artist of stories and much can be gleaned from his work through his skilful rendering of dress: an individual's personality and status can be pinpointed, a moral about society elucidated, or a corrupt social practice pointed out.

Gravelot was the teacher of two of the leading English exponents of the Rococo style, Francis Hayman and Thomas Gainsborough. Hayman's charming Rococo conversation pieces influenced the early small portrait groups of Gainsborough who almost certainly worked with him in Gravelot's studio. Gainsborough's move to Bath in 1759 made him the most stylish society portrait painter of his day and he was also unofficial court painter to George III and Queen Charlotte.

While his rival Sir Joshua Reynolds could indeed paint portraits where costume is accurately and exquisitely rendered, as in his *Portrait of Nelly O'Brien*, Gainsborough was, in general, superior to Reynolds in the actual handling of dress. Gainsborough's elegant manner of rendering fashions can be appreciated not only in his paintings but also in his drawings. The exhibition,

Drawings from the J. Paul Getty Museum, held at the Royal Academy of Arts in London in 1993-94 had this caption for Gainsborough's *Study of a Seated Woman* (see p64):

This drawing was made about 1765-70 either from life or from a costumed doll. The intentionally vague features of the sitter and the elaborate, highly worked drapery indicate this was a costume study.

The sitter's costume is similar to that worn by Mary, Countess Howe in the portrait Gainsborough painted of her c. 1763-64. The Iveagh Bequest, Kenwood, London holds both the painting and a replica of the costume

'An English Lady and Gentleman', drawn by Hubert-François Gravelot and engraved by L. Truchy, 1744-45.
This study, annotated as being drawn *ad vivum*, from life, combines English informality with French elegance. She wears a fitted English gown with plain robings and with sleeves that have winged cuffs permitting the ruffles of her shift to show underneath. A plain linen neckerchief covers her bodice, held in place by a band across the robings, matching her long apron. A small linen cap and a hat are worn over her French *tête-de-mouton* hairstyle. The English gentleman wears a long coat and long waistcoat. With informal dress the frills on the shirt take the place of the cravat. His hair is arranged in the curly *aile-de-pigeon* (pigeon wing) style over his temples and is worn with a *queue*. (Victoria and Albert Museum, London)

complete with *fichu*, apron and undergarments, and accessories of shoes, pearls, and black wrist bands. The *oeuvre* of Gravelot which is most insightful for his crucial link with Anglo-French fashions and fashion illustration is his series of engravings of English fashions published in London in 1744-5. They are studies of English men and women drawn after three lay figures wearing clothes that cover the gamut of social occasions from city-life to the theatre. As English fashions were far more informal than French ones, Gravelot was

Portrait of Maurice Greene, painted by Francis Hayman, 1747. The nightgown, or banyan, was highly fashionable for informal wear. Hayman's portrait shows the Professor of Music at Cambridge (on the left) in the 'undress' of a fine red damask banyan. Loose and straight-cut, it was a style favoured by artists and intellectuals. Turbans or nightcaps were worn indoors to keep the shaven head warm when the wig was removed. *(National Portrait Gallery, London)*

Portrait of Nelly O'Brien, painted by Sir Joshua Reynolds, 1762-64.
The gown of this famous eighteenth-century beauty is made of crisp, striped silk, a material and pattern much in favour in the 1760s. The bodice is laced across in front fastened by metal eyes rather than backlaced, contributing to both her comfort and the informality of her dress. A typical English feature is the very expansive quilted silk petticoat. The fine brocaded silk gauze apron was a luxury object for chic women and a little shoulder mantle made of black Chantilly lace was very *soignée*. Her hair is unpowdered and worn with a winged, wired cap edged with lace and a straw hat known as a mushroom or shepherdess hat, trimmed with blue silk ribbons, another English fashion. The necklace may be of imitation pearls called French beads. *(Reproduced by permission of the Trustees of The Wallace Collection)*

but were in fact produced by European manufactories, notably Lyon and Spitalfields. Bizarre silk designs were always exotic and oddly shaped, hence the name given to them by contemporaries, and had a marked diagonal movement, a manifestation of the Rococo taste for asymmetry.

Lyon had a whole school of talented illustrators-designers. By about 1730 the most outstanding of these artists was Jean Revel. Revel invented a process called *points rentrés* which consisted of mixing and blending colours making it possible to 'paint' on the loom, that is, to weave blurred colour effects. This technique allowed the silk weaver to simulate the shading and volume that objects have in real life. Another was Jean Pillement, an imaginative artist whose impact on silk design was conveyed through his books of engravings, one of the most influential being *Fleures idéales*. He drew Eastern-inspired floral designs and *chinoiseries*.

Because of the trend for informal styles and the craze for *chinoiserie*, printed cottons and fine muslins also became fashionable textiles. Printed textiles were established at Marseille, the French port in proximity with the East. Opposition from the silk weavers and the East India Company had always been intense and as far back as October 1686 Louis XIV had issued a decree prohibiting the manufacture or sale of painted cloths. However, as fashions simplified and printed cottons flourished due to the development of the techniques of the protected manufacturers, the ban on fabric painting in France was lifted on 5 September 1759. The most celebrated of all the printed textile manufactories was the Manufacture Oberkampf de Jouy-en-Josas near Versailles. The first Oberkampf-designed, engraved, printed and dyed cotton was produced in May 1760. Success was immediate and Jouy became the outstanding centre of artistic creativity for motifs, colours, and technique. The German-born Christophe-Philippe Oberkampf, director of the printed fabric works at Jouy, invented wooden blocks that had to be laid on by hand so as to make the design of a *toile de Jouy* continuous. He used engraved copper plates, rollers and dyes of such high quality that the distinctive, richly-coloured *toiles* had a veritable countrified look. Jouy *indiennes* form graceful, unified compositions distributed on the *toile* with technical virtuosity. What Oberkampf achieved was truly remarkable, the re-invention of techniques originally employed in India but banned in France to protect the home textile industry. The

instrumental, when he returned to Paris in 1746, in introducing the English mode which would turn into Anglomania later in the century. Gravelot is also a catalyst for the great revival of the graphic fashion record that ensued in the second half of the century when arbiters on both sides of the Channel, many of them highly specialized, really come to the fore. An early example is Jean Le Gros with his *Livre d'estempes de l'art de la coiffure des dames françoises* which was published in Paris in 1765.

Fabrics, Pattern Books and Specimens of Dress

An experimental and effervescent transitional phase in fabric design had set in against the austerity of the Late Baroque style. Bizarre silks, popular as dress materials and waistcoats, were believed to have come from India

Study of a Seated Woman, drawn in chalk by Thomas Gainsborough, c. 1765-70.
While the features of the sitter are vague and she has the pose of an articulated doll, the costume is a graphic *tour-de-force*. Her gown, which is voluminously cut, suggests it was made for a hoop petticoat. It has plain trimmings with ribboned robings down the side. A shoulder mantle covers the bodice. (*Collection of the J. Paul Getty Museum, Malibu, California*)

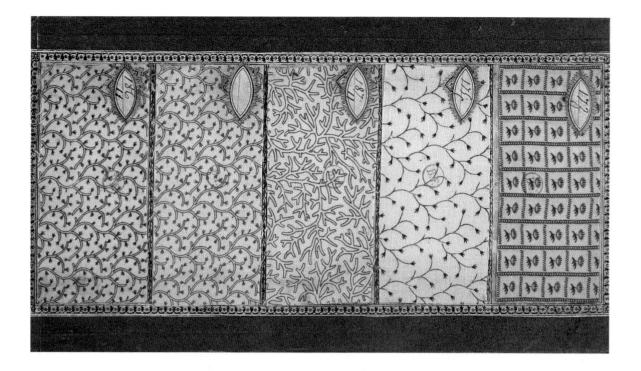

Manufacture Oberkampf was created a *manufacture royale* in 1783. Oberkampf shrewdly survived the French Revolution and his manufactory continued under the Consulate and Empire.

In England, designs in silk for the Court and fashionable society were woven at Spitalfields, a district just outside London. Lyon's output was rivalled only by Spitalfields. During the early part of the eighteenth century most motifs were influenced if not slavishly copied from French silks, but by around the middle of the century Spitalfields underwent a quest for three-dimensional floral naturalism exhibited with the same Rococo asymmetry. And, again like its French counterpart, it encountered around 1760 competition with printed cottons.

Pattern books compiled by individuals during the eighteenth century provide a good deal of information on the interaction of fabrics and fashion. One of the most accomplished was assembled by Barbara Johnson (1738–1825), daughter of a vicar of Olney, Buckinghamshire. She began collecting samples of fabric from her dresses in 1751, when she was only thirteen years old. She often noted full details of the lengths and

widths of the fabrics used together with their prices. Diaries, letters and accounts also give the styles of the dresses, their cost and their number, as well as the names of the fabrics. The album is in the collection of the Victoria and Albert Museum, London. Miss Johnson provides an invaluable link between fabrics and fashion illustration for she often interspersed fashion engravings from pocket books amongst her samples of fabrics. Appearing in pocket books from the 1750s onwards, these fashion engravings have often been overlooked, perhaps because they are small in format and uncoloured.

However, pocket books enjoyed a large circulation in the eighteenth and early nineteenth century and the fashion illustrations contained in them are 'a surer guide to what was generally worn than the more elaborate plates and they relate more closely to much surviving dress.'[6] Even though pocket books gave their information only from year to year, the number issued meant that collectively they provide a good deal of information on fashion at a time when fashion journalism was in its incipient stage.

In France dress was a ritualized way of life. A rigid line was maintained between formal and informal dress. At

Toile de Jouy, with the distinctive dense patterns of richly-coloured floral motifs, from the Manufacture Oberkampf de Jouy-en-Josas. Although many superb designs of different types were produced at Jouy, the most glorious are the early floral motifs, so reminiscent of their Indian cousins. These *toiles* were produced in the factory by wood blocks. Oberkampf's emphasis was always on quality of design, engraving, dyeing and printing. *(Bibliothèque Forney, Paris)*

The Flowering of Fashion Illustration in the Eighteenth Century

the apex of the social structure was the court of King Louis XVI and Queen Marie-Antoinette, the court firmly established once again at Versailles after the interval following Louis XIV's death. The strong leadership in fashion and taste was provided by Queen Marie-Antoinette. Mme Campan, *première femme de chambre de Marie-Antoinette*, has left detailed descriptions of the Queen's daily life. The conservation of her dresses, of which Mme Campan relates that the Queen ordered on average 150 per year, and their daily use according to her engagements, called for meticulous attention in themselves.

Every morning the wardrobe valet on duty presented to the principal *femme de chambre* a book, to which were attached samples of the dresses, formal robes, informal dresses, etc . . . a small portion of the material showed of what kind it was. The principal *femme de chambre* presented that book to the Queen on her awakening, together with a pin-cushion. Her Majesty put pins in everything she wanted for the day: one in the formal robe she wished to wear, one in the informal dress for the afternoon, one in the decorated dress for the hours of play or for supper in the *petits appartements*. The book

(p66) *Robe volante* of embroidered muslin, 1730s. Naturalistic flowers were favourite embroidery motifs. Books of engravings of flowers were sources useful to embroiderers and embroidery patterns began to appear in periodicals such as *The Lady's Magazine* of the early 1760s. This was a completely new departure anticipating the giving away of embroidery patterns with *The Lady's Magazine* from 1770. (*Museum of Costume, Bath*)

(p67) Double sleeve ruffle of white embroidered muslin, c. 1750. Whitework was another form of embroidery in vogue during the eighteenth century. These fine muslin sleeve ruffles are embroidered in white thread in small, delicate floral designs. Light ornamental fillings have also been added. Such airy white embroidery enhanced the colour of the garments

and was also a fashionable alternative to lace. (*Museum of Costume, Bath*)

Blue satin shoe and paste and metal buckles, c. 1750. From the *Régence* to the French Revolution the style of women's shoes changed very slightly. The fashion was for shoes which were high-heeled with the toe pointed and slightly turned-up. Shoes were made either of satin or silk as leather was not at all common until the end of the eighteenth century. Both women and men fastened their shoes over the instep with buckles. Buckles were the focus of interest of footwear and were made in various sizes and materials. Considered as pieces of jewellery in their own right, buckles were completely removable and interchangeable and kept in specially-made satin-lined boxes. (*Museum of Costume, Bath*)

was taken back to the wardrobe, and there soon appeared, in large sheets of taffeta, everything that was necessary for the day.[7]

These books were in the care of Madame la comtesse d'Ossun. One of them, for the year 1782, still exists, and is located in the Archives Nationales in Paris. Stuck on every page are samples of the fabric from which every one of Marie-Antoinette's garments has been made. By examining the swatches of material, not only can a better idea be gleaned of the Queen's taste, but also of how closely that taste is mirrored in the paintings and engravings.

A large number of surviving specimens of dress and their accessories admirably compensate for and offset the dearth of fashion illustration for the early part of the century. Admittedly, many garments have been altered.[8] However, this disadvantage is far outweighed by the information that can be obtained from their cut, construction, fabrics, colours and trimmings.

Costume Books

A new feature marked the costume book of the eighteenth century. This was antiquarian research stimulated by the quest for even more exact knowledge of the historic past. It was Dom Bernard de Montfaucon who pioneered the rediscovery of the Middle Ages in general and its dress in particular. One interesting facet of Montfaucon's work is the cult of personality and dress, as he gives faces and costumes to celebrated people who were hitherto little more than names. This made Montfaucon's *Le Monumens de la monarchie françoise* (5 volumes, 1729-33) indispensable to the development of the artistic style called *le style troubadour*.

Although with the inception of *le style troubadour* interest in France's medieval and Renaissance past was already growing, with important influences on fashion, there was still a dearth of books on medieval costume and Neo-classicism continued to be the dominant artistic style.

In England, too, there was a growing eagerness to research and document the dress of the historic past. What particularly fascinated English people across the social spectrum was their discovery of the romance of the historical past, exemplified by the popularity of the masquerade. Antiquarian research was placed on a sound, academic ground with the founding of the Society of Antiquaries in London in 1717. One of the most scholarly studies to emerge was Thomas Jefferys's monumental four volume work, the first history of costume in English. Volumes one and two, published in

1757, contained 240 plates and another two volumes published in 1772, also included 240 plates. Its full title gives some idea of its artistic scope: *A Collection of Dresses of Different Nations, Ancient and Modern, Particularly Old English Dresses. After the designs of Holbein, Vandyke, Hollar and others, with an account of the authorities from which the figures are taken, and some short historical remarks on the subject.* As the title implies, the bulk of the illustrations are of historical dress, although there are many plates of contemporary dress too. Also included are Oriental costumes, and examples of stage costumes, for Jefferys intended his book as an aid for theatre designers and masqueraders as well as a guide for artists. Undoubtedly its most salient feature is Jefferys's attempt to define a chronological history of dress.

Amongst the 'others' mentioned in Jefferys's title may be included Boissard's costume book of 1581 and the marquis Charles de Ferriol's *Recueil de cent estampes représentant différentes Nations du Levant* which was published by Mm. Le Hay and Duchange in Paris in 1714. The marquis de Ferriol was French ambassador to the Sublime Porte between 1699 and 1709. The plates in his volume were engraved by eight artists in 1712 and 1713 after drawings by Jean-Baptiste van Mour, who lived and worked in Constantinople for many years. De Ferriol's book, with its finely hand-coloured plates of Turkish court and noble costume, heightened with gold, with mica chips added to simulate jewels in the buckles and the finery, stimulated various kinds of excursions into *turquerie*. The book went into two further printings to meet popular demand in Europe. As for van Mour himself, 'if he did not initiate, he at least developed the fashion for Europeans having themselves portrayed in Oriental costume.'[9] The publication had a romantic effect on artists, even those who had never visited Turkey such as François Boucher, Jacques Aved and Carle van Loo. Even the great Joseph-Marie Vien was inspired by *turquerie*. In 1748, while a student at the French Academy in Rome, Vien compiled a series of drawings entitled *La Macarde Turque*, based on a Turkish procession which had traversed the Roman streets in triumphal cars. Another French artist passionate about *turquerie* was Jean-Etienne Liotard who had accompanied Lord Ponsonby and John Montagu, the 4th Earl of Sandwich, on an expedition to Constantinople. In Liotard's baggage when he returned to Europe in 1742 were a number of Turkish clothes which he later used to dress his sitters. Liotard's experience in Constantinople is also reflected in his self-portraits in Turkish costume and in the way he signed his pastels as *le peintre turque*.

Turquerie even penetrated the French court. Turkish costumes became very fashionable and in 1755 Mme de Pompadour commissioned a series of portraits of herself dressed as a sultana from Carle van Loo. In England, the inclusion of van Mour's drawings in Jefferys's book guaranteed that they would have an effect on fashions. English fashions often took their inspiration from masquerades, with the masquerade *en turque* particularly in vogue by the mid- eighteenth century. Jefferys's volumes were easily available in shops and dress-making establishments as masquerade pattern books.[10]

The chief exponent of *turquerie* was Lady Mary Wortley Montagu, who, a mere two years after the publication of the marquis de Ferriol's book, was travelling extensively in Turkey by dint of her husband's appointment as Ambassador to Constantinople. On her return to England in 1718 she started a fashion for wearing

Turkish dress. She was painted *en turque* many times, by artists including Jean-Baptiste van Mour, Charles Jervas, Jonathan Richardson and Sir Godfrey Kneller. The English were captivated by her knowledge, gleaned over her two year stay, of the life and customs of the Turks, and, in particular, the dress of Turkish women. Her letters were widely disseminated before becoming a best-seller when published in book form on her death in 1763.

English dress was the subject of the antiquarian Joseph Strutt. *A Compleat View of the Manners, Customs, Arms, Habits, etc . . . of the Inhabitants of England, from the Arrival of the Saxons to the Present Time* was the first important work

Portrait of Lady Mary Wortley Montagu and Her Son, attributed to Jean-Baptiste van Mour, c. 1717.
A vivid illustration of fashion *à la turque* popularized by Lady Mary Wortley Montagu. Lady Mary wears a striking gold-coloured caftan. It is a garment exactly fitted to her shape providing a natural silhouette. She wears it tucked up into her jewelled girdle allowing her smock of fine silk gauze to be shown off to advantage. Her loose overgown is the *curdee.*

Hers is made of a luxurious blue brocade, is gold-embroidered and is trimmed with ermine. Lady Mary's wearing of the *curdee* had a considerable impact on the fashionable English, being widely worn by women and men. It was a robe that could be both functional, rather like the banyan, and also exotic, touching the fancy of English society. *(National Portrait Gallery, London)*

to concentrate on the history of English dress, illustrated 'by engravings taken from the most authentic remains of Antiquity'. It was published in three volumes from 1774 to 1776. Strutt followed this study with *A Compleat View of the Dress and Habits of the People of England*, published in London in two volumes in the period 1796-9. His inspiration was the great, indefatigable French antiquarian-scholar, Dom Bernard de Montfaucon. Strutt's works on the history of dress in England were to influence the quest for the romantic past in the nineteenth century, when the Artists-Antiquarians searched them for models.

'Le Rendez-vous pour Marly', drawn by Jean-Michel Moreau le jeune and engraved by Carl Güttenburg. From the *Seconde Suite d'Estampes pour servir à l'Histoire des Moeurs et du Costume des François dans le dix-huitième Siècle, année 1776*. Céphise and her friend the marquise are depicted in the gardens of the Tuileries with a cavalry officer who is about to accompany them to Marly. The lady on the right wears a black hat with feathers, the *chapeau à la Henri IV* and a Médicis collar mounted on her *robe à la polonaise*, the new walking dress made in plain and striped fabrics. Here the Médicis collar is transformed into a sheer tucker-style, suitable for a walking dress. Its delicately fluted edges run into the *parfait contentement*, a bow designed in the manner of a neckline. The bodice emphasizes the breasts, a small waist and a rounded torso in between. The gentleman wears a cutaway coat fastened at the broad, turned-down collar, echoing the style of his companion and equally suitable as a walking costume. The children wear simple clothing under the influence of Jean-Jacques Rousseau's book *Émile* (1763), in which he advocated comfortable, health-conscious dress for their active lives. *(Victoria and Albert Museum, London)*

'Les adieux', drawn by Jean-Michel Moreau le jeune and engraved by de Launay le jeune. From the *Seconde Suite d'Estampes pour servir à l'Histoire des Moeurs et du Costume des François dans le dix-huitième Siècle, année 1776*. Here the lady wears a *robe de cour* or *grand habit*. The smoothly rounded bodice follows the traditionally curved lines of French court dress which prescribed a stiff-boned bodice, layered lace sleeve ruffles, long train and *paniers à coudes*. A very low neckline was another feature of ceremonial dress. Behind stands the Médicis collar, a narrow lace frill mounted into a deeply standing collar. Her hair is dressed high over pads, widened at the top by sausage curls, and surmounted by plumes, gauze and ribbons, as court etiquette demanded. The men are the epitome of aristocratic grandeur in the embroidered silk *habit à la française*. At court, formal dress also required the *chapeau bras* and a powdered wig. *(Victoria and Albert Museum, London)*

parts (*Année 1775, Seconde Suite d'Estampes . . . Année 1776; Troisième Suite d'Estampes . . . Année 1783*) of twelve plates each by the publisher M. Prault. In 1789 they were published again, this time collectively, under their better-known title, *Le Monument du costume Physique et Moral de la fin du XVIIIe. Siècle, ou Tableau de la Vie*. With a racy, witty text by Restif de la Bretonne, and the bulk of the 36 engravings from drawings by Jean-Michel Moreau le jeune, one of the great visual chroniclers of the society of late eighteenth-century France, *Le Monument du costume* affords an unmatched insight into the period. The first *suite* recounts the life of Céphise, *une femme de bon ton*, from her *début* into society to the birth of her first child; the second *suite* extols the joys of her motherhood, reflecting the sentiments of Rousseau; and the third *suite* relates the activities of a well-heeled *gentilhomme*. M. Prault published this superb work at the suggestion of M. Eberts, a well-known banker and connoisseur, signifying that in France at least, fashion was being taken seriously as an art form, social force and economic source. The *Préfaces* of the first and second *suites* stress other aims of the engravings, namely, their use as models for artists and theatrical designers, and as a pattern book.

Marie-Antoinette's real achievement was securing the adoption of important elements of the Henri IV style into fashionable dress. Fashions in the time of Henri IV were relaunched by Marie-Antoinette and recorded in the volumes of *Le Monument du costume*, one of the most notable being the *chapeau à la Henri IV*. With her promotion of these fashions she made one of the most important and lasting contributions to this romantic revival of the Middle Ages and the Renaissance which came to be known as *le style troubadour*.[11]

Les poupées et la mode

From the sixteenth century Paris had determined the way fashion would go. While countries such as Germany and Holland produced and supplied wooden dolls, it was the exclusive domain of the French capital to attire them, anticipating a tradition that belongs to the seventeenth, and even more so to the eighteenth century.[12] For, before the advent of the true fashion plate in fashion journals, the means by which French fashions were publicized

Attention to purely French dress was the theme of several important works published in Paris in the 1770s and 1780s. Guillaume-François-Roger Molé's *Histoire des modes françaises*, published in 1777, was the first book on the history of fashion in France. *Les Costumes François représentans les différens États du royaume avec les habillemens propres à chaque état et accompagné de réflections critiques et morales* was published by Le Père et Avaulex in 1776. With an engraved title by Arrivet and eleven engraved plates by N. Dupin, it depicts various echelons of society, ranging from members of the court, the professions and labourers, to the poor. Each is represented by a figure in typical dress with an explanatory text.

One of the most charming series of engravings produced during the eighteenth century in France was the *Suite d'Estampes pour servir à l'Histoire des Moeurs et du Costume des François dans le dix-huitième Siècle*. It was issued in three

'La petite toilette', drawn by Jean-Michel Moreau le jeune and engraved by P.-A. Martini. From the *Seconde Suite d'Estampes pour servir à l'histoire des Moeurs et du Costume des Français dans le dix-huitième Siècle, année 1776*.
Here the gentleman is swathed in a night-shirt and dressing gown and holds an invitation while his barber attends his hair and his assistant heats up the curling papers with tongs. A

tailor shows a new coat, held up by his assistant whose striped stockings were made on the new machine which knitted ribs. In the background stands a running footman. The ceremony takes place against a magnificent Neo-classical interior typical of the period of King Louis XVI. (*Victoria and Albert Museum, London*)

the French dolls could never be replaced. Such was their standing that they were not rendered obsolete even when fashion plates first started appearing in fashion magazines. As late as 1773, *The Lady's Magazine* expressed annoyance at their still being sent out when fashion plates were readily and speedily available.[13]

It was Rose Bertin who kept *la mode* going at the height of the French Revolution. As *marchande de modes* to Marie-Antoinette, her fame was such that she had sent out her own dolls and the Queen, too, often sent Mlle Bertin's dolls to her female relatives in Austria. Nothing less than a *femme d'enterprise*, Mlle Bertin was also shrewd enough to have established a business in London, from whence, during the Reign of Terror, she sent forth her *poupées*.

The First Fashion Plates

Even before the middle of the eighteenth century there was a demand for magazines specifically devoted to the needs of the lady of fashion. Just after the half century this fashion literature started to become illustrative. Three similarly-titled such periodicals were published in London: *The Lady's Magazine or the Compleat Library*, 1738–39; *The Ladies Magazine* by Jasper Goodwill, 1749–53; and *The Lady's Magazine* edited by Oliver Goldsmith, 1759–63. It is Goldsmith's *The Lady's Magazine* that can boast the earliest fashion plate. The issue for December 1759 published a full-page black-and-white engraving entitled 'Habit of a Lady in 1759' with accompanying editorial text.

> . . . I have engaged the ingenious Mr Walker to execute a design of a Lady in a perfectly genteel undress; and for the assistance of those in the country who, as they have not opportunities of seeing the originals may dress by that figure, I shall endeavour to accommodate to it certain plain instructions.

The appearance of these ladies' magazines met the requirements of an ever-growing female readership of the periodical press. As early as 1758 *Le Courier de la nouveauté*, which styled itself a daily paper for ladies, announced in the Prospectus its intention to provide female customers with accurate and up-to-date information under six comprehensive headings.

were the exportation of *les poupées*. They had many appellations: 'Pandoras', 'French babies', 'Joined babies' and *Mademoiselles*. *La grande Pandora* travelled in court dress, while her sister, *la petite Pandora*, was garbed in fashionable dress. The celebrated *marchande de modes*, Rose Bertin, by dint of being first Master of the Corporation of the Marchands de Modes, dressed *la grande Pandora* for her peregrinations across Europe.

Although France dictated fashion through the travels of the Parisian dolls, it should be mentioned that other dolls were sent out, notably from England, with Russia and the American colonies being two popular venues. However,

Doll's French court dress, 1770s.
Made of French brocaded silk, this gown is woven with cloth of silver and yellow stripes, interspersed with knots of pink and yellow roses, elaborately decorated with silver lace, fly braid and ribbon *mignardises*. The boned bodice is bound in white silk and the long train falls from the waist. Such an elaborate, stiff-bodied gown, the *corps de robe* style, would have been reserved for a member of the Royal Family or her immediate attendants and worn only on the most formal state occasions. (*Museum of Costume, Bath*)

Two Ladies in the newest Dress.

From Drawings taken at Ranelagh. May 1775.

Published by G. Robinson June 1. 1775.

1. Wigmakers and hairdressers, their inventions and discoveries, perfume, skin lotions, powders, creams, pomades, rouge, hats, bonnets . . .

2. Fashion suppliers, tailors, *couturières*, corset-makers

3. New jewels, use and properties, suppliers and artisans . . .

4. Names and addresses of florists . . .

5. All the new events in which ladies participate; including public festivals and unusual diversions . . .

6. Names and addresses of able tutors for the young . . .[14]

Even if the *journal* floundered – and there is no evidence beyond the lack of subsequent references to it – the attempt to launch it is itself indicative of the status of women in France.

The group who really gained in fashion importance at this time were the *marchandes de modes*. Fabrics, as has already been noted, had become increasingly plain and the decoration of fashionable women's dress was transferred to the *agréments* or trimmings, especially lace and ribbons. Haberdashery, not just of dresses, but also of hats and items that did not require specialized tailoring such as mantillas, pelisses and capes was the exclusive domain of the *marchandes de modes* in the fashion industry.

Fashion journalism in France had gained some measure of social acceptance by 1768. *Le Courier de la mode ou journal du goût* was cited that year by two of France's leading periodicals: neither Grimm's *Correspondance Littéraire* nor Bachaumont's *Mémoires Sécrets* would have paid tribute to a rival if it could easily have been avoided. In England, on the other hand, it took the fourth *Lady's Magazine, The Lady's Magazine or entertaining Companion for the Fair Sex* to bring 'what perhaps may be regarded as the first objective and professional effort to create a

'Two Ladies in the newest Dress'. From drawings taken at Ranelagh, May 1775. Engraved fashion plate from *The Lady's Magazine*, June 1775.
The fashion plates of *The Lady's Magazine* are useful for showing the complicated, flamboyant hairstyles and dresses in the period before the French Revolution and the ensuing simplicity. The ladies, at an outing to Ranlagh in Chelsea, wear open gowns with the skirts draped in the *polonaise* style, tight sleeves to the elbow finishing in a cuff and ruffles. Their hair is dressed high off the forehead and set with small roll curls at the sides, the back mounted over horse-hair pads. Artificial hair was a necessary supplement to the ladies' own hair. Concoctions such as feathers and long pendant lace lappets were considered part of the total art of hairdressing. *(Victoria and Albert Musuem, London)*

English costumes, c. 1795, of the Most Hon. The Marquess of Lansdowne.
The most distinctive vagary of an English woman's high fashion was her very large hat. As this fine specimen shows, it was worn tilted to one side and embellished with ribbons and feathers. Large hats were the most decisive fashion import from England into France with the taste for pastoral life and the *anglomanie* of the 1780s and 1790s. For French ladies these hats were designed as part of their *coiffures*. The inventiveness of the *marchande de modes* and the *coiffeur* made the most of this enthusiasm. *(Museum of Costume, Bath. The costumes are on display at Bowood House, Calne)*

appeared regularly month by month. In addition the fashion plates at the end of the eighteenth century often show French fashions that were copied directly from the fashion plates in French magazines.[17]

French fashion plates were decades ahead of their English counterparts both in artistic skill and technology. French society had a taste for extravagance, as *Le Monument du costume* so elegantly portrayed, and was ever ready to receive new fashion stimuli. Fashion flourished too, because of the growth of the middle classes. The result of this was that a whole group of French fashion journals burst forth on to the scene, which are the germ of the specialized fashion press of today.

Two *hommes d'enterprise*, Jean Esnauts and Michel Rapilly, realized the illustration of fashion could be a source of economic prosperity. A specialized fashion press would spur on women to acquire fashionable dress and accessories. *La Maison d'Edition Esnauts et Rapilly* published *La Gallerie des modes et costumes français dessinés d'après nature gravés par les plus Célèbres Artistes en ce genre, et colorés avec le plus grand soin*, containing the first comprehensive set of fashion plates keeping women abreast of current fashion tastes. It was published in *cahiers* of six pages between 1778 and 1787. Intended to form four volumes, each *cahier* of *La Gallerie des modes* had six exquisitely hand-coloured engravings of female fashions, including hairstyles and headdresses. In addition, fashion plates of male and children's fashions were also included and some theatrical and operatic costumes. All the clothes illustrated had captions containing full descriptive texts by Guillaume-François-Roger Molé.

In all, 70 *cahiers*, with a total of 342 plates, appeared. There appears to be no complete set in any public or private collection. Because of its inaccessibility, many bibliographical questions are thorny, authorities differing on the total number of volumes into which the engravings were collected, their sequences and so forth. In addition, Esnauts and Rapilly also issued an alternative series of uncoloured fashion plates. Perhaps the easiest way to look at the plates is the reproduction in the exact hues of the originals published in Paris c. 1912,

magazine acceptable to women'.[15] While still not a true fashion magazine, more an amalgam of amusement and improvement, it nevertheless had a special fashion department giving more descriptive space to dress than its predecessors. Its avowed aim was to provide the most far-flung subscribers 'with every innovation that is made in the female dress' but to avoid the 'fleeting whimsies of depraved elegance.'[16]

The first English fashion plate in 1759 had been uncoloured and subsequent 'Habits of the year' were equally unrefined. *The Lady's Magazine or Entertaining Companion for the Fair Sex* published black-and-white fashion plates with little artistic merit with the exception of one that was hand-coloured that appeared in its issue of April 1771. It was not until 1794 that fashion plates

'Jeune Dame en Circassienne', drawn by Claude-Louis Desrais and engraved by E.-C. Voysard. Fashion plate from *La Gallerie des modes et costumes français*, Plate 44 (Plate 8 of Lévy edition), 1778.
The young lady wears a lilac satin *robe à la circassienne* trimmed with blonde lace and ornamented with spotted ribbons. Of Oriental inspiration, the *circassienne* was very short and gathered up into three bunches *à la polonaise*. It also had very short sleeves trimmed with fur and often decorated with tassels which exposed the longer sleeves of the underbodice or *soubreveste*. The young lady's headdress is an elegant 'parasol hat' worn over a tall *coiffure* with a loosely plaited *chignon*. (Victoria and Albert Museum, London)

by Emile Lévy under the editorship of Paul Cornu. What is not in question is the extreme accuracy of the fashions, drawn by some of the most celebrated artists of late eighteenth-century France: Claude-Louis Desrais, Pierre-Thomas Le Clère (or Le Clerc), Augustin de Saint-Aubin, and François-Louis-Joseph Watteau, great nephew of Jean-Antoine Watteau. They drew costumes that they had seen in fashionable society homes or at gathering places like the theatre or as supplied to them by tailors and *marchandes de modes*. This was up-to-the-minute *rapportage* of the fashionable ideal to be followed and purchased by the lady of *bon ton*, the purpose of the fashion plate *per se*. Particularly innovatory was the naming of some of the most sought after *marchandes de modes* and tailors. The very animated attitudes of the figures in the plates suggest that there was probably a close working alliance among the artists, tailors and the *marchandes de modes*.

The woman who achieved the most eminence of all the *marchandes de modes* was Rose Bertin, the first Master of their Corporation. Starting out in 1763 at the age of 16 as an errand-girl to the popular *couturière*, Mlle Pagalle, she quickly established herself, attracting aristocratic *clientèle* such as the duchesse de Chartres and the princesse de Lamballe. Such was her flair that in 1770 she branched out and opened her own business at the sign of the *Grand Mogol* in the rue de Saint-Honoré. Through her networking she was introduced to Marie-Antoinette in about 1772. The new *dauphine*, who had been renowned for her simplicity, soon developed a passion for fashion under the aegis of Mlle Bertin. Being *marchande de modes* to Queen Marie-Antoinette, Rose received the soubriquet of *Ministre de la Mode*.

In the realm of tailoring France also held pre-eminence. The work of the royal tailor, P.-N. Sarrazin, is mentioned in several of the captions of the fashion plates in *La Gallerie des modes*. Two of his most arresting designs appear in *cahier* 18 (plates 103 and 104). They show the *Henri Quatre* costume for court balls worn at the request of Queen Marie-Antoinette: for men, trunk hose, slashed doublets, soft, triple ruffs, waistcoats, cloaks, sashes, felt hats trimmed with ostrich feathers, and flat shoes with rosettes, and for women, Médicis collars, looped-up

overskirts trimmed with ermine, slashed, puffed sleeves held in place by jewelled bands, and velvet or gauze hats decorated with ermine and ostrich feathers.

Another interesting feature of *La Gallerie des modes* is the incredible amount of fashion terms that are mentioned and illustrated, demonstrating that this newly established Parisian magazine had given a significant boost to fashion. One can learn about such curiosities as *noeuds d'amour* (love knots), the ties and bows used for decorations on *robes*; *compères* (godfathers), the inner panels of bodices that had eyelets for lacings; *bonshommes* (pleasant fellows), the sleevelets at the elbow; or *parfaits contentments* (perfect contentments), the bows that covered the pins or clasps at the centre of the *décolletage*. These were romantic terms which were overtly erotic.

The most salient innovation of the 1780s was the fashion for dresses, such as the *robe en chemise*, all made in one piece, which could be put on directly over the head. This was an important development, indeed a revolutionary development, as previously the fashionable lady had to step sideways into her dress. The version worn by Queen Marie-Antoinette in her portrait painted by Mme Vigée-Le Brun, the *chemise à la reine*, caused a scandal and the portrait had to be withdrawn from the salon of 1783 where it was exhibited. It is significant that Bachaumont, in his *Mémoires Secrets*, has an entry for 1785 stating that Marie-Antoinette let it be known to Mlle Bertin that she

'Costume de Dame de Cour sous le règne de Louis XVI en usage pour les bals de la Reine en 1774, 1775 et 1776 … executé par le Sr P.N. Sarrazin, Costumier de la Famille Royale'. Drawn by Claude-Louis Desrais and engraved by Dupin. Fashion plate from *La Gallerie des modes et costumes français*, Plate 103 (Plate 65 of Lévy edition), 1779.
This design, based on fashions of the time of Henri IV, was worn at formal court balls from 1774 to 1776 at the request of Queen Marie-Antoinette. With a companion design for male courtiers, it underlines the Queen's important role in the development of *le style troubadour*. *(Victoria and Albert Museum, London)*

'Robe à l'anglaise de Pékin verd pomme', drawn by Pierre-Thomas Le Clère (or Le Clerc) and engraved by Dupin. Fashion plate from *La Gallerie des modes et costumes français*, Plate 76 (Plate 39 of Lévy edition), 1778.
This *robe à l'anglaise* of apple green Pékin, a silk textile of the nature of taffeta, has a fitted back bodice and corseted waist. The neckline is fastened and covered by a bow, the *parfait contentement*. The back fullness of the skirt and petticoat is extended and supported by the new fashion for a 'false derrière', the *cul postiche*. The skirt and petticoat are short enough to show off the feet and ankles. The huge headdress, called a *pouf*, is a veritable framework of gauze decorated with floral ornament echoing the dress. The lady keeps her balance on her silk high-heeled shoes because of the position of the heels under the arches of her feet. A fob watch, mirror, bracelet and fan further embellish her coquettish ensemble. *(Victoria and Albert Museum, London)*

would no longer be wearing informal attire, including *chemises*, and 'that the imposing gown with pleats' that is, the *robe à la française*, would be worn again.[18] However, from fashion's stand, it was too late. The comfortable, relaxed shapes of these various *chemises* had widespread appeal to the *haute bourgeoisie* of Paris. What these items of dress reveal is not only sensual overtones, but also individuality, and the movement of fashion's leadership away from the court of Versailles to the city of Paris. To compare the fashion plates in *La Gallerie des modes* across the years of its publication is to discern how fashion reflected the dynamic forces of social, economic and political change that would eventually culminate in the French Revolution.

Such was the success of the fashion plates in *La Gallerie des modes* that they were exported and much copied or pirated in various formats. *The Lady's Magazine* frequently re-engraved and reproduced them under the heading 'New Paris fashions'. However, fashion and fashion illustration in France was not just an economic source. The superb artists through their fashion illustration promoted and secured France's superiority in elegance of style and taste which others could copy but never excel.

French Fashion Plates from the Reign of Louis XVI and Marie-Antoinette to the French Revolution

The 1780s was a decade of feverish excitement evidenced by the launching of high quality fashion magazines that were quick to spot the changing feelings in society. *Le Cabinet des modes, ou les modes nouvelles, décrites d'une manière claire et précise, et représentées par des Planches en taille-douce, en luminées,* was the first magazine of French fashions to be published with regular frequency. Launched on 15 November 1785 by M. Le Brun-Tossa, it appeared every 15 days. Each *cahier* was composed of eight pages and contained three fashion plates, coloured by hand, of female, male and children's costumes, accessories, hairstyles, headdresses, hats, jewellery, as well as the status symbols of the *haute bourgeoisie*, interior decorations, furniture, silver and

carriages. The audacious claims in the title, far from exceeding the resources of eighteenth-century French skill and technology, were fulfilled with remarkable success. An editorial reported that each fashion plate took a day to draw, that the etching was finished by dry-point and that it was coloured not in watercolour but in gouache. This was both a painstaking and costly process. The bulk of the drawings are by Pierre-Thomas Le Clère (or Le Clerc), Claude-Louis Desrais and A. Pugin, and all the engravings are by A.-B. Duhamel. In some cases Duhamel has done all the work himself. Subscriptions could be taken out in Paris through the bookseller, Buisson. Amongst the illustrious subscribers was the American ambassador to France, Thomas Jefferson, who 'sent the fashion plates to feminine friends in America, and relayed goings on about

'Jeune Homme "en chenille"'. Engraved fashion plate from *Le Cabinet des modes*, No.1, 15 November 1785, Plate 10. To be 'en chenille' was to be 'like a cocoon', that is, in informal morning dress before turning into a butterfly later in the day. As an example, *Le Cabinet des modes* in its first issue featured this young man in English fashion. His *fraque* is made in dark green cloth. Indispensable accessories are the *chapeau en Jocquay* with a steel buckle, striped stockings, shoes with shoe laces, cane and watches. His hairstyle is *en catogan*. (*Cabinet des Estampes, Bibliothèque Nationale de France, Paris*)

Mademoiselle Rose Bertin, the dressmaker to Queen Marie-Antoinette'.[19]

The high reputation of *Le Cabinet des modes* was secured and its international standing assured when its number for 20 November 1786 was issued under a new title, *Le Magasin des modes nouvelles, françaises et anglaises*. Of great importance was the undertaking on the part of the editor to inform French readers of the latest developments in English fashions. In the Prospectus announcing the change of title, he acknowledged his debt to the London publication, *The Fashionable Magazine*, which first appeared in June 1786 and lasted until December 1786. However, not content with relaying news from *The Fashionable Magazine*, he sent a special reporter to ensure that any developments which escaped the English journalist would be noted by its rival.[20]

A wave of *anglomanie* characterized the 1780s. *La Gallerie des modes*, from its beginnings in the late 1770s, had explored two major trends in France: the formality of court dress and silk; and, the informal styles and cotton, particularly from England. In England the upper classes had never been content to cluster around their court in the manner of their French counterparts. They preferred to spend much of their time on their country estates, for which they had to adopt a simpler form of dress. English dress in France became associated with English social, artistic and political attitudes. In his *Letters concerning the English Nation*, based on his visit to London in 1727, Voltaire expressed admiration for these values. A new middle-class morality, which demonstrated against the aristocratic traditions of hypocrisy and insensibility, had risen in England, manifesting itself in self-reliance and independence in politics and art. Jean-Jacques Rousseau, who, in his writings, stressed the unease with which French society was structured, singled out in particular the hypocrisy and corruption of the nobility. Rousseau admired the writings of English philosophers of the seventeenth century, especially John Locke and found much to enthuse about English life: a comparative lack of privilege and a simplicity. All of this had an effect on dress. English styles were associated with liberty, social cohesion, and a love of nature and the countryside. This was further underscored by the English preference for wool, linen, and cotton. What the French did was to take English informal fashions and endow them *élan*.

Frenchmen began to wear the English *fraque* or frock coat with its turned-down collar and pared-down look. The *chapeau jockei*, derived from the hats worn by jockeys and horsemen, sporting boots in place of shoes and unpowdered hair were in the English taste. Another English fashion, the black suit, was adopted by professional men such as doctors, lawyers, businessmen, and officials. It would become in the nineteenth century the stalwart dress of the urban dweller. By the end of the 1780s the tug of war between the sumptuous French day clothes, and the simplicity and variety of their English counterparts was won by Anglomania, for Frenchmen had become almost completely *à l'anglais* with the *habit à la française* reserved for formal court ceremonies.

'Femme portant une longue veste croisée et un jupon de drap vert naturel', drawn by Claude-Louis Desrais and engraved by A.-B. Duhamel. Fashion plate from *Le Magasin des modes nouvelles, françaises et anglaises*, No. 12, 10 March 1787, Plate I.
The matching jacket and skirt in dark green cloth show the simpler style of fashionable female daywear which *anglomanie* brought into vogue. The outfit is masculine in appearance, but the prominent large hat with its decorative confections is very feminine and shows the degree to which feminine fashion was concentrated on headwear. *(Cabinet des Estampes, Bibliothèque Nationale de France, Paris)*

Frenchwomen stricken with Anglomania favoured the *robe à l'anglaise* (see page 78), relegating the *robe à la française* to ceremonial court dress. The *robe à l'anglaise* brought together the fitted back bodice of the mantua with the back pleats of the *sacque* which were so reduced that they became seams. The usual style in the 1770s was the *corsage en fourreau*, a way of cutting the back bodice in one with the skirt. This was achieved by means of a central panel at the back where the pleats were sewn down and the panel continued into the skirt. The style of the 1780s, however, was different, featuring a complete division at the waist. *Paniers* were discarded and replaced by pads, called amongst other frank terms, a 'false *derrière*'. Nicknamed in French the *cul postiche*, this precursor of the bustle was made of horsehair, wool or cork and shifted the hip emphasis to the back rather than the sides as *paniers* had done. It provided the necessary support to achieve fullness at the back of the skirt. While the back of the bodice was quite distinctive, the front was more varied, featuring a stomacher, *compères*, or perhaps a closed front. The *robe à l'anglaise* was first noted in *La Gallerie des modes* in 1778. Another English fashion was the *redingote*. Although based on the Englishman's riding-coat it was first and foremost a long-sleeved gown. There were also many variants. The *redingote* could be completely closed and buttoned all the way down the front, imitating the English-tailored male style. It could also incorporate other masculine details such as a wide-cut collar, a caped collar or large revers. The *demi-redingote* was fitted to the waist, then opened out to reveal a petticoat or underskirt in a matching or contrasting fabric. The vogue for *redingotes* is attested by the very precise engravings in *La Gallerie des modes*, where it first appeared drawn by Watteau de Lille in 1787, and in the many examples in *Le Cabinet des modes* and *Le Magasin des modes nouvelles, françaises et anglaises*. Another trim outfit was a skirt and jacket distilled from the English riding-habit, the forerunner of the modern, tailored, two-piece suit. The fashionable accessory to wear with these ensembles in the 1780s was a *fichu*, a large, soft, transparent piece of material made of muslin or fine gauze. The *fichu* was worn on the bodice puffed out above the small waist giving, a pouter-pigeon effect to the silhouette and counter-balancing the amplitude of the back projection of the skirt.

Le Magasin des modes nouvelles, françaises et anglaises lasted until 21 December 1789, the editor showing an enlightened awareness of the impact of the Revolution on dress. Fashionable lady's attire proved surprisingly responsive to the vicissitudes of a revolution which undermined its position. One of the most revealing indices of political and social tension was the vestimentary tournament that replaced earlier consensus about costume. On the one side were those dressed for the Revolution. For them, the editor of *Le Magasin des modes nouvelles, françaises et anglaises* produced in the number for 21 September 1789 a reproduction, a trifle top-heavy perhaps, of a lady's hat on which traversed crosier, sword, and spade were embroidered to symbolize the unity of the three orders of the Estates General, the national assembly that met on 5 May 1789 at Versailles in the presence of Louis XVI. Headdresses, going back to the reign of Mlle Bertin, had always echoed current political affairs. A particular political novelty was the *bonnet à la Bastille* in the shape of a tower and trimmed with a tricolour ribbon and rosette. Topical political comment was also a source for jewellery. Bastille buckles to simulate the crenelatted towers of the fortress provided further means by which fashionable women might flaunt their patriotism. Yet, as these rather jejeune efforts that appeared in issues of *Le Magasin des modes nouvelles, françaises et anglaises* for 21 September, 11 November and 1 December 1789 show, the female leaders of fashion, like everyone else, were caught off balance by events.

They were quicker than others, however, to recover their nerve, and to express support for the Revolution in their costume as a whole, as well as in its accessories, as the sequel to *Le Magasin des modes nouvelles, françaises et anglaises*, entitled *Le Journal de la mode et du goût ou Amusemens du Sallon et de la Toilette par M. Le Brun* demonstrates. It ran from 25 February 1790 to 1 April 1793. *Le Journal de la mode et du goût* is a model of what an enterprising editor like M. Le Brun-Tossa, who this time is cited in the title, could achieve with the aid of an outstanding artist. Although the fashion plates are not signed, M. Gaudriault assigns them to A.-B. Duhamel,[21] who had worked for M. Le Brun-Tossa on the two earlier fashion magazines. A pupil of the great fashion illustrator, Augustin de Saint-Aubin, Duhamel was noted for his specialist work in fashion publishing, his strongly researched costumes and *coiffures*.[22] No one could accuse *Le Journal de la mode et du goût* of a lack of political reticence, still less of topicality.[23] Those described euphemistically as freed by the Revolution were encouraged to dress specially for the part. Soon after the disbandment of religious houses in 1790, the *Journal* depicted the *robe à la Vestale*, a special dress for a nun who had been restored to lay society. She was to be robed in white to resemble a Vestal Virgin. At the same time gold lace, fine buckles and a 'passion' hairstyle with five rows of curls forming a diadem hinted that Diana might soon lose one of her retinue.

The larger party, especially after the euphoric efforts of the Fall of the Bastille on 14 July 1789 and the 'abolition of feudalism' on 4 August 1789 had worn off, were opposed to the Revolution. Those who remained after the first *émigrés* had left were more intransigent and inclined towards sartorial bravado. *Le Journal de la mode et du goût* for 15 April 1790 showed a fashionable woman 'vêtue à la constitution'. The ensemble consisted of a fine Indian muslin *robe* embroidered with tiny red, white and blue bouquets over which was worn a linen *fichu en chemise*. Her headwear, a *demi-casque* made of black gauze with a red ribbon and aigrette suggested a slightly military air. The 'femme patriote avec le nouvel uniforme', dashingly shown off in the magazine for 25 August 1790, underlined her revolutionary support with a royal blue cloth *jupe* (skirt) and *coureur* (jacket), the jacket having red facings piped with white, a *gilet* (waistcoat) made of white bazeen, and a wide-brimmed black felt hat decorated with a ribbon cockade and band 'aux couleurs de la nation' over her unpowdered hair.

The ladies outshone the men. To quote the editor of *Le Journal de la mode et du goût* from the issue of 15 April 1791:

> Among the nobility it is the women who lose most through the Revolution: they are the ones barred from all posts by their sex. Now that they are deprived of imposing names and titles, and no longer share with their husbands the honours of their posts, are they going to devote themselves humbly to the practice of the domestic virtues? . . . What difficulties in attracting the public's attention. Youth . . . would pass away in retirement before notoriety were achieved. There remains, therefore, for those who wish to enjoy themselves straight away and bask in other people's attention, only the eccentricity, luxuriousness and elegance of dress.[24]

That shrewd judgement goes far towards explaining one of the most puzzling features of fashionable attire during the first years of the Revolution: the sartorial extravagance at a time of political uncertainty and declining revenues among many of the nobility, and after the emigration had already started. The dresses are defiant in their opulence. It was not long before the Revolution produced fashions which outdid those of the *ancien régime* in elegance, if not opulence. There are many examples offered by the magazine such as the fashionable lady wearing a bonnet the sides of which were adorned with diamonds and trimmed with a black silk band scattered with diamonds. Her *fichu* of white gauze, her *robe* and *jupe* of royal blue Indian taffeta were all bordered with gold lace.

That the pre-Revolutionary and Revolutionary periods had increased the opportunities for fashion journalism is

attested by *Le Journal de la mode et du goût* and its two predecessors, *Le Cabinet des modes* and *Le Magasin des modes nouvelles, françaises et anglaises*. The three together, covering the period 1786–1793, issued a total of 356 fashion plates. With the exception of a few early ones, all were hand-coloured. *Le Journal de la mode et du goût* is especially important for traversing the crucial years of the Revolution. It is also extremely rare: only the Bibliothèque Nationale de France and the Bibliothèque de l'Opera in Paris possess a complete run between them. Yet the very concept of fashion was increasingly riskworthy during the last years of the Revolution, being irreparably anti-revolutionary.

'Officier de chasseur'. Engraved fashion plate from *Le Journal de la mode et du goût*, No. 7, 25 April 1790, Plate I.
A large number of military uniforms appeared from the autumn of 1789, each decorated with a tricolour. This young *élégant* wears the glamorous *chasseur* uniform: a dark blue cloth coat and pantaloons, a white waistcoat, a red belt, a hat with a tricolour cockade and black hussar buskins. *(Cabinet des Estampes, Bibliothèque Nationale de France, Paris)*

21 September 1792 marked the abolition of the monarchy and the start of Year I of the Republic. *Monsieur* and *Madame* were replaced by *citoyen* and *citoyenne*. The *couturières* celebrated this event with the *costume dit à l'égalité* which appeared in *Le Journal de la mode et du goût* for 20 November 1792. A Persian *pierrot* with rose-coloured flowers against a green background was worn with a very full *jupe* that had a train made up in the same material. The matching shawl reached up to the ears. A lawn *polisson* was tied with a small knot of yellow ribbons. The hairstyle with this outfit was short in front and curly behind. The hat, reported to be especially fashionable among republicans, was made of lawn and adorned with yellow ribbons, red plumes and yellow and green flowers. The red-orange shoes completed the meticulously colour-coordinated ensemble. A glance at other fashion plates in the *Journal* of the same time shows that elaborate fashions, far from being the exception were the rule.

It is hardly surprising that visual records of dress worn by the rich are practically non-existent during the Reign of Terror (1793–94) when costumary sobriety appeared necessary for survival, and for some time afterward. There can be little doubt, however, that historians of costume have underestimated the richness of female apparel that continued to be worn during this period. Vestimentary advertisements for the most resplendent female attire appeared in *Le Journal de Paris*. A certain *couturière* who styled herself citizeness Raspal, *ci-devant* Teillard of the Palais *ci-devant* Royal of the street *ci-devant* Richelieu, the place in Paris for the most fashionable *boutiques*, inserted a long advertisement in *Le Journal de Paris* for 19 October 1793. Her sartorial wares included dresses of *pékin velouté lacté, en ray de soie française, en chinoises satinées*, as well as *chemises à la prêtresse, ceintures à la Junon, robes à la Psyche*, and in case it should be forgotten, a most necessary precaution in such a luxurious list, *l'habillement à la républicaine*.[25]

Was the dress of fashionable men as sensitive to political events as that of their womenfolk? The links between cause and effect are certainly less readily discernible. The permissible range of masculine fashion was narrower, change both slower and subtler. Within those parameters, however, much can be gleaned about shift in political and

social outlook from a study of men's attire. In his diary and letters, Gouverneur Morris, an American lawyer resident in Paris, commented upon the extravagantly fanciful military costumes decorated with a tricolour that appeared in the autumn of 1789.[26] The fashion plate that appeared in the issue of *Le Magasin des modes nouvelles, françaises et anglaises* for 1 October 1789, depicting an officer of the National Guard, signalled a seminal influence that was to last for many years. For much of the Revolution membership of this citizen's militia carried

'Petit-maître en habit brun rougeâtre, collet cramoisi, gilet blanc brodé de carreaux tricolores, culotte de peau de daim'. Engraved fashion plate from *Le Journal de la mode et du goût*, No. 27, 15 November 1790, Plate I.
Simplicity characterized the garments of the *petit maître*, a young man obsessed with fashion as a way of life, at this date. The cloth coat has some distinctive features for the period: it is cut very short at the front, opening high to the waist, with the revers at right angles. It could not possibly close, the large gilded copper buttons serving as the only ornamentation. The collar is cut very high and made in a colour contrasting with the rest of the coat. The fashionable man with democratic leanings wore boots. Masculine support for the Revolution was also indicated by an unpowdered and short haircut.
(Cabinet des Estampes, Bibliothèque Nationale de France, Paris)

enormous social cachet. To judge from the countless portraits of National Guard's officers that were shown at the *salons* over many years, the uniform was a common sight in Paris right up to the Empire. As for the uniform itself, the Parisian version had a coat of royal blue piped with crimson. Also of crimson was the collar, while the buttons were gold and bore the arms of the city of Paris and numerals of the wearer's section and regiment. Under the coat were white cloth breeches and a waistcoat with gold buttons like those on the coat. Costume accessories consisted of stockings of white cotton fastened with copper buckles and white gaiters and plain shoes unadorned with buckles. This costume amounted to a quasi-official dress at the beginning of the Revolution, elements of which would be borrowed by civilians

For 15 February 1790 *Le Journal de la mode et du goût* illustrated 'un homme vêtu d'un habit de drap noir à la Révolution'. His garb consisted of a black cloth coat, a red casimir waistcoat and yellow knee-breeches, although the magazine hastened to point out that black knee-breeches could be equally fashionable.

Black, indeed, was a colour that could be worn by both sides of the political divide but with subtle distinctions: silk for those aligned to the monarchy and cloth for those with democratic compassions mirrored in the black cloth costume of the Third Estate. For fashionable aristocrats, the wearing of black was associated not just with mourning for royalty, but for the demise of royalty itself, and an expression, too, of sorrow for the reduced powers of the monarchy.

It is hardly surprising that revolutionaries so sensitive to vestimentary discrimination should have devised uniforms to raise themselves beyond sartorial criticism. The result was almost too successful. In its issue for 5 May 1790 *Le Journal de la mode et du goût* pointed out that town councillors were instructed in a decree of 20 March 1790 to wear a tricolour sash, differentiated with yellow fringe for the Mayor, violet for the Procurator of the Commune and white for the others.[27] From these beginnings the dress of revolutionary officials became increasingly resplendent until the uniform of the *Directoire* could bear comparison with that of a court chamberlain under the *ancien régime*.

From the Spring of 1793 fashion magazines ceased publication and did not resume until the Summer of 1797, when a middle-class society based on property and money had been established and firmly governed France. From 1795 to 1799 France had a bourgeois Republic called the *Directoire*. It was the Directory period which saw a remarkable proliferation of fashion journals which gave dress its finest expression. There was J.-J. Lucet's *Correspondance des dames, ou journal des modes et des spectacles*

de Paris and *Le Tableau général du goût, par une société d'artistes et gens de lettres*, both of which maintained high standards. There were periodicals dealing with literature and the arts in which substantial coverage was given to fashion as in *L'Arlequin* and, to judge from a survey of rivals in *Le Mois*, several others. But the period's outstanding, indeed, key, source for the study of fashion is *Les Journal des dames et des modes* under its great editor, the Oratorian priest and Professor of Philosophy, Pierre de La Mésangère (1759-1831). From June 1797 when the periodical first appeared as *Le Journal des modes et nouveautés* (which gave way on 16 September 1797 to the better-known name above), it supplied readers unfailingly with at least one hand-coloured fashion plate, a *Costume Parisien*, every five days. The accompanying texts, which were written mainly by La Mésangère himself, are models of lucid exposition. His draughtsmen, who, over the long run of the fashion magazine, included a large proportion of the period's minor masters, depicted the fashions with engaging charm and remarkable clarity. Among them were E.-C. Voysard, P.-L. Baquoy, C.-L. Desrais, J.-F. Bosio, M. Deny, Ph.-L. Debucourt and the Vernets, Carle and his son Horace.[28] In June 1798, La Mésangère announced the addition of a second fashion plate in each edition, of which there were two every *decadi*, so that readers could keep abreast of the rapid changes in fashion. The dress of the *élégantes* of the *Directoire* as the fashionable women were called (although the term goes back to at least 1759), proved so fertile that a month or even a week saw greater changes in fashion than several decades under the *ancien régime*.

La Mésangère's primacy in the field of fashion illustration and journalism seems never to have challenged until well into the nineteenth century. (The *Journal* lasted until 1839). Despite the understandably high cost of a magazine that appeared so frequently and contained so many hand-coloured engraved fashion plates it was very well-received, La Mésangère increasing his subscriptions and even feeling obliged to warn his subscribers of the circulation of counterfeits. Naturally loathe to allow others to profit at the *Journal*'s expense, he announced in the Prospectus for the fifth volume a reprinting of numbers for the first two years. Although no reliable figures exist for the circulation of eighteenth-century journals, there can be little doubt that *Le Journal des dames et des modes* was widely read in the fashionable world of the time. The police in their report of 1810 credited it and *Le Mercure* with the highest circulation of the Parisian papers: 830 copies of each were said to leave Paris for the provinces, while it is safe to assume that at least a third as many again remained within the capital.[29]

The large circulation of *Le Journal des dames et des modes* goes far toward guaranteeing the accuracy of the fashion plates. The editor himself staked his reputation on it. La

Mésangère explained at length, for instance, that aesthetic considerations had been sacrificed in one of the fashion plates, where the model's gesture might seem strained, in order to obtain a clear view of the lace ornamentation of the mantelet. The fashion plates were sketched from life, and the models were easily recognizable by those who moved in society. The few challenges to the *Journal's* accuracy and accusations of publishing caricatures were answered and rebutted convincingly from the outset.

We have again received a letter in which our comparisons are faulted for exaggerating the character of Parisian costume to the point that they amount to caricature. People claim that they cannot possibly portray the dress of respectable women. We dare to protest that our figures are all taken from life and that we take trouble to select our models from highly considered balls, the most respectable society, in short from gatherings where no is admitted whose dress arouses suspicion of her morality.

La Mésangère went on to argue cogently that his correspondent had been shocked by the lady's *décolletage* because he had not known that bare necks were accepted

'Femme en robe d'étoffe de printemps couleur de chair, ornée par les bas de petits sujets peints, fichu en chemise de linon blanc'. 'Femme en pierrot et jupe d'étoffe de printemps, dont le fond est coquelicot et les mouches noirs, fichu de linon orné de guirlande de feuilles vertes. Engraved fashion plates from *Le Journal de la mode et du goût*, No. 7, 1 May 1792, Plates I and II.

These ensembles are good examples of contemporary awareness that fashionable dress continued to prosper despite political events. The *Journal* advertised a postal service which shows the scale of operation to supply the sartorial needs of fashionable republican ladies. *(Bibliothèque de l'Opéra, Paris)*

were included) is how little feminine and masculine costume have in common: Periclean Athens is paired incongruously with Georgian London. La Mésangère often remarks that he is at a loss to make any new comments about masculine attire, for the basic style of men's fashions changed very little during the *Directoire*. The fashion plates reveal to the sedulous eye minor alterations in the details, for example, ways of tying the cravat, the height of collars, the shapes of pockets, and the size and materials of buttons. The editor lays out the standard, everyday garb of *élégants* in January 1799: a dark cutaway coat, pantaloons, and boots, with shoes and knee-breeches reserved for balls. With the coat and pantaloons or knee-breeches a light-coloured *veste* or *gilet*, a starched white linen or muslin cravat, and a white linen shirt were worn. For outerwear, *élégants* favoured a *redingote* or a cloak, artistically draped *à l'antique*. By the end of the century the cloak with its voluminous cut and dark colour was dramatically swathed to create a Romantic air. The most fashionable hairstyle was the short, curly *cheveux à la Titus* and the most popular hat was the English round style.

For women, the fashion plates of *Le Journal des dames et des modes* reveal protean variety. La Mésangère himself admitted that his draughtsmen sometimes represent only one of 20 variations on show at Tivoli or Frascati. His meticulous inventory has the effect of making the parts appear greater than the whole. Yet he appears to have had few doubts that he was charting the progress of a fashion rather than assisting at its birth.

A pronounced sculptural quality was what practically all the dresses of the *Directoire* had in common. They were Neo-classical in style, designed in the manner of classical drapery to reveal, sometimes with amazing frankness, the shape of the body beneath.[31] The dress of the *élégantes* reflected the contemporary taste for classical antiquity, also evident in architecture and interior decoration. In the aftermath of the Reign of Terror society was yearning for an order that the classical world symbolized and the *Directoire* was seen as the heir of the classical republican tradition. Aided by the opening of the Musée du Louvre in 1793, which included many works of classical statuary

in polite society as they were always modestly veiled in the street from public gaze.[30]

The first impression from the fashion plates in *Le Journal des dames et des modes* (in spite of its title, men's fashions

'Cheveux à la Titus. Habit dégagé. Pantalon à la hussarde'. Engraved fashion plate from *Le Journal des dames et des modes*, 15 germinal an VII, 4 April 1799, Plate 99.
This plate was based on Carle Vernet's *homme dégagé*. He wears a double-breasted coat, tight-fitting across the chest, with the skirts cut away in front and hanging to the bend of the knees in the back. The coat has a waistline seam and no pockets. A dark colour was preferred for the coat which was

made in broadcloth, a fine woollen cloth of plain weave made in a wide width, hence its name. French tailoring was at its most perfect during the *Directoire*. The *pantalon à la hussarde*, which hugged the legs, also required expert tailoring to create a quasi-antique look. A contrasting light-coloured *veste* or *gilet* was fashionable, the main detail being the large lapels. *(Bibliothèque Doucet, Paris)*

which La Mésangère urged artists to study for women's dress, the Neo-classical *chemise* was a symbol of the new times. Ladies would go to memorable lengths to exhibit figures worthy of serving as models for the Greek

sculptor Phidias, La Mésangère noted.[32] Sometimes they appeared in tulle so light over muslins that were so transparent that enraptured onlookers could tell the colour of their garters. Others highlighted the display by circling their legs and thighs with diamonds. In *Le Journal des dames et des modes* for 9 pluviôse an VI (28 January

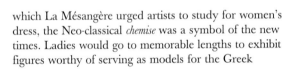

'Robe relevée sur le côte, chapeau spencer violet avec plumet blanc à pointes violettes, schall rose à bordure d'anneaux noirs fermé sur la poitrine par une barrette. Spencer violet à collet rabattu et à revers. Engraved fashion plate from *Le Journal des modes et nouveautés*, July 1797, Plate 4.

One of the *Directoire*'s main achievements in fashion was to transform the shawl into a kind of long, narrow stole called the *schall uni*. This *élégante* wears a rose-coloured *schall uni* of transparent lawn which is decorated with the Grecian motif of interlocking black rings which complements perfectly her white Neo-classical *chemise*. The *élégante*'s spencer does not impair the line of her dress except for the oddity of the turned back cuffs of the long sleeves. (*Bibliothèque Doucet, Paris*)

'Capote anglaise garnie en crêpe, Bandeau de velours guilloche en or, petite fichu croisé, rubans en cothurnes'. Hand-coloured engraved fashion plate from *Le Journal des dames et des modes*, No. LV, 25 vend. An VI, 16 October 1797, Plate 8.

The orange *fichu* and other trimmings serve to enliven the simple Neo-classical chemise. While the *fichu* before the French Revolution had been designed, at least ostensibly, as an aid to modesty, here it enlivens the *décolletage* and, through being fastened around the high *Directoire* waist, helps to make the breasts still more prominent. Fans had simple geometrical motifs that were designed to catch the light and sparkle, and above all to complement the dress as this fashion plate clearly shows. (*Private Collection*)

1798), Mme Tallien, it was reported, favoured flesh-coloured stockings spangled with gold which glittered under her diaphanous *chemise*.

The fashions of the *élégantes* can also be appreciated in terms of colour. Louis Sébastien Mercier held that white suited all women and that white muslin, artistically draped, looked like marble. Although white predominated in the case of the Neo-classical *chemise*, other colours appeared and disappeared with startling rapidity. Violet, slate, rose, red, yellow, even coffee colour, all had their vogue. Delicate pastel shades, however, were preferred to strong colours for the principal outer garments in the interests of preserving the draped effect. The popularity of white derived, apart from the way it set off shapely limbs beneath, from its advantage as a background for striking bands of colour in so many of the fashion plates of *Le Journal des dames et des modes*.

Fabrics made their own contribution to the development of *Directoire* fashions. Without diaphanous muslins would the sculptural affect of classical statuary have been within the grasp of the *couturières* of the *Directoire*? Cheapness, as distinct from availability, is unlikely to have been a recommendation. The vogue for simpler attire, encouraged by Queen Marie-Antoinette's example before the Revolution, was essentially a reaction against sumptuous apparel on grounds of taste, not of cost. The expense of dressing in fashion was enormous, and was almost certainly used as a means of limiting entry to the Parisian *élite*. Besides, even if muslins were comparatively cheap, some types were expensive. Furthermore, lace, velvet, silk, tulle, lawn, taffeta, fur and cashmere were all too often used to enhance the appearance of the *élégantes*. The richer fabrics frequently provided the materials for the resplendent hats worn by ladies of fashion. Silk ribbons, either loose in comet tails, or as edging for dresses were, of course, extremely common. White silk stockings for ladies, as for men, were also regulation attire. In short, the fabrics served the fashion, but, beyond, perhaps, the initial inspiration, did not create it.

La Mésangère's plates show a fashion that had achieved definition in essentials, while exhibiting much uncertainty over accessories. Of the 40 odd fashion plates of gowns in full length illustrated between 1797 and 1799 only four failed to evoke the fall of classical folds.

A most serious distortion of the fashion was wrought by the widespread adoption of the incongruous spencer, an English fashion which first appeared in Paris in 1789. A waist-length jacket with or without lapels it was generally in a dark colour to contrast with the white gown. Parisians gave it many variations such as short sleeves and a tight-fitting effect with thick braiding on the seams emphasizing its constrictions and restraining the figure.

Aprons, which were first worn during the *Directoire* in May 1798, also had the effect of detracting from the fashion's classical appearance. An impetus from the theatre, they sprang from the short-lived craze for an opera which also encouraged the wearing of the *chapeau à la Primerose*. Yet again classical costume showed its powers of absorption by reducing the independent function of the apron, like the spencer, to the barest of accessories.

Shawls were a favourite accessory of Josephine Bonaparte, and would turn into a real passion when she became Empress. Shawls themselves seemed to have entered the wardrobes of fashionable ladies as part of the Neo-classical style of dress pioneered in the 1760s. Shawls were mentioned in *Le Journal de la mode et du goût* for June 1790 as being a fashion taken from the English. Soon academies were opened for fashionable ladies to acquire the grace necessary for wearing them. With the advent of the *Directoire* and the Egyptian Campaigns of Napoleon in 1798–9, cashmere shawls really came into their own both as an enhancement of the classical appearance and as an aid to warmth.[33] Cashmere was the most highly prized fabric for shawls because of its soft, supple properties which could be draped most becomingly to attain the style *à l'antique*. One of the great sartorial victories of the classical style was the transformation of the shawl in to a kind of stole that was named the *schall uni*. This accessory naturally met with La Mésangère's full approval. The *schall uni*, if anything, tended to enhance the classical effect. As it tended to be coloured it contrasted with the white of the dress to emphasize the sweep of the drapery, thus adding to the general simplification in shape and movement.

Croisures à la victime were another challenge to the classical influence. They were a form of criss-cross lacing with ribbons on the back of the dress from shoulder to waist and down the sides of the sleeves. In *Le Journal des dames et des modes* for 19 May 1798 La Mésangère wrote that this

Embroidered muslin dress, *fichu* and *réticule*, 1790s. Muslin proved to be the most popular fabric for Neo-classical styles because it had soft and transparent properties and also could be easily washed and cared for, an important factor when only white or pale colours were fashionable. Muslin was woven in a variety of textures, shades and patterns and was often embroidered with small designs. Silks continued to be worn but those with a light, papery texture were preferred. The new slim-line gowns did not allow pockets. Their absence led to the use of the *réticule*. (Museum of Costume, Bath)

(24)

indeed, especially when worn with *chemises* that had delicate fan-like pleating on the back.

The statuesque character of the dresses clearly set ornamentation at a discount. There is, in particular, a notable restraint in the use of jewellery: many *élégantes* disdained all jewellery except pearls and diamonds.

curious millinery affectation was a symbolic way by which *élégantes* advertised that there was no mark of devotion or sacrifice which they would withhold from their lovers. The *croisures à la victime* looked regrettable

'Chignon en poire double Bandeau de Jais blanc. Schall de Laine à Franges'. Engraved fashion plate from *Le Journal des dames et des modes*, No. LXXIII, 7 ventôse an VI, 25 February 1798, Plate 24.
Long woollen shawls, particularly of cashmere, became the rage as the material could be draped in a manner becoming to the antique style of dress. The Egyptian expedition and fascination with the Orient provided the *marchandes de modes* with an opportunity for making exotic turbans and headdresses fashioned like turbans, with the addition of a striking *aigrette* serving admirably to enhance the height of the figure. *(Private Collection)*

'Elégante en Costume de Bal, les cheveux relevés à la Grecque; à l'instant du repos après le Tournoiement d'un Valse'. Engraved fashion plate from *Le Journal des dames et des modes*, No. V, 4 floréal an VI, 24 April 1798, Plate 16. The waltz, which was German in origin, was the dance-mania of 1797-98. This *élégante* is singled out both for her modesty and romantic disorder. Her ample gown and her headdress are heavily laden with diamonds. Her partner wears a green coat with a high collar, buff knee-breeches, white stockings and black pumps. Pantaloons and boots were worn for everyday fashion. *(Bibliothèque Doucet, Paris)*

was given a more stylish *entrée* in what was called the *balantine*. It was attached rather awkwardly with cords to the waist, as if the world of fashion were waiting unavailingly for the discovery of the shoulder bag. After these self-conscious introductions the handbag appears to have become commonplace.

Classical inspiration barely held in check the anarchical impulses that threatened a chain reaction of sartorial metamorphoses. Changes in accessories, at least, came at a bewildering pace that outstripped language's development. The constraint of the Neo-classical style elsewhere, made the *marchandes de modes* the safety valve of repressed fantasy. The extraordinary headdresses of the time provided a rallying point for all those with nothing in common beyond a search for the unusual and exotic. Turbans from the East, the famous comet, and ballooning, which so stirred imaginations, as well as plays, operas and ballets, struck the fancy of the fashionable world. Hats seemed to be suffused by the romantic outlook of *le style troubadour* that was gaining ground. That is not to say classical elements were altogether lacking. A close look at the fashion plates of *Le Journal des dames et des modes* shows examples of headdresses with classical overtones. Some *élégantes* wear laurel wreaths which no doubt would have won sartorial acclaim in antiquity. The *chapeau à la Minerve* hints at the helmet shape seen in the sketchbook that Jacques-Louis David made in Rome of antique statues of Minerva.

Correct footwear was also a test for those who aspired to recreate the antique. Most of the models in the fashion plates wear flat shoes made in green moroccan leather. In the period 1797-9 only four of the fashion plates in *Le Journal des dames et des modes* show *élégantes* wearing sandals, called by La Mésangère *cothurnes*. Some *élégantes* wear sandals which have thick soles and laced ribbon straps that reach to the ankle. Others wear green moroccan flat shoes with ribbon straps laced well above the ankle. The open lacework has the purpose of emphasizing the delicacy of the leg and evoking the classical spirit.

The sculptural qualities of the dress, by outlawing the use of pockets, had brought upheavals to households through ladies leaving their private correspondence about and losing their keys. A variety of handbags were brought onto the fashionable scene with some bravado. Some handbags were carried that were prominently inscribed 'R', standing less for *réticule*, than its nickname, a *risicule*, or as it came to be known more widely, a *ridicule*. For those who wished to be, if anything, more Roman than the Romans, the handbag

'Cheveux à la Titus. Écharpe agrafée sur l'épaule. Manteau sur le Bras. Gants froncés'. Engraved fashion plate from *Le Journal des dames et des modes*, No. XXVI, 5 fructidor an VI, 22 August 1799, Plate 57.
The *écharpe agrafée*, a closed scarf, lent variety to the classical line. In spite of its velvet border decorated with gold spangles,

the classical idea was there, the drapery reminiscent of a Roman toga. The complementary nature of *Directoire* accessories is also illustrated by the long, plain dark gloves simply tied at the elbows. *(Bibliothèque Doucet, Paris)*

In short, the French Revolution proved no more than a temporary setback for fashion and in the long run provided a fertile source for inspiration.[34]

Late Eighteenth-Century French Artists and Fashion

In the eighteenth century costume conspired with wealth to place all the other arts under its thrall. All the great artists from Watteau to Ingres delighted in reproducing the texture of fine materials, whether silk, tapestry, velvet, satin, damask or plain wool or cotton. The sharp, hard lines of David, François Gérard and other artists gain from the softening effect of the Neo-classical *chemise* to the point that an austere, pure style was born.

The immediate cause of the trend towards informal attire can be traced to changes at the French court. The alteration of the *bouffant* hairstyle seems to have originated from Queen Marie-Antoinette's mishap of losing some of her hair during a pregnancy. The simple muslin *chemise* that came into fashion in the 1780s has also been traced to the Queen who sensibly required a simpler attire when she and her ladies-in-waiting affected the role of milkmaids at Versailles's small *hameau* and at the *laîterie* at Rambouillet in what must have been the most elegantly appointed dairy in the world.

It was the *chemise à la reine*, worn by Queen Marie-Antoinette in her portrait painted by Mme Vigée-Le Brun and introduced formally to fashionable society at the *Salon* of 1783, that was to have the most profound repercussions on future developments in fashion. Mme Vigée-Le Brun, the daughter of a portrait painter and a hairdresser, was *the* artist at the epicentre of fashion. Her memoirs leave no doubt that she was something of an aspiring *couturière* and *coiffeureuse*. This is underpinned by the fact that all the great fashionable ladies of influence wanted her to paint them, wearing her costumes and hairstyles, such was their trust in her taste.

> As I had a horror of the current fashion, I did my best to make my models a little more picturesque. I was

delighted when, having gained their trust, they allowed me to dress them after my fancy. No-one wore shawls then, but I liked to drape my models with large scarves, interlacing them around the body and through the arms, which was an attempt to imitate the beautiful style of draperies seen in the paintings of Raphael and Domenichino . . . above all I detested the powdering of hair and succeeded in persuading the beautiful duchesse de Grammont-Caderousse not to wear it when she sat for me. Her hair was black as ebony, and I parted it on the forehead, arranging it in irregular curls. After the sitting, which ended around dinner time, I did not alter her hair at all and she left directly for the theatre; being such a pretty woman she was quite influential and her hairstyle insinuated itself into fashionable society and eventually became universal.[35]

Mme Vigée-Le Brun is an example of an artist who created fashions as well as recorded them. Yet, the origins of the *Directoire chemise* can be traced back as far as Joseph-Marie Vien. The teacher of Jacques-Louis David, Vien was the interpreter of the new finds at Herculaneum and Pompeii. Vien was particularly admired by Mme Vigée-Le Brun as the artist 'who first gave us the exactitude and style of the ancient Greek and Roman costumes.'[36] In the 'us' she included David and his pupils. In Vien's *La Marchande d'amours* of 1763, the dress of his concupiscent ladies is practically identical with the Neo-classical *chemise* of the *Directoire*. Both are designed to set off the youthful lines of tall statuesque girlish wearers, with no sartorial restraint beyond the high waist which itself helped the breasts to mould the garment's shape. The low *décolletage*, bare arms, simple hairstyle or modest turban, together with unfussy sandals are all more *Directoire* than the *Directoire* itself. They represent the simplification which artists held out as the ideal to the creators of fashion. That their ideal was accepted in its essentials can be seen from the review just undertaken of *Le Journal des dames et des modes*. Beside it, the influence of English fashion, of the theatre, even of comet tails and feminine caprice is far less marked.

Mme Vigée-Le Brun also participated in recording Spanish dress, a sartorial facet of *le style troubadour* that was especially popular during the reign of Louis XVI and Marie-Antoinette.[37] By now, Spain was a political and economic backwater. Yet the country still evoked for the French a sense of the romantic and the exotic, especially

Portrait of Queen Marie-Antoinette, painting attributed to E.-L. Vigée-Le Brun, c. 1783.
This portrait is a veritable icon of fashion history. The Queen evokes a pastoral mood in a muslin *chemise à la reine* and straw hat. The *chemise à la reine* is cut full and loose and is

tied with a silk gold-striped sash round her waist, while the full sleeves are held in place by ribbon ties. The origin of this style was the *robe à la mode en Créole* which came from the French West Indies. (*The National Gallery of Art, Washington, D.C., Timken Collection*)

in regard to dress. What the French loved so much were its details, such as rosettes, ribbon lacings and trimmings, lace collars and cuffs, and large hats bedecked with feathers. These details appealed to Rococo artists because of their asymmetry and the three-dimensional effects they could achieve. French *commedia dell'arte* characters of Spanish origin such as Crispin and Scaramouche were painted by Watteau. Watteau also drew fashionable French ladies wearing the distinctive *espagnolette* costume which consisted of a corset, a tight black silk bodice, and a long, full, black skirt set off by rosettes of brightly coloured taffeta. By the middle of the eighteenth century Mme de Pompadour patronized the painting of figures in Spanish dress. The outstanding practitioner was Carle Van Loo, his most celebrated paintings in the genre being *La Conversation espagnole* (1755) and *La Lecture espagnole* (1761). Indeed his output was so vast that contemporaries

gave him the soubriquet, *Vanloo d'Espagne*. A fashionable portraitist who brought out the Arcadian quality of Spanish dress was Drouais, seen, for example, in his group portrait of the marquis de Sourches and his family, painted in 1756. Besides creating a pastoral mood and providing a masquerade costume, Spanish dress was also linked with the theatre. By being painted in Spanish dress the sitter was indicating that he or she was well-educated and well-read, with a knowledge of the historic past.

By the time Mme Vigée-Le Brun was painting, details of Spanish dress had merged with contemporary French fashion. For women this meant a tight black bodice in the form of a jacket, and a long, full, black skirt, an updated

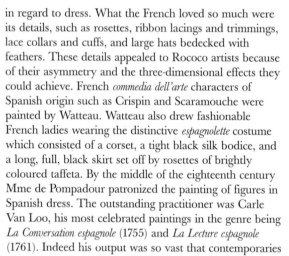

Portrait of Madame Molé-Raymond, painted by E.-L. Vigée-Le Brun, 1786 and 'Femme en habit de promenade du matin; redingote écarlate, gilet et jupon blancs garnis de queues de martre'. Engraved by A.-B. Duhamel. Fashion plate from *Le Magasin des modes nouvelles, françaises et anglaises*, No. 1, December 1788, Plate 1

This portrait, dated 1786, seems to have been borrowed by *Le Magasin des modes nouvelles, françaises et anglaises* in 1788,

for the pose and the fashions of the pair are very similar. Both subjects wear their hair only slightly powdered, falling wide and loose, under immense hats. They both wear wide, flat-collared *demi-redingotes* simple in cut, of unpatterned material, and opening onto plain skirts. They make a point of displaying their large fur muffs, a major accessory of the 1780s. *(Musée de Louvre, Paris/Cabinet des Estampes, Bibliothèque Nationale de France, Paris. © Photo: RMN-H Lewandowski)*

Portrait of Madame Adélaide Perregaux, painted by E.-L. Vigée-Le Brun, 1789.

The sitter wears the very fashionable Spanish costume, important in the development of *le style troubadour*. Madame Perregaux wears an updated, chic version of the old *espagnolette* costume consisting of a corset, a tight black bodice, here in the form of the fashionable jacket known as the *caraco* or *pierrot* and a long, full black skirt, all dramatically set off by red rosettes, red buttons and red piping. Her very full white muslin *fichu* has a delicately-edged lace collar which matches the cuffs of her sleeves. A black *béret* topped with a profusion of red plumes completes this ravishing outfit.
(Reproduced by permission of the Trustees of the Wallace Collection, London)

version of the *espagnolette* costume. The basic garments for men were the *pourpoint*, knee-breeches which followed the cut of the eighteenth-century *culottes*, and a *manteau*.

The portrait of Mme Perregaux wearing Spanish dress is Mme Vigée-Le Brun's most lavish statement in this aspect of *le style troubadour*. Dated 1789, this portrait, with the sitter clothed in a lush black jacket and skirt set off by red rosettes and ribbon trimmings, shows how rich Spanish dress was on the eve of the French Revolution. Mme Perregaux was the daughter of the comte de Praël and married Jean-Fréderic Perregaux, a wealthy banker whose many English clients included the 3rd Marquess of Hertford, one of the founders of the Wallace Collection in London, where the portrait is located.

Mme Vigée-Le Brun, in her *Self-Portrait in a Straw Hat*, also paid tribute to the kind of seventeenth-century Arcadian costume popular in the Spanish-ruled

Netherlands. Althought she wears the fashionable French *chemise*, her portrait was clearly inspired by Rubens's *Chapeau de Paille* which she had admired on a visit to the Low Countries in 1782. Mme Vigée-Le Brun painted herself on several occasions in various styles of dress. They are fashion illustrations in their own right. Self-portraiture had become very popular from the late seventeenth century. In 1664 Leopoldo de' Médici established the collection of self-portraits at the Uffizi Gallery in Florence. During the following centuries artists travelling to Italy visited the collection and were often invited, as Mme Vigée-Le Brun was, to contribute a self-portrait to it.

Another woman artist who deserves to be far better known and consulted for the documentation of dress is Marguerite Gérard. Sister-in-law of Jean-Honoré Fragonard, whose celebrated *portraits de fantasie* are another facet of *le style troubadour*, she responded like him,

A Musical Evening in a Salon, gouache by J.-B. Mallet, 1793. Mallet illustrates the softer feminine fashion line and the greater tightness and slimness of the male silhouette during the French Revolution. Female fashions emphasize the large hats, loose *fichus* and full skirts which show that both silk and muslin were popular. Interesting male details are the wide lapels of the *veste* overlapping the emerging lapels of the coat. (*Sale, Sotheby Parke Bernet, London, 27 June 1974, lot 44*)

to the changing tastes in fashion. Her interest in and promotion of fashion is indispensable to fashion illustration. She was one of the first artists to note the romantic revival in fashionable dress featuring troubadourian costume and accessories. Above all, Marguerite Gérard should be studied for fabrics and their relationship to dress, for instance, for the way the skirts of dresses fell. Her inventory contains a description of four 'extremely' worn *mannikins* of different sizes which she used to achieve the 'hyper-realistic reproduction of the cascading fabrics of ladies' skirts'.[38]

Antoine-Louis-François Sergent-Marceau aspired during the Revolution to re-design feminine costume. He was reported to have declared the need for a dress which at once freed women's limbs while not detracting from the beauty of their bodies.[39] A pupil of Saint-Aubin, he also continued the tradition of costume books with his *Les Costumes des peuples anciens et modernes*.

During the first years of the Revolution Jean-Baptiste Mallet set fashionable *élégants* and *élégantes* against classical interiors in a *salon*, usually engaged in a musical evening. By dint of their clothes, deportment and setting they could just as easily have stepped out of fashion plates. His work is also essential for consultation during those years when fashion magazines were in abeyance. Mallet was both a painter and an engraver with wide-ranging tastes. He was renowned for his historicism in promoting troubadourian costumes and accessories.

Another artist fundamental to the story of the development of fashion and its illustration is Jacques-Louis David. The last great *chef d'atelier* before Ingres, David counted among his pupils François Gérard, Anne-Louis Girodet, Antoine-Jean Gros, and Ingres himself, all of whom were fashionable portrait painters. With his painting of *Psyche* in 1798, Gérard also made popular the fashion for white face. David's paintings, particularly the *Oath of the Horatii* and the *Brutus*, inspired historically-accurate classical costumes, and were rapturously received in the *salons* as well as reproduced upon the stage as *tableaux vivants* during the Revolution. In May 1794 the Committee of Public Safety invited David to produce designs for a national civilian costume and for government officials. David directed the revolutionary festivals and clothed the women who took part in simple, antique-style white

gowns which helped to make the white *chemise* the most important gown of the 1790s. David was profoundly convinced of the importance of women's dress in the 'return to the antique', and in his portraits he helped both to pioneer and reflect the latest fashions. His influence on fashion as its leading painter, and as what was effectively Minister of Fashion, was enormous during the Revolution and the *Directoire*.

Finally, a glance at some of the outstanding caricaturists must be included. The justification for their inclusion is the exceptional skill with which these artists managed to reconcile the demands of caricature with accurate portrayal of dress. These artists were perceptive enough to fasten onto the essentials of fashion, often down to the smallest details. There were so many able artists in this group: Philibert-Louis Debucourt, Carle and Horace Vernet, Louis-Léopold Boilly, Claude-Louis Desrais, Antoine Chataîgnier and Jean-Baptiste Isabey. Carle Vernet's drawings of *incroyables* and *merveilleuses* may seem preposterous distortions of fashion, but a clear indication

of Vernet's accuracy was the indignation of the *incroyables* themselves at his caricatures of them.[40] The strongest proof that Carle Vernet's caricatures gave an authentic rendering of their subjects is the appearance of the fashion plate in La Mésangère's *Journal* based on his notorious *homme degagé* and the endorsement by La Mésangère that the fashions were actually worn (see p85). Carle Vernet's *homme degagé* enjoyed the status of a model for aspiring men of fashion - so caricature suffered the indignity of being turned inside out to become a new reality. In fact, a close look at Vernet's *incroyables* and *merveilleuses* serves to dispel much of their sartorial grotesqueness: it is far less the costumes than the wearers who are distorted. The prints of Debucourt, Boilly, Isabey, and Desrais show that all these fashions, far from being the monopoly of a few eccentrics, were worn at the very top of society.

The words *incroyables* and *merveilleuses*, along with others such as *inconcevables* and *impossibles*, were coined to express the public's sheer astonishment of the new fashions rather than as precise sartorial labels. Until

their resurrection under the First Empire, they were used, as the dates of most of the caricatures show, at the beginning of the *Directoire*. While it is true that a vein of folly ran through the headdresses of *Directoire merveilleuses*, frizzy wigs after the first few months gave way to close-cropped hairstyles *à la Titus* and *à la Caracalla*. Most important in their attire was the simple, Neo-classical *chemise*, even amongst those who chose to hitch them up to show off their legs. Horace Vernet's popular series, *Incroyables et Merveilleuses, Paris, 1810–1818*, had the effect of reviving the terms almost after they had died out. These later *merveilleuses* represent an almost complete reversal of their *Directoire* namesakes, and, prefigure some of the worst vestimentary excesses of the mid-nineteenth century.

Fashion Illustration Outside France to the End of the Eighteenth Century

High fashion almost all over Europe took as its source of inspiration Parisian models. Hand in hand with the copying of French fashions went the copying of French fashion plates. Copyright laws were slack and piracy was widespread.[41] In England *The Lady's Magazine* just after 1785 started to reproduce French fashion plates. This was in spite of the fact that England had some excellent fashion-plate artists such as Thomas Stothard whose anonymous work had appeared in that periodical.[42]

The influence of the theatre on fashion illustration must also be noted. The exhibition entitled *Mrs Jordan. The Duchess of Drury Lane*, held at Kenwood House, London, in 1995 featured prints of the actress wearing the costumes in which she performed some of her famous roles. The exhibition and catalogue emphasized how a deluge of these prints found a ready market amongst her loyal fans who wanted a cheap image to remind them of a favourite performance. Some of these prints also appeared as fashion plates in ladies' magazines.

London continued to flourish, with the publication of more magazines towards the close of the eighteenth century. Occasionally a title displays a tendency towards overstatement, for example, *The Lady's Monthly Museum, or Polite Repository of Amusement and Instruction: being an Assemblage of what can Tend to Please the Fancy, Instruct the Mind or Exalt the Character of the British Fair. Edited by a

Montgolfière lancée à Tivoli, le 15 thermidor, engraved by Philibert-Louis Debucourt, c. 1799-1800.
Ballooning was a popular craze since the early 1780s. The first unmanned balloon ascent took plate in 1782. Debucourt's print captures so many of the fashions recorded in *Le Journal des dames et des modes*: the *croisures à la victime*, the *récticules*, fans, the Grecian hairstyles, the great variety of headwear, the Neo-classical *chemises* of the *élégantes* and the streamlined dark coats, short, striped waistcoats, pantaloons, embryonic top hats, and classical hairstyles of the *élégants*. Debucourt, who perfected the process of printing in colour, is regarded as one of the supreme masters of engraving. *(B.T. Batsford Ltd Archive)*

Welladay! Is this my son Tom!, engraving after S.H. Grimm, c. 1770.
Here, the old father, arriving in London to see his son, expresses disbelief at his becoming a 'macaroni'. Fashionable young men, as part of their education, went on the Grand Tour. From Italy in the 1760s they introduced the word 'macaroni', which meant stylish, elegant. It soon came to be appropriated to an effeminate young man who wore a brightly coloured, tight-fitting coat, a nosegay of flowers, a huge powdered wig, and a tiny Nivernois hat, named after the French ambassador in London. *(Victoria and Albert Musuem, London)*

On the principle of saving the best till last, Niklaus Wilhelm Innocentius von Heideloff's *The Gallery of Fashion* (1794-1803) is undoubtedly the highlight of late eighteenth-century fashionable English women's periodical publication. Of quarto size rather than the tiny octavo size of French fashion magazines, it is the first English magazine to be devoted entirely to fashion, and the first also to be issued with all the fashion plates in colour. Printed on fine quality paper and with an elaborate title page, *The Gallery of Fashion* appeared in monthly parts with two fashion plates each, the total number of plates being 217. Each fashion plate showed either one, two or three figures and was accompanied by full descriptions of the costumes they wore. The cost of subscribing was three guineas a year. The fashion plates are hand-coloured aquatints. Aquatint was invented around the middle of the eighteenth century and enjoyed much popularity for the rest of the eighteenth century in England. It is a process whereby a metal plate is sprinkled with acid-resistant varnish, which then is fused to the plate by heating. When the plate is placed in an acid bath, the acid bites between the tiny particles of resin and produces a surface which is evenly granulated. The artist can create his design by drawing on the plate with acid-resistant varnish. Aquatint is a technique admirably suited to the rendering of the transparent effects of dress, for a great variety of tone can be obtained by immersing the plate in acid and varnishing in turn. An added attraction of Heideloff's fashion plates is that details of the costumes are highlighted in gold, silver and other metallic tints. Sacheverell Sitwell has written that Heideloff would have employed not more than three or four artists for the hand-colouring at his premises and that the work of gold, silver and other metallic tints would have been the work of one person who did nothing else.[43] An interesting feature of *The Gallery of Fashion* was the great number of pursuits, mainly outdoors, of late eighteenth-century fashionable women, and the great variety of dresses needed to carry them out. Groups of women are shown out driving in a berlin, riding, at the seaside (a new preoccupation),

'Society of Ladies' (1798–1832). This magazine precisely outlined its objectives: a woman's domestic duties were her first priority. Instruction included languages, maths, philosophy and history, while music, art, poetry and gardening were among the recommendations for amusement. For the fashion-conscious a Cabinet of Fashion was featured every six months which contained coloured engravings. The editor pointed out that the Cabinet of Fashion only recorded what fashionable society women were wearing and did not prognosticate future styles. In the first issues the illustrations are of a poor quality, although those of the nineteenth century are of a higher standard. In format, *The Lady's Monthly Museum* was small, measuring only seven inches by five inches, and bulky, being usually made up of about 85 pages.

taking tea, playing and singing at the harpsichord or harp, and in evening dress and court dress. English court dress was most peculiar, for wide hoops continued to be worn with the newly fashionable Neo-classical line. Another curious English fashion was the wearing of two or three enormous ostrich feathers in the hair. Fashionable ladies were provided with a whole host of accessories, fans, gloves, parasols, watches and even telescopes! Heideloff did not design the costumes and accessories but copied what he saw at court and in high fashion circles, for his subscribers were not in trade, but from the upper strata of society, with lists published at the end of each copy. Many of his subscribers came from the German Royal Family. Heideloff himself was born in Stuttgart in 1761 into a family of artists and worked as an engraver there before emigrating to Paris in 1784 where he worked as a miniature painter. Like so many of his clients, he fled to England at the time of the French Revolution.

English and French fashion plates were both copied and exported all over Europe.[44] *Le Journal des dames et des modes* was published in a legitimate edition at Frankfurt from 1798 to 1848, with the text for a time both in French and German. Yet, as the superb exhibition, *German Printmaking in the Age of Goethe* (British Museum, 1994) showed, the German states enjoyed a period of extraordinary achievement in literature, music, art and printing during Goethe's lifetime (1749–1832). Indeed, the *Papierkultur* of the second half of the eighteenth century in Germany, due to rigorous education and the recruitment of artists which served the practical self-interests of the German rulers who founded or re-modelled numerous academies, had important repercussions for fashion illustration.

Berlin, under the aegis of the intensely Francophile King Frederick II the Great, rapidly advanced its position in the second half of the eighteenth century as a political and cultural centre. Many artists were closely involved in the intellectual life of the city, making a salient contribution to the printing renaissance, largely through book illustration. Few artists had the necessary skill to execute line engraving, the most prestigious form of print production which had Paris the principal centre, so they gravitated toward the more spontaneous medium of etching. The artist with the most distinctive style was Daniel Nikolaus Chodowiecki, the 'German Hogarth'. Born in Danzig (Gdansk) in 1726, Chodowiecki settled permanently in Berlin in 1743. He was admitted to the Berlin Academy in 1764 as a miniature painter, but it was as a printmaker in the field of book illustration that he achieved his reputation from 1768 onwards attaining such renown that he played an important part in the Academy, rising to become its Director in 1797. Chodowiecki's etchings were often executed in connection with the pocket calendars and almanacs which were a popular and prominent feature of German book production in the latter part of the eighteenth century. They provided an ideal vehicle for conveying didactic moral cycles, and also, fashions. His two series of etchings entitled *Natural and Affected Behaviour* published in the Göttingen pocket calendar for 1779 and 1780, were a commission Chodowiecki received from Lichtenberg, who supplied the text but gave Chodowiecki free rein in his choice of images. The conflict between 'natural' and 'artificial' man was central to eighteenth-century philosophy and literature. In this case the satire was directed in general against all forms of exaggerated self-expression and more specifically against the manners of Francophile court culture, which was particularly dominant in Prussia. Chodowiecki's figures for calendars and almanacs were generally executed twelve to a plate in two rows of six back to back, corresponding to the months of the year. The small-scale format combined with his lively, graceful style soon made the copying of English almanacs redundant, as they do not stand aesthetic comparison with Chodowiecki's *oeuvre*, or with that of Johann August Rossmässler and Ernst Ludwig Riepenhuisen who worked in a similar vein.

Chodowiecki is important to the study of fashion both as an illustrator and as a designer. The damage to women's health caused by their constricting clothing was an on-going debate throughout the eighteenth century. In the

1780s the debate accelerated in the German-speaking world. Emperor Joseph II of Austria issued a decree in 1783 banning the wearing of the voluminous French *paniers*. Ladies at the Berlin court loved them so much that regulations had to be imposed on their wear. In 1785 Chodowiecki was called upon by Franz Ehrenberg, publisher of *Frauenzimmer-Almanach*, to design a reform dress. The designs of Chodowiecki's gowns were based upon the simple *chemise* in the classical Greek style.

The development of printing techniques and fashion illustration continued apace in the German-speaking world. Johann Georg Wille was the most famous and successful German line engraver of the late eighteenth century. He worked his way to Paris and became the key link between Germany and France. The last two decades of the eighteenth century saw the blossoming of German fashion magazines, providing the first important competition to England and especially France. With the worsening political situation leading to the collapse of the *ancien régime*, German publishers, now in a strong position, seized their opportunities.

One of the most important and widely read fashion magazines was the *Journal der Luxus und der Moden* (1786-1825) founded in Weimar by the publisher Friedrich Justus Bertuch, a friend of Goethe's and the painter Georg Melchior Kraus. Correspondents were sent to Paris and London to report on the fashions. Tinted etchings were accompanied by detailed descriptions of the garments, their colours, materials and patterns, and the accessories which set them off. German fashions were methodically covered as the aim of the *Journal der Luxus und der Moden* was 'to raise the standards of taste in Germany and not slavishly imitate everything foreign'. The *Journal für Fabrik, Manufaktur, Handlung und Mode* (1791-1808) was founded in Leipzig and had amongst its distinguished publishers Christian Adolphe Hempel and Johann Friedrich Gleditsch. It was innovatory in affixing to each issue small squares of fashionable textiles. However influential these journals were, artistically they could never match the delicacy and refinement of line and colour found in the fashion

plates of *Le Journal des dames et des modes*. Paris still set the tone, with French tailors travelling throughout the German-speaking world to propagate French models.[45] German copying of the far superior originals is only too obvious in their fashion magazines.

Goethe's *Travels in Italy* is the most famous literary testament to the fascination Italy exerted on German artists and there were few who from the 1770s did not visit the country at some point in their careers. Invaluable for fashion illustration is the work of the society artist Friederich Rehberg. His series of twelve etchings entitled *Drawings faithfully copied from Nature at Naples . . . dedicated to the Right Honourable Sir William Hamilton*, dated 1794, studied Lady Emma Hamilton in twelve different poses. She had married Hamilton, the first British ambassador at Naples, a few years earlier.

'Lady Hamilton as a bacchante', engraved by Thomas Piroli. After *Drawings faithfully copied from nature at Naples . . . dedicated to the Right Honourable Sir William Hamilton* by Friederich Rehberg, 1794, Plate 8.
Lady Hamilton in her 'attitudes' delighted to recreate *bacchantes* in the frescoes of the villa of Cicero. (*Victoria and Albert Museum, London*)

A Meissen Crinoline Group of the Handkiss, modelled by J.J. Kändler, c. 1740.
The lady, with a pug perched on her lap, sits on a gilt-pierced chair taking tea from a page. She wears a black bodice, a bright yellow underskirt with an elaborate *indianische Blumen* border, voluminous *paniers*, and a pink overskirt gracefully turned back to reveal its fine turquoise lining. Her suitor wears a gilt-edged iron-red coat, black breeches, shoes and bag wig. (*Department of European Ceramics, Christie's, London*)

Her evening entertainment for her husband's guests was to strike classical poses in Greek costume.

In Germany, another medium of recording fashion, figures of porcelain, must be singled out. Porcelain is a neglected form of illustration but one of importance to the broader development of fashion illustration throughout Europe. The outstanding porcelain factory was at Meissen, where J. J. Kändler was the first modeller to realize the creative possibilities of depicting fashion on porcelain figures. Born in Dresden in 1706 and apprenticed as a sculptor, he was appointed *Modellmeister* at Meissen in 1733. As chief modeller for the next 40 years, he was arbiter of the types of figures made and of the fashions they wore. Imitations, copies and adaptations of his work were made at various rival factories both inside and outside Germany.[46] The most celebrated of Kändler's porcelain figures are generically described as 'crinoline' groups. This is a modern term for

porcelain figures where a fashionable lady is attired in a dress worn with voluminous *paniers*. (The crinoline is a mid-nineteenth fashion.) She is courted by a fashionable dressed gentleman and attended by a servant. Crinoline groups show fashionable society engaged in frivolous pursuits and pleasures of the court. The penetrating influence of French court culture including dress is keenly felt. The crinoline groups are a superb vehicle for studying the spirit of an age of elegance in dress, and beyond, for Kändler's impact on fashion was considerable.

In the absence of Spanish fashion plates it is the work of Goya that is indispensable for viewing Spanish fashions. Goya's paintings, tapestry designs, drawings and etchings show the whole gamut of the dress worn in Spain. His fashionable women wear Parisian-inspired costumes, but their gowns are always shorter and tighter than their French counterparts. Their accessories are also different with a preference for brilliantly-coloured shawls, and white or black lace mantillas mounted on tortoiseshell combs, with an occasional flower over one temple. Exotic fans and parasols were also favoured by Spanish ladies. For fashionable men, the differences from their French equivalents consisted in shorter, tighter garments, flapping lapels, and wide cravats.

Italy was fragmented politically, being, like Germany, a conglomeration of states. Italian dress was affected by two factors: regional influences and sumptuary legislation which tried to control foreign fashions and to govern the dress of the noble class in the old city states. However, sumptuary legislation was only partially effective and by the second half of the eighteenth century French fashions were worn. French fashion plates were copied in various Italian cities. It was in the large cities, Venice having pride of place, that French dress was introduced. Two key artistic sources which show how luxurious French costume was interpreted in Italy are the *oeuvres* of the Maestro di Ridotto and Pietro Longhi. The former is excellent for elucidating how fashionable Venetian ladies took their Parisian-inspired models and imposed upon them bright colours and fabrics suitable to their climate. His most insightful scenes are the *levées* of noblewomen where merchants are showing them samples of fabric. The manufacture of fine textiles continued to flourish in eighteenth-century Italy: Genoa and Milan produced velvets, Milan and Turin concentrated on the whole

Portrait of Don Sebastián Martínez y Pérez, painted by Francisco de Goya, 1792.
Men's coats made in a narrow, striped material are popular in Europe in the last decade of the eighteenth century. However, what makes this coat distinctively Spanish is the way the stripes are used to enhance the tight, cutaway line and flapping

lapels of the coat. The large, ornate buttons are also characteristically Spanish. This portrait is a magnificent example of Goya's sensitivity for fashion. The reflections of the sunlight on the blue silk, white-striped coat bring out the shimmering quality of the fabric. *(The Metropolitan Museum of Art, New York, Rogers Fund 1906)*

gamut of silks from satin to gauze, while many cities wove woollen cloth of various weights. The genre scenes of the everyday life of patricians and rich merchants painted by Pietro Longhi are also of much value. His forte was the combined details of the manners, settings and costumes of the Venetian nobility and wealthy. In Longhi's paintings men too indulge themselves and pay much attention to their fabrics and their tailoring.

Italy, and in particular Venice, maintained prime position as a publisher of costume books. The outstanding costume book of the late eighteenth century is Teodoro Viero's *Raccolta Di 126 Stampe rappresantano Figure ed Abiti di varie Nazione . . .* published in Venice in 1783. Viero illustrates all types of regional dress. The widescale use of black for all classes in Italy is also well documented. The effect of sumptuary legislation upon the clothing worn by

the distinctive patrician class is well-observed especially for Genoa and Venice. Towards the end of the eighteenth century a few fashion magazines were launched in Florence, the most successful being *Giornale delle Mode* (1788-95). It confirms that for the upper classes the essential line was French for both men and women. And at the end of the century Giovanni Domenico Tiepolo observed the ludicrous pretensions of society in his series of drawings, *Scenes from Contemporary Life*. His biting humour is matched by his delight in rendering fashions. While Tiepolo's drawings convey a sense of the ridiculous, they are excellent for studying the minutiae of fashion and have a spontaneous quality often lacking in fashion plates.

'The Milliner's Shop', pen and brown ink drawing with brown, ochre and tawny-coloured washes over black chalk on white paper, by Giovanni Domenico Tiepolo, c. 1791.
Interest in the milliner's shop is provided by the employees, the customers and their companions, and a crowd of children playing games. On the table on the right perched on a milliner's dummy is a bonnet in the latest fashion. This drawing comes from the series, *Scenes from Contemporary Life*. The series constitutes a kind of *comédie humaine* of late eighteenth-century Venice where fashion plays a prominent part. *(Courtesy Museum of Fine Arts, Boston, Sir Frederick Wedmore; Henry Oppenheime)*

Children's Dress

Throughout this chapter there have been many references to 'revolution'. It is a salutary reminder of the great changes which took place in children's dress in the third quarter of the eighteenth century. Many of the ideas on the subject of the rearing, education and clothing of children advocated by eighteenth-century philosophers had already been popularized by John Locke in his *Thoughts on Education* written in 1693. Locke was of the opinion that, as man had been born free, he should not be wrapped in swaddling clothes as a child. While swaddling was on the decline in England by the middle of the eighteenth century, it was still widespread in Europe. In France, Rousseau took up the thoughts advanced by Locke. In his *Émile*, written in 1762, he advocated loose-fitting clothes for children. In 1787 children's dress was the subject of one of the fullest and best-informed treatments in any fashion periodical of the late eighteenth-century. *Le Magasin des modes nouvelles, françaises et anglaises* accorded great importance to children's dress:

> It is a long time since we last depicted children. They also have their fashions, as fathers and mothers will not be displeased to learn, for they are often at a loss to know how to clothe them. Small girls almost invariably follow women's fashions, but small boys who are dressed as sailors have their own.[47]

The fashion magazine illustrated a girl in a simple white muslin frock that was also worn by women in the 1780s. Both styles were reflections of the new feeling for naturalism and informality, with the *chemise* going on to fashion dominance during the French Revolution. The new garment for boys, the *matelot* or sailor's outfit, described and illustrated in the fashion magazine, was called a 'skeleton suit' in England. There its fashion roots were laid in the 1770s when the trend for informality commenced. Consisting of trousers whose provenance was not only sailors but also peasants, and a short jacket, it was the ideal ensemble for the comfort and well-being

of children. With the skeleton suit boys wore a fine cotton or linen shirt with the collar open and their hair loosely arranged and unpowdered. By the end of the 1780s English-style dress for boys was the subject of discussion not only in the leading French fashion magazine but also the leading German fashion periodical, the *Journal des Luxus und der Moden.* Boys had not only effected a revolution in their own dress, but also anticipated the attire of the *sans-culotte* and contributed to the advancement of fatherly sartorial elegance by foreshadowing the pantaloons of the 1790s and the Romanticism of the early nineteenth century when gentlemen would adopt a similar style of dress.

Portrait of Don Manuel Osorio Monique de Zuñiga, painted by Francisco de Goya, 1784.
Goya's charming portrait shows how Spanish formality was combined with the new, easy, functional clothes for boys. This little boy wears a red silk skeleton suit, fastened round the waist with a wide, lace-trimmed silk sash. Typically Spanish details are the open collar with a gold and silver *faja* and slippers with bow knots. The jacket and suit while fitted is simply cut. The skeleton suit was worn by boys all over Europe. (*The Metropolitan Museum of Art, Jules Bache Collection 1949*)

Portrait of Miss Haverfield, painted by Thomas Gainsborough, c. 1780.
New fashions for girls at the end of the eighteenth century were a fine linen or muslin dress and a wide silk ribbon sash. The rigid boned bodice disappeared as did the powdered wig. (*Reproduced by permission of the Trustees of The Wallace Collection, London*)

4: The Growth of Fashion Illustration in the Nineteenth Century

A New Silhouette and a New Monopoly on Fashion

If one were looking for a word to characterize the silhouette of costume at the beginning of the nineteenth century it would be simplicity. In the aftermath of the stirring events of the French Revolution the map of fashion had changed dramatically and permanently. Well established by the end of the eighteenth century and the beginning of the nineteenth century were dresses falling vertically from a waistline just under the bust, with a *décolleté* neckline which emphasized a sexuality that did not hark back to the eighteenth century but anticipated the twentieth. Called the 'Empire line' after the French First Empire (1800-14) when this style of dress was so popular, it has undergone continuous revivals up to the present day. Men's clothes, too, evoked a simplicity at the turn of the century, with a sober and streamlined appearance bereft of fussy details and decoration, characteristics that are still adhered to today. In addition to its influential role as a catalyst in the evolution of modern dress, the French Revolution also brought about a shift in social attitudes to fashion by breaking the privileged grip of the nobility. In the nineteenth century fashion was arbitrated by the middle classes. It became the prerogative of those who wanted to expend their time and money on it, thus accelerating the growth of fashion illustration.

French Influences on English Fashion Plates

The nineteenth century was the heyday of the fashion plate. Even in time of strife French fashions led the way and were eagerly sought after. Fashionable English society was heavily dependent on the high calibre of the *couturières* and *marchandes de modes*. The fashionable English lady in any case felt that French fashions were superior to English ones.

Fashion journals dedicated to women snowballed, for, right from the beginning of the new century, fashion was largely a female preoccupation. The reason for this was the very different roles assigned men and women's dress in the newly established social order where the *nouveaux riches* were in the ascendant.

Men adopted a form of three-piece suit, consisting of a morning coat, trousers and waistcoat. The coat and trousers were made of good quality cloth in plain, subdued colours. Only the waistcoat offered a modicum of dash and colour. It was this standardized, uniform mode that symbolized their new economic position. Whilst various new overcoats and accessories were shown in the fashion plates of women's fashion magazines, female finery was the way of showing off newly acquired wealth and social standing.

Many of the new fashion magazines were given a French title as the publishers thought that would give them an added cachet. Thus there appeared *Le Miroir de la Mode*, published in London by the Bond Street dressmaker, Madame Lanchester, from 1803 to 1806. A committed francophile, Madame Lanchester purveyed her own designs which English ladies, who wanted to be as purist as possible in their emulation of the French Neo-classical

'Le Prétexte'. Fashion plate engraved by Philibert-Louis Debucourt. From his series *Modes et manières du jour à la fin du dix-huitième et au commencement du dix-neuvième*, published by Pierre de La Mésangère, Paris, No. 1, 1800. This simple white muslin chemise dress and a dark velvet short sleeve spencer defining the silhouette shows the enduring passion for the Neo-classical style. Debucourt's refined style in this series was still reflected in the fashion plates of the early twentieth century. (*Victoria and Albert Museum, London*)

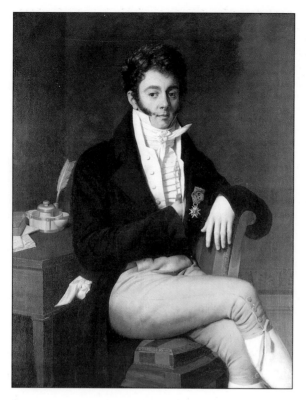

February 1806 entitled *La Belle Assemblée*; sub-title, 'Bell's Court and Fashionable Magazine, Addressed Particularly to the Ladies'. Bell is thought to have been influenced by the success of Le Brun's *Le Journal de la mode et du goût*,[1] and his magazine followed much the same format, combining fashion with a literary content, as well as encouraging communication and correspondence. Because of its *franglais* character, 'elegance of display' was also of primary concern. Considered the ancestor of the glitzy fashion magazines of today, it was royal octavo in size. Fashions were delineated in two black-and-white engraved fashion plates, folded face to face, or, in one fashion plate folded to equal two fashion plates. Bell employed the best fashion artists in England, including Arthur William Devis, the son of the celebrated portrait painter, James Mitan, John and William Hopwood, and Richard Corbould. Many of the fashion plates were anonymous, and it was thought Bell called upon the services of Thomas Stothard who had worked on *The Lady's Magazine* during its most successful period in the late eighteenth century. Bell also had French fashion plates copied, many of the fashion plates being English copies of French originals. One of Bell's most exciting innovations was the addition of two supplements. One supplement was concerned with literature, the second devoted to advertisements. Here ladies found items such as dressmaking and dress materials, cosmetics and perfumery. Some of these ads could be quite lengthy, such as the four pages selling Urlings Lace, which included an engraving of Urlings shop in the Strand and samples of real lace appended to the shop windows. It was John Bell's son, John Browne Bell, who in October 1806 launched the aforementioned *Le Beau Monde*. The rivalry prompted Bell *père* to bring out *La Belle Assemblée* in two forms after November 1806: one priced at half-a-crown which had black-and-white fashion plates and one costing three shillings and sixpence which contained hand-coloured fashion plates. Luckily for Bell senior, *Le*

style of dress, studied intently. John Browne Bell published *Le Beau Monde* in London from 1806-10, offering his subscribers hand-coloured fashion plates with every issue. He also aimed to attract a male readership with articles on male sporting attire, newly-designed coaches and equipment and accounts of race meetings.

The seminal importance of French fashion publishing was confirmed when the London publisher John Bell founded a monthly fashion magazine for ladies in

Portrait of Louis-Charles-Mercier Dupaty, painted by J.-A.-D. Ingres, c. 1805-10.
Ingres's rendering of the line and texture of clothing brings out both the simplicity and the Romantic qualities evident in fashionable men's dress at the beginning of the nineteenth century. M. Dupaty's plain dark-green coat has full upper sleeves gathered into armseye, a high-rolled collar and notched lapel and is impeccably cut back into the tails to show off the pearl-grey form-fitting breeches that button on the knee and are decorated with red ribbons. The smallest attention to detail is seen in the gleaming white shirt which has a stiff, high collar and finely pleated ruffles down the front. Equally faultless is the cravat which holds the shirt collar in the distinctive funnel-shape at the neck. *(Philadelphia Museum of Art, John G. Johnson Collection)*

Self-Portrait, miniature, painted by J.-B. Isabey, ivory, c. 1805. This self-portrait points the direction in which men's fashionable dress was heading. Black is worn with dramatic effect against a stark white neckcloth, heightening the painter's Romantic appearance. Sombre colours heralded the coming of the Industrial Revolution and a more utilitarian outlook when the majority of men wanted to project an image of sober respectability as though dressed for work of a professional nature. *(Reproduced by permission of The Trustees of The Wallace Collection)*

Beau Monde did not flourish, eventually folding in 1810. Thus commenced what would be *La Belle Assemblée*'s finest decade. The fashion section came under the aegis of Mrs Mary Ann Bell, who it is thought was related in some way to John Bell.[2] She was a leading dressmaker with a string of successful shops in London. From 1810 to 1820 *La Belle Assemblée* went upmarket, offering two illustrated pages in each issue featuring morning and evening dresses, town costumes, walking attire, seaside bathing dresses, headwear, spencers, pelisses and corsets. Each item had a detailed description with the accreditation, 'the sole inventions of Mrs M.A. Bell'. In 1821, when John Bell was 76, he sold *La Belle Assemblée* and, sadly, the name of Mrs Bell disappears. A 'New Series' began under J. P. & C. Whitaker of Paternoster Row. In 1832 *La Belle Assemblée* became known as *The Court Magazine and Belle Assemblée* under the editorship of the Hon. Mrs Norton. In 1837 the title was absorbed into *The Lady's Magazine* and *Museum of Belles Lettres* which in turn became from 1838 to 1847 *The Court Magazine and Monthly Critic and Lady's Magazine and Museum of Belles Lettres*.

The Repository of Arts, Literature, Commerce, Manufactures, Fashions and Politics was another rival to *La Belle Assemblée* when it began publication under Rudolph Ackermann in 1809. Ackermann was born in Stuttgart, where he studied engraving, and had gone to Paris as a designer, carriages being his speciality. He came as a refugee to England during the French Revolution, putting his artistic flair and entrepreneurial acumen into action. *The Repository of Arts* was issued monthly in a large octavo format, about 10 x 6 inches, and each number contained two or more anonymous fashion plates, engraved in aquatint and coloured by hand. Each plate showed only one or two figures but they were always posed very gracefully, often with a piece of fine furniture, and the plate was accompanied by a detailed description of the costumes. In this connection it is interesting to conjecture how much Ackermann had been influenced by French fashion magazines, especially the instructive, artistic and journalistic policies of *Le Cabinet des modes*. His enlightened fashion plates totalled around 450 from the inception of *The Repository of Arts* in 1809 to its demise in 1829. The fashion plates themselves were designed for women of fashion and their dressmakers. In several of the earlier issues of *The Repository of Arts* Ackermann invited British textile manufacturers to submit patterns of new dress fabrics, saying that 'if the requisites of Novelty, Fashion and Elegance are united, the necessary quantity for this magazine will be ordered.' The fabrics chosen were pasted on to settings in the magazine which were described as 'allegorical' woodcuts. The origin of this device was German, for small squares of fashionable materials had been affixed to the *Journal für Fabrik*.

Meanwhile, the redoubtable Mrs Mary Bell surfaced again in close collaboration with a new publication entitled *The World of Fashion and Continental Feuilletons Dedicated Expressly to the High Life, Fashionables, and Fashions, Polite Literature, Fine Arts, the Opera, Theatre, etc.* Founded in London in 1824 as a monthly it obviously owed much to the pioneering work of John Bell and Rudolph Ackermann. Mary Bell transferred the rights to reproduce her designs solely to *The World of Fashion* thus making it exclusively a woman's fashion magazine. *The World of Fashion* also had a large format with the fashion plates containing up to six figures. The best of the plates were engraved by William Wolfe Alais, but the bulk were copies of French fashion plates. The publishers of *The World of Fashion* have always been shrouded in mystery. On publication they were given as Mr Anderson and Mr Bell. By 1830 the magazine was 'edited by several Literary and Fashionable Characters'. What is clear is that the fashion plates in the magazines discussed in this section did their best to emulate the Neo-classical style of dress of the Parisian *élégantes*.

Le style troubadour

The foundations of what came to be known as *le style troubadour* had already been laid by Queen Marie-Antoinette and were raised to exquisite heights by the Empress Josephine. During the First Empire contemporaries spoke of *le genre chevaleresque* or *le genre anecdotique*. *Le style troubadour*, as a term, was unknown to contemporaries. It was Émile Littré, in his great *Dictionnaire de la langue français* (2 vols., 1863-72), who first defined *le style troubadour* as the prevailing taste of the First Empire. It is a useful term for bringing out the inter-relationship of different elements associated with the cult of the Middle Ages, such as *le bon vieux temps*, *les moeurs chevaleresque*, the idealization of women and the mystery of the Gothic. The Middle Ages, for the early Romantics, embraced everything that was thought to lie between the twelfth and the sixteenth centuries.[3]

Portrait of the duchesse d'Abrantès, painted by Jean-Baptiste Isabey, c. 1806.
The duchesse d'Abrantès wears one of Josephine's favourite accessories *à la style troubadour*, the long veil. The duchesse has opted for draping a sheer version around her face, with the sinuous lines of the veil offset by the carefully contrived 'negligence' of her curly hair, enhancing the Romantic feeling of the portrait. (*Private Collection*)

The Empress Josephine was the outstanding patron of *le style troubadour*, and advanced its cause through painting. She not only patronized the *troubadour* painters, she also helped to provide them with the very context in which they worked. They gleaned much of their inspiration from the Musée des Monuments français under its curator, Alexandre Lenoir. By appointing Lenoir to the post of *conservateur des objets d'art de la Malmaison*, Josephine strengthened her links to the *troubadour* painters.

Josephine's outstanding achievement was to introduce *le style troubadour* into both fashionable and court dress. Many of the details of her costume were inspired by *troubadour* paintings. The editor of the leading fashion periodical of the time, *Le Journal des dames et des modes*, in the number for 27 September 1804, singled out Jean-

Baptiste Isabey, Robert Lefèvre and François Gérard as the three most sought after artists by Josephine and the *élégantes* of the First Empire for painting portraits of them showing off their historically-inspired costumes.

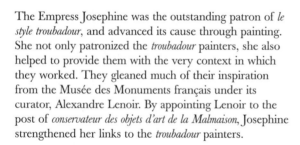

Portrait Miniature of the Empress Josephine, ivory mounted on a gold box, painted by Jean-Baptiste Isabey, c. 1806.
Isabey's miniature shows the Empress Josephine wearing a close-fitting, dark velvet coat called a *pelisse* which she made fashionable. The *pelisse* is set off by a high-standing embroidered Médicis collar. The Empress also wears a *toque*, in the style of François Ier, made of velvet and topped with ostrich feathers. *(Private Collection)*

Joueur de hautbois, painted by J.-A. Laurent, 1806.
This painting by Jean-Antoine Laurent, one of Josephine's favourite *troubadour* painters, was bought by her when it was shown at the *Salon* of 1806. Laurent was considered the *troubadour* painter most akin to the seventeenth-century Dutch masters in the precision of his costumes and for his ability in bringing out the tactile qualities of velvet, satin and fur. *(Location unknown)*

Headwear occupied a privileged position. One of the most favoured items of headgear was the *toque*. The form of the *toque* owed much to Josephine's principal *couturier*, Louis-Hippolyte Leroy, who often found inspiration for his fashion designs in the work of contemporary artists. Josephine herself liked to offset her dishevelled Romantic curls by the simple lines of the small velvet *toque* in the style of François I, as seen in the portrait miniature of her by Jean-Baptiste Isabey. In Pierre Révoils's *L'Anneau l'Empereur Charles-Quint* both François I and Charles V

wear them. The same *toque* can be seen in a *troubadour* painting Josephine purchased, the *Joueur de hautbois*, by one of her favourite *troubadour* painters, Jean-Antoine Laurent. Another favourite headdress of Josephine's was the long veil, made of lace or muslin, that is often seen in *troubadour* paintings, such as *Le Départ du chevalier*, a watercolour painted by her daughter, Hortense de Beauharnais, a *troubadour* artist in her own right, having studied under the great Isabey.

Portrait of Pauline Bonaparte, painted by Robert Lefèvre, 1806. Even though she had a strong aversion to her sister-in-law, the Empress Josephine, Pauline Bonaparte copied her innovatory dress. Her Romantic taste is expressed in the use of Renaissance-style jewellery, the *ferronnière* worn across her brow, the gold bracelets at her wrist, and the gold braid wound around the long, puffy sleeves of her dress and echoed in the headdress. Her dress retains the high, Empire waist through the use of an exquisite belt bound like the military belts of the *chevaliers* of the fourteenth and fifteenth centuries. The shawl is draped on her shoulder with a swaggering bravado that underlines how it was *the* fashion accessory of the Romantics. (*Wellington Museum, Victoria and Albert Museum, London*)

Portrait of a Woman, painted by Henry-François Mulard, c. 1810.
This portrait brings out the full extent of Scottish influence on dress in *le style troubadour*. The lady wears a silk Scottish scarf, knotted with almost Byronic abandon, and held in place by a matching sash around her high Empire waist. Other *troubadour* features are the small Médicis collar and long sleeves puffed out at the shoulders and edged with delicate peacock-eye embroidery. The Romantic feeling of the portrait is enhanced by the circuituous lines of the shawl and the naturalistic rendering of the flowers, while the short, regular fringe has a rather machine-made look. (*French & Company Inc., New York*)

The Growth of Fashion Illustration in the Nineteenth Century

periodicals was *redingote*. During the First Empire the two names were interchangeable, the common denominator being that, because of Josephine, the style was of *troubadour* inspiration, as *Le Journal des dames et des modes* pointed out.[4]

Josephine often wore a *parure* consisting of pearl bracelet, a double strand of pearls on her bodice, and a pearl hair ornament. Also in keeping with the spirit of the Renaissance were pearls and precious stones worn across her brow in the manner of a *ferronnière*. It was very popular for artists such as Ingres and Girodet to copy Leonardo da Vinci's painting, *La Belle Ferronnière*.

An extension of *le style troubadour* in fashionable dress was the influence of Scotland. Josephine's *inventaire* at Malmaison compiled by M. Grandjean lists six dresses with Scottish trimmings.[5] As early as the summer of 1806 *Le Journal des dames et des modes* carried two fashion plates showing ladies wearing Scottish scarves. In the Spring of 1807 the *Journal* reported that Scottish ribbons were much in use on hats. And exactly a year later the editor of the *Journal* wrote that the use of Scottish ribbons had multiplied and they were more in vogue than ever.[6]

Perhaps the most magnificent icon of sartorial elegance in *le style troubadour* in portraiture is Ingres's *Vicomtesse de Senonnes*. Ingres often used fashion plates as the basis for his portraits, thus depicting the real and the particular in dress and capturing the immediacy of fashion. He has posed vicomtesse de Senonnes in front of a mirror, a device often used in fashion plates so that a good back view of the fashions could be rendered, in this case vicomtesse de Senonnes's hairstyle *à la Madonna* with its jewelled comb and the gossamer quality of her lace *collerette à la Médicis*. This portrait also affords the opportunity to study jewellery both from the point of

In her portrait miniature by Isabey, which is mounted on a gold box, Josephine wears her fetching *toque* with a dark velvet coat fastened across the front and with long, tight, sleeves slashed at the top in an elaborate cutwork design in the Renaissance manner. It is set off by a high-standing Médicis collar. In contemporary fashion literature these coats were called *pelisses*, a dress term dating back to the Middle Ages. An alternative name in the fashion

Portrait of vicomtesse de Senonnes, painted by J.-A.-D. Ingres, 1816.
Vicomtesse de Senonnes wears a dress of lush red velvet elaborated by a fringed white satin sash and by long sleeves that are slashed in the style of the Renaissance to reveal puffs of white satin material. Her dress has a very wide neckline, typical of the Renaissance, is filled in with a sheer white silk *chemisette* and set off by a blonde lace *collerette à la Médicis*. A fine cashmere shawl with a floral pattern continues to be an important accessory. Her fingers have clusters of rings whose pale red and green jewels reverberate in the shawl's floral embroidery. She wears drop earrings set with rubies or garnets, and around her neck are two lockets and a cross which hang below her sash. Religion had always played a part in *le style troubadour* and the cross was the favourite devotional jewel. *(Musée des Beaux-Arts, Nantes. © RMN-P Bernard)*

Paolo and Francesca, painted by J.-A.-D. Ingres.
Ingres painted his portrait of vicomtesse de Senonnes at the time that he was also reading Dante and drawing and painting the poignant circumstances of the death of Paolo and Francesca. Francesca da Rimini's red dress is the style of the sixteenth century with the neckline cut straight across and with the long sleeves slashed allowing white puffs of material to show through. Vicomtesse de Senonnes's dress was clearly linked to the Renaissance dress of Francesca. A particularly interesting detail is the similarity in the fullness of the pleated material of their gowns and in the looping rhythms of the fabrics. *(Musée Bonnat, Bayonne. © Photo RMN-R-G Ojeda)*

view of the craftsmanship of the period and in its relation to dress in *le style troubadour*. Ingres's *oeuvre* further shows the close links between art and dress. His exquisite *troubadour* painting, *Paolo and Francesca*, with its romantic story, diminutive scale and delicate touch, especially in the closeness of Francesca's costume to vicomtesse de Senonnes's, was the kind of work so much admired by Josephine.

The Fashion Plates of Horace Vernet

It is not surprising that Horace Vernet should have an excellent eye for the wonders of French fashionable life, culminating in his series *Incroyables et Merveilleuses*, published between 1810 and 1818, and *Le Bon Genre*, first published in 1817. His grandfather was Moreau le Jeune, who was largely responsible for *Le Monument du costume* and his father Carle Vernet, the source of the original *Directoire incroyables and merveilleuses*. Father and son designed fashion plates for *Le Journal des dames et des modes*, and it was the editor, Pierre de La Mésangère, who commissioned Horace Vernet's series of *Incroyables et Merveilleuses*. These watercolour drawings were engraved as a set of 36 fashion plates by Georges-Jacques Gatine and show Vernet's superb draughtsmanship and mastery of the parameters of fashion illustration: especially the elongation and stylization of the silhouette to set off the fashions to the best advantage. In commissioning a separate series of fashion plates Pierre de La Mésangère was developing a new format and style in French fashion plates, and offering specific details on fashionable themes.

Horace Vernet continued the convention of representing *le beau monde* with his society figures of both the nobility and the *parvenus* who prospered under Napoleon's First

Empire. Notwithstanding wars taking place all over Europe, Paris continued to flourish as the centre of fashion, in the process underpinning France's economic well-being and extending her social and cultural influence.

'Merveilleuse: Chapeau de paille d'Italie. Pardessus à la chinoise'. Fashion plate drawn by Horace Vernet and engraved by Georges-Jacques Gatine. From Vernet's series *Incroyables et Merveilleuses*, published by Pierre de La Mésangère, Paris, No. 16, c. 1812.
China provided the fantasy of this embroidered 'Chinese' tunic decorated with tassels. The new *merveilleuses*, while retaining the high Neo-classical waist, opted for short puffed sleeves and a short skirt which showed off to advantage petite shoes with coloured-ribbon lacings. For headwear the *merveilleuses* were spoilt for choice. Amongst the diversity was this Italian straw hat bedecked with lilies and foliage. Vernet's fashion plates show the movement away from Neo-classicism to Romanticism in dress. *(Victoria and Albert Museum, London)*

'Manches en Spirale. Profusion de Garnitures. Mouchoire Servant de porte-Clef', 1811. Fashion plate engraved by Horace Vernet, from his series *Le Bon Genre*, Paris, 1817. Horace Vernet, always the witty chronicler of the latest fashions, shows how eclecticism could sometimes be carried to exuberant lengths: sixteenth-century-style puffs on the sleeves and high ruff at the neck, accompanied by the cashmere shawl, the principal vestimentary symbol of Romanticism. The 'profusion of trimmings' reduces the fine cashmere shawl to just one of many Romantic traits. *(The Metropolitan Museum of Art, New York)*

The details of Vernet's costumes, seen in front and back views, are sharp enough to inform the *tailleur* and the *couturière* while the élan and wit with which he conveys the fashions make his series a work of art in its own right. For the *incroyables*, tight-fitting cutaway coats are made of fine cloth in muted shades of green, buff, dark blue and brown. Back-view details of the coat, such as the seams, the sleeves cut full at the shoulders and set well in towards the centre back, and sharp vertical pleats, are all clearly delineated. The coats are worn with short, trim, square-cut waistcoats which are usually striped and double-breasted. A new emphasis was placed on the legs which were tightly enveloped in form-fitting pantaloons, usually made from a clinging material such as stockinet or soft doeskin, or in the increasingly popular long, slim, sleek trousers. The shirt and cravat continued to be important. Both were made of brilliantly white and heavily-starched linen. A shirt pin, a cane or sporting whip, a high-crown black hat and seals at the waist completed the male outfit.

The new *merveilleuses*, while keeping the high-waisted dresses of their *Directoire* sisters, returned to wearing the corset, which had been re-introduced in French dress in about 1804. The bodice was very fitted with the bosom pushed upwards, and the waist slimmed by means of a laced corset, the lacing so tight that Napoleon exclaimed the corset to be the murderer of the human race! The dresses of the *merveilleuses* featured many details of *le style troubadour*: puffed and slashed sleeves, Médicis collars, velvet *toques* topped with ostrich feathers and Scottish ribbons, scarves and trimmings. The most eye-catching part of the dress was the new shortened skirt which was very full. This was made possible by gores, wedge-shaped inserts that provided width and flair. Voluminousness was further enhanced by the lavish embellishment of the hem with pleating, tiered flouncing and padded trimmings like *rouleaux*.

'Costumes anglais', 1814. Fashion plate drawn and engraved by Horace Vernet. From his series *Le Bon Genre*, Paris, 1817. The French view of English dress as depicted by Horace Vernet. He has made fun of English fashionable women's dress by highlighting the fussy details on the bodices and sleeves, the ungainly headdresses and above all the boned stays which emphasize the stiff bust and waist. The lady separated from the others wears the most rigid bodice of all, made even more prominent by the decorative trimming. The English gentleman wears a long, informal coat with frogged trimming. (*Private Collection*)

Horace Vernet's gift of immediacy of observation was also displayed in *Le Bon Genre*, a series of 104 engraved fashion plates which was first published in 1817. A second edition, published in 1822, included a further eleven plates. A third edition followed in 1827. The charming plates are accompanied by lively accounts of fashionable life in Paris at the beginning of the nineteenth century.

Regency Romance

Just as the classical style was on the wane, there appeared in England three costume studies which were quite separate from the fashion magazines. One was Thomas Hope's *Costume of the Ancients* published in 1809, another was *Designs of Modern Costume*, illustrated by Henry Moses for Thomas Hope in 1812, and finally came *An Illustration of Egyptian, Grecian and Roman Costume* by Thomas Baxter, published in 1814, which contained 40 outlines from the Antique. Baxter's work had a dedication dated July 1810 to Henry Fuseli, the artist who was fascinated, if not fetishly obsessed, by the fantastically coiffeured hair of fashionable ladies of the late eighteenth and early nineteenth centuries.

The changes in women's fashionable garments in England were transitional, fluttering on the verge of Romanticism. By 1809 the Gothic taste was gaining ground, impinging on the purity of the classical line. The classical style was now being disrupted by ornamentation on the bodice, sleeves and skirt of the dress. Then the high waistline began to fluctuate, and from 1808 to 1814 lowered considerably. The gown took on more frills and tucks to the hem which soon began to spread up the skirt, becoming increasingly elaborate. The artist who most clearly noticed the eccentricity of English Gothic taste was Horace Vernet. For several years England had been cut off from fashion developments in France. The protracted war, the blockade and the breaking of the Peace of Amiens had taken their toll on English fashions and a characteristic English style had emerged.

The peace treaty of 1814 brought an influx of English visitors into Paris. *Le Bon Genre* for 1814 and 1815 contains satirical illustrations and caustic comments about

'the disgrace of English women's little flat hats, long lank corsets, and badly cut skirts', maintaining it is only necessary to set them beside the contrast of 'our Parisiennes' to have a ready-made caricature. Vernet also ridiculed the quasi-historical components of their dress such as the square necklines and bodices which protruded and appeared ungainly because of the stiff-fitting corsets and excessive decoration, the fussily beribboned short, swollen sleeves and the long sleeves *à la Mameluke*, that is arranged in puffs of material. It is a tribute to Vernet's influence on fashion that English women took his criticisms to heart by jettisoning their dowdiness and embracing the new, exuberant Romantic French fashions, turning themselves into the full-blown dandyesses of the Regency, or 'monstrosities' as the caricaturist George Cruikshank labelled them. In his engravings, Cruikshank drew attention to their close-belted waists, wide skirts, drooping shoulders, and puff sleeves, the whole topped by vast flower and feather-

Three Heads of Young Girls. Pencil and watercolour drawing by Henry Fuseli, 1815.
Important for fashion are Fuseli's groups of female heads combining portraiture with a fetish observation of the elaborately coiffeured hair of the period. The three girls are thought to be Lady Georgiana North, Sophia Burdett and Susan, Countess of Guildford, a great patron of Fuseli, who, although Swiss by birth, was English by adoption. Fuseli has drawn a complex pseudo-Grecian hairstyle of curls mounted to create a conical line seen in Greek vase paintings and then wrapped in a Romantic bonnet. The other two hairstyles are a combination of the more classically simple and romantically natural, parted in the centre with a few curls about the forehead and sides with a soft chignon at the back top of the head. *(Department of Old Master Drawings, Christie's, London)*

An Irresistible Arming for Conquest, Anonymous fashion engraving, 1828-30.

The tight-lacing provided by the corset achieved a 'pouter-pigeon' look of wasp-waist and bosom pushed upwards. A new type of corset appeared early in the nineteenth century: a long underbodice with a front busk and backbones laced at the back. From 1828 corsets had metal eyelets to get extremely tight lacing. The bustle made of cotton flounces at the back was a further aid to the hour-glass figure fashionable till about 1836. The *femme fatale* wears white silk stockings and black squared-toe shoes with ribbon lacings. Her maid, though attired in a cotton cap and plain dress, nonetheless shows off fashionable features such as the fitted waist, *gigot de mouton* sleeves, and full skirt. *(Victoria and Albert Museum, London)*

Pl. 2.   —DANDIES—of—1817—

& MONSTROSITIES of 1818.

Pubd Octr 3 1818 by G. Humphrey 27 St James's Stt.

G. Cruikshank fect.

bedecked hats and bonnets. Headwear was perhaps their most important accessory, the hat or bonnet for outdoor wear and the turban or cap for indoors. By far the most popular bonnet was the 'coal-scuttle' or 'poke' bonnet, which had appeared at the end of the eighteenth century.

The Regency, the period from 1811 to 1820 when George III's son the Prince of Wales acted as Regent, is, however, most associated with the clothes-conscious Dandies. They were the leaders of male high fashion at its most extreme and flamboyant. The style of the Dandy was marked by a coat which had gathered shoulders, padding at the chest, and a high waist, which they nipped in with a corset to achieve tightness. The collars of their shirts and their cravats came up almost to the eyes, their peg-top trousers were cut wide and full around the hips,

and their chosen headwear was either a small hat with a high crown or a tiny flat hat. The Regency Dandy should not be compared to Beau Brummell, but rather to the fop and the *macaroni*. Beau Brummell relied on perfect tailoring, harmony of colour, a discerning selection of accessories and neatness: his sobriety and understated elegance is the antithesis of the Regency Dandy.

However, the changes in style wrought by these clothes-horses are useful for showing the direction of fashion. The caricatures of George Cruikshank provide a wealth of information on cut and construction, and best capture the Romantic silhouette of the Regency Dandies denoted by their puffed-out chests, pinched-in waists and rounded hips, foreshadowing the hourglass figure of both men and women in the 1820s and 1830s.

Dandies of 1817, Monstrosities of 1818. Engraving by George Cruikshank, 1818.
Cruikshank's engraving shows the extravagance characteristic of women's and men's fashionable dress during the Regency. The Dandy style consisted of high shirt collars and cravats, a frock or morning coat with gathered shoulders, padded chests, and high, tight waists achieved by wearing a corset, breeches or trousers, which became fashionable for day wear from

1807. Favourite accessories were sharply-pointed footwear in the form of shoes or boots with spurs and small hats with high crowns or flat hats. Cruikshank mocks the way English ladies have embraced the French fashion for short skirts, heavily decorated hems and semi-circular pads at the back, giving an almost humped-back effect. Large bonnets, reticules, parasols, and neck chains with either watches or scent bottles were popular accessories. *(Victoria and Albert Museum, London)*

The Golden Years of French Fashion Plates

Even during the disintegration of Napoleon's First Empire there was a demand for French fashion. The Spanish ladies wore their mantillas and the Nordic ones their furs but the essential line of their dress was French. Once the Napoleonic Wars ended, the demand for French modes was as insatiable as ever. The primary source, *Le Journal des dames et des modes*, for example, had produced an amazing 3,624 fashion plates by the time of its demise in

Nothing to extenuate, nor aught set down in malice, Anonymous fashion engraving, 1827.
From 1820 the waistline began to drop due to the increasing decorative emphasis on the bodice. A narrow waist was achieved by tight-lacing, making the corset once again an essential item of fashion. Voluminous skirts and sleeves also made the waist look neat and trim. The sleeves, too, grew ever larger, down-filled puffs literally padding the shoulders. The lady's dress has the *gigot de mouton* or leg-of-mutton sleeves, very full but tapering to a narrow waist. To counterbalance the wide shoulders and skirt, women's fashionable hats were large and decorated with many yards of ribbons and other ornaments. If the fashion shape of 1827 appears caricatured, the surviving specimens of dress show that this was just about the reality, confirming the broad outline of changes seen in fashion engravings. *(Victoria and Albert Museum, London)*

Portrait of Benjamin Disraeli, drawing after Daniel Maclise, 1833. Disraeli displays the elegant English dandy image of the 1830s. He wears a plain morning coat, a tail coat cut with a high waist and with the front edges sloping back in a curve and the skirts hanging back at the sides. It has brass buttons, a roll collar and M-notch lapels to allow them to lie flat. His waistcoat is very short and has a shawl collar. His trousers reach the instep and are kept in place by straps passing under the foot, over which are square-toed shoes with ribbon bows. Disraeli wears a variety of jewellery including studs, pins, rings, watch and chain. Short curls with a side parting is the fashionable hairstyle. *(National Portrait Gallery, London)*

Germany. In London, *Townsend's Quarterly* (later *Monthly*) *Selection of Parisian Costumes*, which started in 1823, imported fashion plates of *Le Journal des dames et des modes* and accompanied them with English descriptions. At the turn of the century *The Lady's Magazine* was copying fashion plates from *Le Journal des dames et des modes* with the details of the dress often altered for modesty. *The Lady's Magazine* finally gave up the ghost of issuing its own fashion plates and imported them from the French fashion magazine *Le Follet* which began publication in 1829.

In the wake of the Napoleonic Wars France cemented its position as the fashion leader of Europe and its publishing industry in Paris answered with a veritable explosion of fashion magazines with high-quality fashion plates. One of the most prominent and successful fashion magazines largely devoted to dress for women was the *Petit courrier des dames* which started in 1821 and ran until 1868 when it was absorbed by *Le Journal des demoiselles*, becoming *Le Journal des demoiselles et petit courrier des dames réunis*. As the *Petit courrier des dames*, it was subtitled *Nouveau journal des modes, des théâtres, de la littérature et des arts*. Of octavo size, it appeared every five days with eight pages of text containing fashion news, theatrical reviews, fiction, poetry, historical sketches, and one or two fashion plates on a heavier paper. The fashion plates were meticulously numbered hand-coloured copperplate engravings with the captions underneath a cornucopia of advertisements with name and address of the dressmakers, hairdressers, *marchandes de modes*, jewellers, florists and tradesmen. Sometimes the dressmakers were given separate credits for their designs. No artists signed the fashion plates of the 1820s and 1830s; indeed, it is only with the issue beginning 10 May 1833 that the fashion plates start to be dated. A number of artists contributed to the journal, amongst them Mme Florensa de Closménil, who usually signed her name in full, or sometimes simply, Florensa, Hervy, Gabriel-Xavier Montaut, Emile Préval, A. de Taverne, Mlle. A. Pauquet, François-Claudins Compte-Calix, and Laure Noël. At the bottom of the fashion plates the publisher's Paris address was given as the Boulevard des Italiens. Most of the artists mentioned above also drew for other fashion magazines, which had their editorial offices at No. 1 Boulevard des Italiens. Also given at the bottom of the fashion plates were the Brussels, Amsterdam and London offices. The London publishers were S. and J. Fuller, thus

1839. Its erudite editor, Pierre de La Mésangère, so accurately recorded the fashions over such a long time (he died in 1831) that Georges Vicaire says *Le Journal des dames et des modes* was referred to simply as 'Le La Mésangère'.[7] French fashions were an important part of the country's export trade and it now became common for French publishers to have foreign editions of their fashion magazines, or to enter into an agreement with a foreign publisher to have their fashion plates reproduced. Copyright laws were still little enforced and so many French fashion plates were simply being reproduced with the details of the dress often changed in foreign fashion magazines. In the case of *Le Journal des dames et des modes* legitimate editions were produced in Belgium and

'Carrick à collets rond'. Engraved fashion plate from *Le Journal des dames et des modes*, No. IX, 15 February 1812, Plate 1206. A notable feature of male attire was the carrick. It was a long, ample overcoat made of heavy fawn-coloured cloth and had several caped collars. Originally it had been a coachman's coat worn for warmth when riding outside the coach. Men began to replace their cloak with a carrick as fashionable outerwear from the late-eighteenth century. The carrick in various styles remained popular to the end of the nineteenth century. *(Private Collection)*

31 Décemb. 1836.　　　　Thierens sc.　　　　1315.

Modes de Paris.

Petit Courrier des Dames.

Boulevart des Italiens, N.º 2, près le passage de l'Opéra.

Redingote doublée en bison du Canada. Habit à bouton d'or mat. Pantalon en casimir.

acknowledging the continued English dependence on French fashion plates. In fact a short-lived English version of the *Petit courrier des dames* appeared in London in 1823 as *Fashion as it Flies* or *The Ladies Little Messenger of Parisian Fashions*. *Townsend's* also imported fashion plates from the *Petit courrier des dames*, and around 1826, finding it expensive, economized for a short time by issuing badly executed French fashion plates. This proved to be a false economy and the real thing was soon restored.

The fashions depicted in the *Petit courrier des dames* are for the well-to-do middle classes of the Romantic era who had become firmly entrenched firstly under Louis XVIII and then under Louis-Philippe, the 'citizen-king'. The well-dressed bourgeois man wore trousers inherited from the French Revolution, and a top hat. He was also distinguished by his elaborate cravat, either in white or a dark colour, tied around his neck in a highly starched fashion and worn with an immaculate white shirt of the finest linen. Colours, apart from the waistcoat, were sombre and showed already the trend for respectability. Very important was his beard, which formed a fringe around his chin, giving him a Romantic appeal. The French dandies, led by the comte d'Orsay, set the tone to follow, and an outpouring of brochures provided enlightenment on the intricacies to be mastered, such as *Theorie de l'art de coiffeur* by Professor Croissart which appeared in Paris in 1846.

For women the *Petit courrier des dames* provided an interesting format and iconography. One primary figure in the fashion plate faced forward, while a secondary figure further back from her faced away acting as a double and displaying the reverse side of the dress and hairstyle. Sometimes a mirror was used, a fashion-plate device that artists such as Ingres borrowed. By the late 1830s, however, it was usual to find two women, or men, side by side, standing rather apart from each other and showing off different styles of dress.

If the clothing of men was predominantly drab, a glance through the *Petit courrier des dames* shows that the garments of women were colourful and novel. Many garments and fabrics were inspired by *le style troubadour* or by the exotica of India and Islamic lands. One of the glories of the *Petit courrier des dames* is the many types of textiles depicted. The new jacquard looms made a much greater variety of weaves available for ladies of fashion.

The circulation of successful magazines like the *Petit courrier des dames* had grown every year by dint of an enormously expanded middle-class readership and by the export of its fashion plates. Consequently, the hand-coloured copperplate engraving process, where the comparative softness of copper limited the number of prints that could be taken from an engraving, to perhaps only about 1,500 good impressions each, was now clearly inadequate for the demand where speed of production was all-important. New mechanized printing methods were introduced by the middle of the nineteenth century where a dramatic increase in sales was matched by a substantial decrease in price. As early as 1820 a process, which had long been kept secret, was discovered in England for engraving images on steel plates. In this technique the finished copperplates are steel-faced. This is achieved by means of electrolysis where a microscopic film of steel is deposited on the surface of the plate, thereby hardening it enough to print large editions. Steel engraving was ideal for fashion magazines because it did not interfere with the finest detail of the plate and could take all the tones of colour. Even in a large print run fashion plates could be reproduced with great precision especially with regard to the tactile qualities of fabrics such as velvet and silk. By the middle of the nineteenth century the *Petit courrier des dames* was using steel engraving and what with the calibre of the fashion artists employed, the fashion magazine in general did not suffer an overall decline in the quality of its fashion plates.

When the *Petit courrier des dames* was launched a debate about the conventions of the fashion plate was already taking place. In response, the publisher Henri de Girardon co-founded *La Mode* in 1829 with Honoré de Balzac. It was another highly successful fashion magazine, in circulation until 1854 under that title before taking on the names *La Revue universelle* and *La Revue du monde élégant*, and finally from 1856-1862 becoming *La Mode nouvelle*.[8] M. de Girardon's worry, which he elucidated in his introductory editorial in 1829, was the 'well-dressed doll' of current fashion illustration. He deplored the lack of relating fashion illustration to contemporary Parisian life. In setting out to redress this issue he had the foresight to collaborate with Honoré de Balzac, whose novels are an acute observation of modern society.

Balzac's *Traité de la vie élégante* (1830) is of seminal importance to the history of costume. His treatise, which

'Modes de Paris'. Engraved fashion plate from the *Petit courrier des dames*, Paris, 31 December 1836.
The man on the left wears a narrow-waisted *redingote* with a shawl collar made of Canadian bison fur. The man on the right also displays an effeminate silhouette with his puffed out 'pouter-pigeon' chest and tiny waist. His dark morning coat has smooth, curving, sloping shoulders and his pinched waist is achieved by a corset or waist-cincher. His skintight trousers in a contrasting light colour further draws attention to the romantic hourglass line analogous to the shape in female fashion. The most common headwear for daytime wear was a top hat which had a narrow curving brim. *(B.T. Batsford Ltd Archive)*

Mode, where Gavarni showed off not just the prevailing fashions but also fashionable women in the complete state of relaxation that the fancy-dress ball afforded. In other fashion plates Gavarni depicted his fondness for children and their dress. He sometimes signed his name, but at other times penned G-I, or Gi; in any case, his flair and touch is recognizable. Amongst the other journals to which he contributed fashion plates are *Psyché, La Sylphide, La Gazette des salons, Le Voleur, Le Journal des gens du monde, Le Journal des femmes, Le Journal des jeunes personnes* and *L'Abeille impériale*. As for *La Mode,* it acquired the services of Mme Florensa de Closménil, Emile Guérard, Numa, whose full name was Pierre Numa Bassaset, Ange-Louis Janet-Lange and Louis-Marie Lanté, who contributed fashion plates to *Le Journal des dames et des modes* and who was closely associated with Horace Vernet.

La Mode was one of the first fashion magazines to promote sports dress. With the Restoration, a new wave of Anglomania hit Paris and *le sport* became very fashionable. It was equestrian sports with their aristocratic connotations that were considered the most prestigious and therefore required special costumes.

first appeared in *La Mode*, put forward the view that *la toilette* is the expression of society. As men of vision, Girardon and Balzac chose the artist Sulpice-Guillaume Chevalier, who adopted the *nom de pinceau* Paul Gavarni, to design the fashion plates for *La Mode*. Gavarni was a brilliant draughtsman who was noted for both his illustrations of Parisian life, in particular *grisettes, lorettes* and opera balls, and for his fashion plates. According to Baudelaire, Gavarni's work was the perfect visual complement to Balzac's *La Comédie humaine*. Indeed, Gavarni was the precursor of the 'painters of modern life'. The humanity of his fashion plate figures can be seen in his series of *travestissements* or fancy dresses for *La*

One of the longest-running of all fashion magazines was *Le Follet*. Commencing in 1829, it flowered with hand-coloured fashion plates right up until its demise in 1892. In the annals of fashion literature it rates extremely high, and no collection of fashion plates can be considered comprehensive without examples from *Le Follet*. Specializing in the fashions worn at the Opéra and at *soirées*, the fashion plates were the work of two of the Colin sisters. Laure Noël and Anaïs Toudouze were adept at choosing just the right delicate background for showing off evening clothes, a technique Anaïs passed on to her daughter, Isabelle Toudouze. Legitimate foreign editions of *Le Follet* were produced in Germany, Italy and England. The English edition is extremely important

'Toilettes du soir', drawn by Anaïs Toudouze. Engraved fashion plate from *Le Follet*, 1863, Plate 2406.
By 1860 very wide "artificial" or "cage" crinolines were the dominant style. The volume of the skirts of dresses was also increased by bold flouncing and ruching. Often they were deliberately stiffened to stand out further from the skirts and create the illusion of an even greater width. The little girl's dress echoes that of the lady seated next to her. The various *coiffures* are advertised as the work of M. Chagot *ainé*. (B.T. Batsford Ltd Archive)

Portrait miniature of Fanny Brawne, painted by an Anonymous Artist, 1833.
Fanny Brawne was engaged to John Keats in 1819 but his early death prevented their marriage. She went into mourning for four years and remained unmarried for another eight years. This portrait was probably painted for her marriage to Louis Lindon. While not a great beauty, Fanny follows the style seen in many fashion plates: the centre-parting hairstyle with side ringlets, a complementing bonnet which always has connotations of softness being made of lace with ribbon and ribbon ties under the chin, and a lace *pelerine*, a wide, flat cape-like collar held in place by an oval portrait-miniature brooch. (Reproduced by permission of The London Borough of Camden from the Collections at Keats House, Hampstead, London)

for showing the links between a fashion journal and *couturiers* and for confirming how complete the French domination of the fashion industry was by the middle of the nineteenth century. We read, for example, of the showrooms where the latest Parisian models were displayed in London, and how dressmakers would travel to Paris in the Spring and Autumn when the best *couture* houses showed their new models to prospective buyers.[9]

During the 1830s, three salient fashion magazines were published in Paris: *Le Journal des demoiselles, Le Musée des familles* (1833-91) and *Le Bon ton* (1834-74). All three employed some of the best artists to design the fashion plates, names already mentioned such as A. de Taverne, E. Préval, Mlle A. Pauquet, Mme Florensa de Closménil, Laure Noël and her sister, Héloïse Leloir. *Le Bon ton* was in fact one of the first fashion magazines to employ Mme Noël when she was unmarried and still signed her fashion plates Laure Colin. This highly accomplished magazine was founded by Louis-Joseph Mariton, a former hairdresser. Within twelve years of its launch, M. Mariton had turned himself into a fabulously successful proprietor of no less than nine fashion magazines. Héloïse Leloir, who had found her niche *chez Mariton,* saw her fashion plates distributed to many French fashion magazines and also to *La Belle Assemblée.*[10] Besides importing Mme Leloir's hand-coloured fashion plates into England, M. Mariton also begot an English version of *Le Bon ton*, subtitled *Journal of Fashions*, which he published in Paris from 1852 to 1853, demonstrating just how bereft England was of good fashion plates in the middle of the century. *Le Journal des demoiselles* was one of the most distinctive of the French fashion magazines. Its fashion plates were noted for their sharp emphasis on the design features of ladies' dresses, for example, in the 1870s, the long, slender waist and the precise mass of skirt folds perched on top of the high bustle. This magazine also retained the hand-coloured method of steel engraving, one of the last of the well-established fashion periodicals to do so, and it was still being published in 1906.

In the 1840s two fashion magazines published in Paris, *Les Modes parisiennes* (1843-75) and *Le Moniteur de la mode* (1843-1913) imbued the fashion plate with the atmosphere of a conversation piece. The chief fashion

artist of *Les Modes parisiennes* was François-Claudius Compte-Calix, who had also designed fashion plates for the *Petit courrier des dames*. He was an artist of some renown, having exhibited his watercolours for many years at the Paris Salon and also illustrating costume books. The fashion plates of Émile Préval, the prolific draughtsman and engraver of the 1860s, also appeared in *Les Modes parisiennes*. In format both its pages and its fashion plates were of the size of a modern tabloid newspaper, the first of the fashion magazines to experiment with this size. However, by the beginning of 1844 it did not prove feasible, and the magazine was reduced to octavo. The change in format perhaps explains the confusion over the date of first issue, variously given as March 1843 or January 1844. Fortunately the fashion plates were numbered consecutively from the beginning, and the fashion plates for the year 1844 are numbered 45 to 96. *Les Modes*

LE MONITEUR DE LA MODE

'Robe à arcades Grande nouveauté de la Maison Gagelin', drawn by Jules David. Engraved fashion plate from *Le Moniteur de la mode,* 1853, Plate 362.

By 1850, Charles Frederick Worth, the founding father of Parisian *haute couture*, had established a dressmaking department in the Maison Gagelin, the famous silk mercers. The extreme width of the skirt of the dress reveals his early experimentation with the 'artificial' or 'cage' crinoline. Features

such as the lace *pelerine* held in place by a brooch, the cross, the slashed sleeves and lace cuffs, and the dark, glossy silk fabric, show Worth's interest in historical romanticism in fashionable dress. The charming hat of feathers and ribbons so carefully arranged on the stand on the fashionable lady's dressing table is advertised as the work of the Melles Bübler Soeurs. *(B.T. Batsford Ltd Archive)*

parisiennes is particularly invaluable for the light it throws on the relationship of the *couturier* with the artist. Dressmakers were not always skilled at drawing their designs, and they therefore often turned to the artist, preferring the drawing to look like a fashion plate found in a fashion magazine. Fashion prints of the artist Charles Pilatte, clearly indicated as the costumes of the dressmaker Mme Alexandre Guys, appeared in *Les Modes parisiennes* for the years 1862-65, thus proving that the dresses depicted actually existed and that the magazine's artists would often go to the fashion houses to obtain all the details.[11] The fashion plates of Compte-Calix for *Les Modes parisiennes* do indeed feature dresses made by Mme Guys.

The painter and lithographer Jules David is so uniquely associated with *Le Moniteur de la mode* that the origins of this substantial fashion magazine are often forgotten. The germ was an advertising publication called *Le Journal spécial des nouveautés de la Maison Popelin-Ducarre* ('magasin de broderies et robes confectionees', 41 rue Vivienne, Paris), which M. Antoine Popelin-Ducarre started in 1839. He issued it free each month to all the courts and foremost families of Europe. Each number was accompanied by prints designed by M. Duboulos and engraved by Sophie Gatine. In February, March and April of 1842 M. Lanté designed them and he was then replaced by Jules David. Out of these beginnings M. Popelin-Ducarre forged a collaboration with the publisher Camille-Adolphe Goubaud in 1843 in the launch of a new weekly fashion magazine entitled *Le Moniteur de la mode* with all the plates to be designed by Jules David.[12] He furnished not only the fashion plates but also the frontispieces to the bound volumes. David was ideally suited for this work for his watercolours and lithographs had been exhibited at the *Salon* of 1834, and he was already celebrated for his book illustrations and for his contributions in the 1830s to *Le Journal des jeunes personnes* and *Le Journal des desmoiselles*. His fashion plates for *Le Moniteur de la mode* are imbued with vitality: life-like figures placed in charming and detailed backgrounds, his interiors themselves a valuable documentation of the décor of the time. David presents a repertoire of drawing-room, dining-room, boudoir, music room, garden, theatre, balls, seaside, racecourse and other ambiences where the fashionable lady both displays her *toilette* and appears involved in the scene. David always signed his fashion plates, which numbered 2,600 at his death in 1892. A complete set would make for an ideal review of the fashions from the 1840s to the 1890s. David's *oeuvre* was quite remarkable, but this is not to disparage some of the other great fashion artists of this period.

While David revitalized the fashion plate he was not the first to put animated figures in real-life situations. The Colin sisters, Emile Guérard and Paul Gavarni had made

great advances, and Ange-Louis Janet-Lange, another outstanding fashion plate designer, was one of the earliest to produce conversation pieces for *Le Cabinet de lecture*, *Le Voleur* (they eventually emerged) and *La Sylphide*. It is because David was so successful that the others are sometimes overlooked. His beautiful watercolour drawings for *Le Moniteur de la mode*, however, show his natural ability and elegance for the precise delineation of dress and for totally real people and places. David's fashion plates were already being copied in the 1840s and it was not until the international agreements on literary and artistic propriety of 1854 that M. Goubaud was assured control over the sale of them. One of his most successful sales was to Mr Beeton, publisher of *The Englishwoman's Domestic Magazine*. *Le Moniteur de la mode* went from strength to strength with eight editions in foreign languages in 1869. From the 1870s it absorbed *Le Bon ton*, *La Gazette rose illustrée*, and *L'Élégance parisienne*.

As it expanded *Le Moniteur de la mode* also underwent changes in typography and format. From 1843 to 1860 the fashion plates were steel engraved.[13] With its circulation growing every year, subscribers numbering many thousands, and so many international editions, lithography became an important method of engraving the fashion plates. Lithography had already been employed for fashion engraving, its real triumph occurring during the 1830s with the fashion plates of Paul Gavarni and Achille Déveria for fashion magazines such as *Le Goût nouveau* and *Le Journal des jeunes personnes* as well as his series *Dix-Huit heures de la journée de la parisienne*. Lithography was invented in 1798 by Alois Senefelder, the process being based on the idea of water running off a greasy surface. The design is drawn with a greasy crayon on stone and then the stone is wetted and rolled with greasy ink. When the greasy ink is rolled onto the stone it will not adhere to the wet parts and sticks only on the parts which are already greasy, from which the water has run. Prints can then be taken in a press and colours applied by hand. This method was ideal for fashion magazines with huge print runs where fashion plates had to be churned out quickly. The fashion artist only needed to draw on the stone and all technicalities could be left to the printer.

From the second half of the nineteenth century, fashion magazines, including *Le Moniteur de la mode*, were also tempted by the copying of the newly-invented photograph, which was achieved by the employment of the *héliochromie* on *papier glacé*.[14] *Le Moniteur de la mode* underwent another evolution after 1880 when it adapted the large format, copying the model of *La Mode illustrée* and using wood engraving for its fashion plates.[15] This was another cheap printing process often associated with the English artist, Thomas Bewick. Though not its inventor, Bewick is called the father of modern wood

engraving because in the late eighteenth and early nineteenth centuries he raised the technique to new pictorial possibilities. Wood engraving is derived from the woodcut, but because of the harder and smoother surface of the block itself, which is of boxwood cut across the grain, and the use of a graver or burin, which is also an implement of copperplate engraving, its overall effect is much finer and more detailed than the woodcut.

From its launch in 1860 'dates the transformation of fashion journals'. The fashion magazine in question, *La Mode illustrée*, (1860-beginning of the twentieth century) was distinctive because of the large format of its fashion plates as noted above, and indeed, forged the way for other fashion periodicals. Fashion plates measured 370 x 260 mm, giving the clothes, their wearers and the settings a new prominence. They were designed by Anaïs Toudouze, her sisters, and her daughter, Isabelle Toudouze. The magazine came out weekly and had a circulation of about 20,000 copies. Published by Firmin Didot, it had a fairly straightforward relationship with its female readership:

> Some of our subscribers who live in the country but in proximity to a city, have asked me to indicate to them which dresses can be worn in the country without inconvenience, and in the city without oddness.

By the middle of the nineteenth century women were increasingly leading more active lives. Fashion plates were now placing them more often outside the house, favourite topical settings being the seaside, riding, walking, in the garden. *La Mode illustrée*'s fashion plates are excellent for showing the appropriate circumstances for the dresses to be worn. *La Mode illustrée* was also one of the first fashion magazines to have a regular report on ladies underwear, albeit very discreetly, for the fashion plates did not show them on fashionable ladies. The garments were neatly arranged to show off details such as embroidery and lace. *Le Petit courrier des dames*, *Le Bon ton* and *La Sylphide* had occasionally featured corsets, but *La mode illustrée* was one of the most important fashion journals of its kind in illustrating this aspect of ladies' dress.

The last important fashion magazine to be launched before the Franco-Prussian War was *La Mode artistique* (1869-early 1900s). This was an expensive publication for its fashion plates signified the full flowering of the *de luxe* lithograph. They were printed in both colour and monochrome on high-quality, durable paper. Although following the cumbersome large format, the fashion plates are exceptional from 1877 when they were drawn by Gustave Lange, brother of Ange-Louis Janet-Lange.

The Franco-Prussian War of 1870-71 is a benchmark in the annals of fashion and fashion illustration. The siege of Paris occurred on 20 September 1870 and ended with the city's surrender on 30 January 1871. Although most of the fashion magazines continued in circulation in Paris, they did not reach the rest of Europe. The publishers of fashion journals found themselves in a difficult position during the war years as the Prussians virtually cut off all means of communication making the dissemination of fashion plates impossible. A few fashion magazines managed to get out and they were badly copied and printed in England, Holland and Belgium for circulation. Descriptions of fashions could also be found in newspapers and on the basis of the written word fashion plates were designed and printed on poor-quality paper. Nevertheless, they were ferreted out of Paris on board balloons to let other Europeans know what was going on in the Parisian world of fashion. These fashion plates are hard to come by as, in the main, they were not considered worthy of preservation. Foreign fashion publications which had printed French fashion plates, like *The Queen* (founded in 1861 and registered as a newspaper), showed the degree to which the war affected the spread of French fashion and fashion illustration. In its number for October 1870 *The Queen* announced:

> We regret to inform our subscribers, that owing to the disturbed state of affairs in Paris and the interruption of external communications, the coloured fashion plate which it has been our custom to publish with *The Queen* on the first Saturday of each month, has not arrived for this issue . . . Although our subscribers will understand that the delay is thoroughly unavoidable, we beg to express our sorrow for any probable inconvenience caused thereby.[16]

The full reinstatement of fashion plates after the cessation of hostilities shows just how elaborate and embellished women's fashionable dress and hairstyles had become. Dresses abounded with ribbons, lace and pleats, and bonnets were perched precariously on enormous stacks of hair. With the new fashion styles came a decline in traditional fashion-plate art and the beginnings of experimentation with fashion photography. Charles

Crinolette, 1875–80.
In the period 1863–67 the crinoline was already becoming smaller, and some ladies dispensed with it altogether, their skirts having little or no support. By the early 1870s some kind of under-structure was required for the new fashion of the backward sweep of the skirt. A crinolette or half-crinoline was devised for this new silhouette which could concentrate fullness at the back of the skirt. (*Museum of Costume, Bath*)

Adolphe Sandoz, a Ukrainian-born painter and illustrator, working in Paris, was one of the few who kept alive the conversation-piece format of the fashion plate in his work for *The Queen* from 1888 to 1898. The breadth of his work can be seen in his fashion plates for *La Revue de la mode*, one of the few fashion magazines to appear after the Franco-Prussian war, albeit for a short time, from 1872 to 1888. Sandoz's style is reminiscent of some of the great fashion artists of late eighteenth-century France such as Moreau le Jeune for *Le Monument du costume*. It appears likely that Sandoz drew the garments for his fashion plates from the photographic records of the great *maisons de couture*.

Amongst the best of the late nineteenth-century fashion artists can be numbered Marie de Solar, who drew fashion plates for *L'Art et la mode*, which started in 1880 and continued, incredibly, until 1967, and has the distinction of publishing the first half-tone illustration ever printed in a fashion magazine in its opening number. It was noted for experimenting early on with fashion photography. In the 1890s technological advances in photography made the inclusion of photographs in fashion journals easier and more economical. *L'Art et la mode*'s black-and-white fashion plates were drawn by artists who must have been influenced by photography, as they mirror the photographic conventions of clarity and sharpness. This magazine is essential for studying women's fashions of the early twentieth century for it concentrated on some of its most salient influences: sport, the automobile, and the *garçonne* look. The developments in *haute couture* for children, which it highlighted, are unique social statements. Published every Saturday and sold on both sides of the Atlantic, it provided bi-lingual captions and commentaries.[17]

Another important French fashion magazine founded near the end and continuing into the twentieth century was *La Mode pratique*. Right at the start of publication in 1892 it contained fashion photo-engravings.[18] Photography had infiltrated into the illustration of yet another fashion magazine of stature. One of the reasons for the general degeneration and decline of the fashion plate at the turn of the century was the great enthusiasm for experimentation with this new medium.

Austrian and German Fashion Plates

Since the time of the Empress Maria Theresa (1740-80), mother of Marie-Antoinette, Vienna had been a cultural centre where architecture, painting and music flourished. Maria Theresa also supported fashion, her encouragement leading to the foundation of an indigenous silk industry. The work of tailors and dressmakers was considered of a high standard, and trades such as the making of boots, shoes, bags, and parasols prospered. In 1815 the Congress of Vienna met to settle post-war boundaries in the wake of the Napoleonic Wars. The Congress made Vienna the political, cultural, and social centre of Europe, and brought together the élite of European society to partake of the social events connected with the Congress. These included a series of sparkling balls at which the newly fashionable dresses with gored skirts and shortened hems brilliantly suited the German dance mania, the waltz. For the first time a Viennese style emerged which concentrated on the details of dress and also on accessories, especially jewellery, so beautifully delineated in the work of Moritz Michael Daffinger, the pre-eminent miniaturist. For a brief, shining moment the accent was on Vienna: hardly any fashions which came direct from Paris and London were shown in Austria and Germany at the time. Indeed, the German fashion magazines, which had copied Parisian fashion journals so slavishly, now turned to Vienna.

An important step in the dissemination of Viennese fashion was undertaken by Johann Schickh, the owner of the fancy-goods shop at the Kohlmarkt in Vienna called *Zu den drey Grazien* (At the Sign of the Three Graces). In 1816 Herr Schickh founded the bi-weekly *Wiener Modenzeitung* (Viennese Fashion Journal). This fashion magazine inaugurated a new era for Viennese fashion, enabling Viennese tailors and dressmakers to publish their creations and thereby reach a wider potential clientele. More than 1,700 fashion plates, coloured by hand, appeared in its long run from 1816 to 1848.[19] This was the era of the Biedermeier style (1815-48), the culture of domesticity, when the middle classes gained power and challenged the old, aristocratic order, including their taste in fashion. Gottfried Biedermeier, a humorous and popular fictional character from the journal, *Fliegende Blätter*, came to symbolize the new bourgeois values, giving his name to the style that would find favour among *nouveaux riches* throughout Europe.

The designs for women's fashions in the *Wiener Modenzeitung* were by Vienna's most renowned dressmakers, Josef George Beer, Friedrich Bohlinger and Thomas Petko. Ladies' hats, headdresses and hairstyles were by Johann Langer and later by the milliner, Josefine Niederreiter. Men's fashion designs were by Josef Gunkel, the most celebrated tailor of the time. In addition to its fashion reports, the *Wiener Modenzeitung* published prose, poetry, travel writing, theatre criticism and news from the world of art, literature, and music.

In 1817 the *Wiener Modenzeitung* changed its name, becoming the *Wiener Zeitschrift für Kunst, Literatur, Theater und Mode* (Viennese Review of Art, Literature, Theatre and Fashion). When Johann Schickh died in 1835, the magazine was taken over by Friedrich Witthauer. By this time the magazine's best years were behind it; the reputation of Viennese fashion was on the wane and the tailors and dressmakers were again taking their direction from Paris. The significance of this fashion magazine lay in the fact that it published only fashion plates from original designs by Viennese tailors and dressmakers. The hand-coloured copperplate engravings were amongst the finest in Europe, setting a high artistic standard.

Viennese women's dress conformed to the Empire line of a high waist, with the skirt having a slight flare and gathered only in the back, and the long sleeves puffed at the shoulder. Decoration was placed on the neckline in the form of silk blonde or cotton lace or openwork which also featured in the cuffs of the sleeves and hem of the skirt. The fashion plates for 1818 show the particularly Viennese penchant for checked patterns, the most popular materials being cotton, silk, and sheep's wool.[20] Cashmere shawls, parasols, fans, gloves and bonnets were important accessories. A distinctively Viennese fashion was the *Kopfmantel* or headwrap. It was made of cotton lace and could measure an incredible four Viennese ells, or ten feet in length.

Another Viennese fashion illustrated and described in the *Wiener Modenzeitung* in 1817 was the first divided skirt.

> When the lady rides astraddle she wraps the sections round and buttons the same above the foot in such a way as to form trousers.[21]

Though a very innovative garment for its time, it failed to make an impact amongst fashionable Viennese ladies.

As with French and English fashions, waistlines dropped in the 1820s and dresses were worn with corsets. Again the Viennese showed their enterprising spirit when Johann Nepomuk Reithoffer discovered that rubber could be combined with flax, wool, or silk to produce stretch fabrics. By 1828 Reithoffer was marketing a seamless corset made of such fabrics.[22] When fashion turned ladies into veritable tea cosies, with the wide, circular shape of the skirt, Josef George Beer was credited with making the first crinoline in 1838.[23]

In the realm of men's dress, questions of etiquette emerged right at the beginning of the Congress of Vienna. A special session was called on the question of should the Holy Alliance adopt the pantaloon or keep the *culotte*? Though the session laid down no definitive code, the Alliance pronounced that the *habit habillé* would be kept for court functions.[24] Pantaloons or long trousers thus become socially acceptable for day, with *culottes*

retained for evening dress.[25] Men's fashionable garments otherwise altered little in this period: a dark frock coat, a waistcoat in a different colour, pantaloons or long trousers and shoes or ankle boots. The male figure of the 1820s and 1830s was hourglass in shape, and men also favoured check patterns.

The Orient inspired both women's and men's informal clothes in the 1830s and 1840s. Herr Beer designed Mandarin-style housedresses made in prints with motifs of pagodas, birds and flowers, and wide, loose coats made of Chinese cashmere with funnel-shaped Chinese sleeves and high collars. The fashion-conscious Viennese male wore a wide, loose morning coat of cashmere printed with palmette motifs, trousers, and slippers with curled-up toes, a shirt with a wide collar round which he would loosely drape a shawl and a little cap, rather like a fez, which often had *passementerie* trimming.

Undoubtedly the most decorative item of clothing worn by men during the Biedermeier era was the waistcoat, which provided the only colour in an otherwise drab outfit. It was not considered over-luxurious to own as many as 50 waistcoats so long as they displayed the latest cut and the fashionable details such as the exact type and number of buttons.[26]

In 1870 Vienna was once again a major centre of fashion. The Franco-Prussian War (1870-71) had serious repercussions for the fashion industry of the participating countries. Viennese entrepreneurship once again came to the fore and fashion magazines appeared which were important in their own right. The most outstanding were the *Wiener Mode*, which appeared in the 1880s, and *Wiener Chic*, which was launched in 1891 and had exceptionally fine fashion plates and a healthy circulation, and *Le Chic Parisien*, a very sumptuous fashion magazine founded by Arnold Bachwitz in about 1899. The last named publication, like earlier English fashion magazines, took a French title, yet had a clearly Viennese flavour.

Germany also developed some interesting fashion magazines. *Charis* (1801-06), launched in Leipzig, was a magazine 'für das Neueste in Kunst, Geschmack und Mode'. In 1803 it published a now-celebrated caricature of a male Janus-like figure which throws into focus the sartorial uncertainty that would confront occasions like the opening of the Congress of Vienna. One half of this figure is clad in pantaloons, a coat with a high collar, a large cravat, boots, and he sports a curly, dishevelled hairstyle. His other half is attired in an embroidered silk coat, waistcoat, *culottes*, *chapeau-bras*, and powdered wig, all associated with France of the *ancien régime*.

The *Allgemeine Modenzeitung*, also out of Leipzig, was launched in 1807 and was published there intermittently until 1894. The great virtue of this fashion magazine is that it contained the fashion plates of Jules David for *Le Moniteur de la mode*. Berlin was the most cosmopolitan of the German cities and introduced itself on the international fashion stage in 1865 with *Die Modenvelt*, a fashion magazine having the important sub-title 'Illustrierte Zeitung für Toiletten und Handarbeiten' (illustrated magazine for costume and needlework). It was a phenomenally successful magazine, lasting until 1909, its circulation encompassing no less than 14 different countries including France, England, America, and Russia, each version of the magazine translated into the language of the individual country. In England it was called *The Season* and it was entitled that in the language of each country of issue. In its first year alone a staggering 17,000 copies were sold, and within a few years ten times as many copies were being sold.[27] Freiherr Franz Lipperheide, the famous collector of fashion magazines and literature on the history of costume, was its editor. The global success of *Die Modenvelt* (it probably had a wider circulation than any other magazine) proved, that by the second half of the nineteenth century, national boundaries in fashion had disappeared.

American Fashion Plates

The first American fashion magazine was published in Philadelphia in 1826. Entitled *Graham's American Monthly Magazine of Literature, Art and Fashion*, it modelled itself on *La Belle assemblée* and contained copies of English and French fashion plates that were made by local artists. Competition was already keen with the appearance of many new fashion periodicals: *Petersons' Magazine*, *The Chicago Magazine of Fashion*, *Frank Leslie's Ladies' Gazette of Fashion* and above all, *Godey's Lady's Book*.

Godey's Lady's Book, another fashion magazine from Philadelphia, was launched by Louis B. Godey, and enjoyed tremendous popularity over its long run from 1830 to 1898. Its first fashion plate, published in July 1830, contained no caption or description. For the next few years fashion plates were sporadic and in the main were crude copies of French fashion plates taken largely from the *Petit courrier des dames*. It was not until January 1837, with the appointment of Sarah Josepha Hale as editor, that a clear, bold philosophy was stamped on the fashion magazine.

First we name dress and personal appearance these in a Lady's Book as well as in real life, are important things. Character is displayed, yes! Moral taste and goodness, or their perversion are indicated in dress.[28]

Mrs Hale was an ardent feminist yet with the demeanour of a proper Victorian lady. For her, fashion was a worthy pursuit, because dress together with good manners were the means by which women could exert great moral influence. Furthermore, her aim was to make her work

national . . . American . . . and a miscellany which although devoted to general literature is more expressly designed to mark the progress of national improvement.[29]

Her first step in this direction was to employ local artists to redraw for *Godey's Lady's Book* the fashions that appeared in the fashion plates in foreign fashion magazines. As a result a single fashion plate in *Godey's Lady's Book* can be from a conglomeration of sources as well as of dates, some as much as a year apart. That is why the fabric scrapbooks of Hannah Ditzler Alspaugh, who lived throughout the second half of the nineteenth century and into the early twentieth century, are so invaluable. She kept scraps of fabric and wrote brief descriptions of her garments, who made them, of what fabrics they were made, what she thought of them, and their eventual remodelling and remaking.[30a]

Yet Mrs Hale was no fool when it came to the business of fashion, and revitalizing *Godey's Lady's Book*. More simplified versions of European day and evening dress in outstandingly realistic black-and-white drawings were presented. The two designated leaders of fashion were Queen Victoria and Empress Eugénie. On her coronation in 1837 Queen Victoria was adulated by American women. Aware of this, *Godey's Lady's Book* had a correspondent who reported on the Queen's activities in London. However, as Victoria's fashions became austere and devoid of ornamentation during the 1840s, American women's interest in her waned. Their attention turned to the Empress Eugénie, who revived the French court in 1852 with Emperor Napoleon III. She put an end to Victorian starkness with her patronization of Charles Frederick Worth, who provided her and her circle with sumptuous gowns of magnificent silks, laces,

'Marie-Antoinette's fichu'. Engraved fashion plate from *Harper's Bazar*, 15 May 1869.
The Empress Eugénie's obsession with the cult of Marie-Antoinette led to a revival of the latter's fashions. These are larger and heavier than their forerunners. They were usually trimmed with lace or ribbon and fastened in front. The fullness

of the skirt is now swept towards the back and draped up over the hips in the style of the *polonaise* of the 1770s, supported by a "dress improver" or bustle. *(Victorian Fashions and Costumes from Harper's Bazaar: 1867-1898, Dover Publications)*

ribbons, feathers, and artificial flowers. While few American ladies could afford these gowns, *Godey's Lady's Book* provided copies of French fashion plates, many of the French gowns illustrated were simplified New York or Philadelphia versions.[31]

With the American Civil War (1861-5) American society changed dramatically. Reconstruction, the growth of industrialization and technology, improved communications and travel facilities, and more leisure time meant the upper middle class expanded and an aristocracy based on money evolved.

A new fashion awareness was stimulated by visits of European royalty to America and rich American women returning from the International Exhibition in Paris in 1867 with their trunks filled with French fashions. To affluent, style-conscious American women, the fashion plates in *Godey's Lady's Book* began to look decidedly provincial and subscriptions fell.

It was in this atmosphere that *Harper's Bazar* was launched on 2 November 1867. Sub-titled 'A Repository of Fashion, Pleasure and Instruction', it was published in New York by Harper and Brothers. *Harper's Bazar* came out every Saturday, selling for ten cents a copy or '$4.00 a year in advance.' The first editorial made clear that this was a fashion magazine largely intended for women. Special arrangements were made with leading European fashion magazines, especially *Der Bazar*, the editorial pronounced, whereby *Harper's Bazar* would receive fashion plates in advance and publish them at the same time as they appeared in Paris, Berlin, and other European cities. *Harper's Bazar* was innovative in that it was different from both American and French fashion magazines. *Godey's Lady's Book* and its lesser counterparts

devoted most of their pages to utilitarian wear suited to the American way of life as it was then conceived. The fashion plates in these magazines were usually redrawn from French periodicals, and were often printed a year or more after their initial appearance. The French magazines . . . were aloof to the practical aspects of life and showed fashions in delicate, highly-idealised colour illustrations. *Harper's Bazar* had a more solid appearance, with carefully detailed engravings, in

black and white. Many of the designs included were directly of European origin, but selected with an American audience in mind. Most of the others were based on European models, but had been altered to meet American tastes and needs.[32]

Harper's Bazar was the best source for high fashion in America until *Vogue* appeared on the scene in 1892.

Painters of Modern Life

An accurate rendering of costume can be found in other types of illustration, for, in the nineteenth century new links were forged between art and fashion. In England one valuable source is what Christopher Wood calls 'modern-life narrative paintings'.[33] This type of painting dates back to the eighteenth century and is seen most

'Bicycle Dress'. Engraved fashion plate from *Harper's Bazar*, 14 April 1894.
Around 1850 Mrs Bloomer, an American dress reformer, advocated that women be allowed to wear trousers instead of cumbersome fashionable dress and promoted her 'Bloomer costume'. It was an important symbol of freedom and was donned by American suffragists, most notable Susan B

Anthony. This elegant costume in brown velveteen consists of Turkish trousers, and a short double-breasted jacket buttoned with a vest, collar and tie. The liberated 'new woman' of the 1890s, indulging in the new cycling craze, made Mrs Bloomer's ideal a fashionable reality. *(Victorian Fashions and Costumes from Harper's Bazaar: 1867-1898, Dover Publications)*

significantly in the work of William Hogarth. The Pre-Raphaelites and individual painters, above all, William Frith, continued in the footsteps of Hogarth, depicting dress in painstaking detail aligned to social realism. It is worth emphasizing how often auction houses selling this kind of painting refer to the dress of the figures in their catalogue entries for dating or setting pictures in their appropriate period.

In France one of the great debates of the nineteenth century was the search for modernity, which placed an emphasis on the painting of contemporary fashion. This debate was inherited from the eighteenth century when critics like Diderot deemed modern dress undignified. Édouard Manet dismissed Diderot's views saying 'we must accept our own time and paint what we see'.[34] His paintings treat new trends in fashion with the carefully observed character of fashion plates. For Manet and his circle, fashion was one of the leading issues of the time. Champfleury, a writer associated with the Realist movement, supported Manet in his demand for paintings of 'present-day people with round hats, black suits, polished shoes . . .'.[35]

It was Charles Baudelaire who furthered the dialogue between fashion and art. According to Champfleury, dress had a central role in Baudelaire's life. At a time when the suit was available ready-made, Baudelaire, in his quest for perfection, demanded fitting after fitting from his tailor, and, when he thought the tailor finally got it right, wanted a dozen suits like it.[36] 'On the Heroism of Modern Life', a section of Baudelaire's *Salon* of 1846, was a plea for the virtues of painting men in their modern black suits.

> And yet, has it not its own beauty and native charm, that victimised suit? Is it not the necessary attire for our sickly time, which bears a symbol of perpetual mourning on its black, skinny shoulders? [37]

Baudelaire's cause was taken up by the critic Théophile Gautier in his book *De La Mode* (1858).

> Modern dress prevents them (artists and sculptors) so they tell us, from producing masterpieces. To listen to them, it is the fault of black suits, paletots and crinolines that they are not Titians, van Dycks, or Velázquezes.[38]

Yet Titian, van Dyck, and Velázquez, as Gautier stated, painted the costume of their own time. Baudelaire's fullest discussion of the dandy and the modernity of dress is found in 'The Painter of Modern Life' (1859), published in *Le Figaro* in 1863. The stark black suit, the bedrock of Baudelaire's dandyism, was the primary dress of the bourgeois male of fashion. This sober attire of the dandy-gentleman was salient to society itself, bearing witness to professional status. Here Baudelaire placed fashion solidly in the context of modernity, indeed, made it the cornerstone of his aesthetic of modernity. The painter of modern life

> has an aim loftier than that of the mere *flâneur* . . . something other than the fugitive pleasure of circumstance. He is looking for that quality which you must allow me to call 'modernity'. He makes it his business to extract from fashion whatever element it may contain of poetry within history, to distil the eternal from the transitory.[39]

The *flâneur* had many permutations in Baudelaire's Paris. Implicit delineations were the 'stroller' or 'boulevardier' who wandered amongst the crowds and observed them. He was a dandy by virtue of his fastidious attention to dress and exquisite manners. He was also an *artiste* who could create lasting work observed from transitory moments of modern life. In his portrait of James Tissot, Degas portrays his subject as an *artiste-flâneur*. Tissot has just called by for a visit after a stroll. He has negligently but elegantly placed his black top hat and cape on the table as good etiquette required. Even though he does not reveal Tissot's occupation, by placing him in his own studio surrounded by his easel and art work, Degas implicitly associates Tissot with the artistic profession, and, as it is his own milieu, Degas hints that he too, like Tissot, is an *artiste-flâneur*.

Baudelaire's own choice to illustrate his definition of the painter of modern life was Constantin Guys. He identified Guys as a *flâneur*, a dandy and an artist, that is, as observer, participant and creator. When Guys sketched dandies 'nothing was missed' because only a dandy himself could appreciate his way of wearing a coat or riding a horse.[40]

Baudelaire was very much inspired by fashion plates, particularly those of the most widely-subscribed and influential fashion magazine of the early nineteenth century, La Mésangère's *Le Journal des dames et des modes*. For Baudelaire, fashion plates continuously offered a re-definition of beauty. The explosion of fashion magazines, and their new, cheap mechanized means of production, meant that fashion plates were available to every level of society. Fashion plates caught the eye of more painters of modern life. John Rewald in his *History of Impressionism* shows fashion plates that correspond to some paintings of Cézanne[41] and Mark Roskill in his article 'Early Impressionism and the Fashion Print' shows the influence of fashion plates on the paintings of Monet.[42]

There are a host of artists who could illustrate perfectly Baudelaire's thesis of capturing the harmonious whole –

the inter-relationship of costume, gestures, pose: Ingres, of course, who Baudelaire likened to a 'fashionable milliner', Édouard Manet, Eugène Boudin, Alfred Stevens, Pierre-Auguste Renoir and James Tissot.

Paris during the Second Empire and Third Republic was the perfect place for them to paint the beauty of women and their fashions. Under the architect Baron Hausmann, Paris was made into an imperial city of grand boulevards and spacious parks, the ideal venue for showing off the opulent clothes of the *nouveaux riches*.

The greatest painter of modern life, in terms of both genre subjects and portraits, was undoubtedly James Tissot. Like Ingres, Tissot's family was in the fashion trade. His father was a *marchand de nouveautés* and his mother ran a hat-making company. Tissot was as

fascinated with fashion plates as the Impressionists, and his *oeuvre d'art* is a valuable historical and social document of the second half of the nineteenth century for the depiction of a variety of customed images of society in numerous settings.

When Degas painted Tissot as an *artiste-flâneur*, he placed Tissot as the dandy who mixed in the world of fashion he portrayed in his paintings. Like Renoir, Tissot enjoyed painting venues where sophisticated, modish people dressed up in *couture* clothing. Such was his focus on fashion that he collected contemporary costumes and kept them in his studio, garbing his models in often identical outfits, as his sketch and painting, *The Ball on Shipboard*, of c. 1874, reveals (see p144). *The Ball on Shipboard* is often seen as a sumptuous dress rehearsal for the series *La Femme à Paris* which Tissot completed some ten years later.[43] *La Femme à Paris* is a series of 15 paintings which was exhibited in 1885 at the Galerie Sedelmeyer in Paris. The group of paintings illustrates Parisiennes of various classes at their vocations and amusements, the common denominator being the emphasis on fashion as an integral element of modern beauty and the increasingly complex role women played in French society.[44] *La Femme à Paris* was an inspiration for the next generation of painters: Jacques-Emile Blanche, Albert Besnard, Giovanni Boldoni and Paul-César Helleu who drew the fashionable women of the *Belle Époque*.

Portrait of James Tissot, painted by Edgar Degas, 1868. Degas shows his painter-friend looking like a model in a fashion plate. Impeccably dressed, Tissot is an exemplar of the *artiste-flâneur*, a painter of modern life. (*The Metropolitan Museum of Art, New York, Rogers Fund*)

Meeting in the Park, pen-and-ink drawing and watercolour by Constantin Guys.
Baudelaire noted how Guys, his designated painter of modern life, attached great importance to backgrounds, and here we get a sense of the open space of Paris created by the Baron Hausmann, the ideal setting for showing off the stylish modes of the Second Empire, especially the crinoline. (*The Metropolitan Museum of Art, New York, Rogers Fund*)

Photography

Photography is another major visual source for the study of fashion. France can be credited as the country where the first photographic images were produced.

Joseph Nicéphore Niepce and the painter Louis Daguerre worked together in the late 1820s on a method of focusing and placing an image onto a metal plate that had already been chemically treated. Daguerre perfected this process after Niepce's death in 1833, and by 1840 had invented the daguerrotype which created small, permanent mirror-image portraits with an exposure time of only two minutes. Each daguerrotype was an individual negative that was not reproducible, and the technique was, needless to say, an expensive process with the market largely the domain of the middle and upper classes. With the cheaper ambrotypes of the 1850s, portraiture was made available to a wider cross-section of society which helped stimulate the dissemination of fashion news.

It was not until the late nineteenth century that fashion magazines such as *L'Art et la mode* and *La Mode pratique* started to make use of photographs and photo-engravings. Photographic records were undertaken by

Will You Go With Me, Fido? (Departing for the Promenade), painted by Alfred Stevens, 1859.
Women of the Second Empire dressed in the finest silks and satins which became Stevens's trademark as well as his means to define modernity both in subject and painting technique. The back view of the figure standing and posed in an elegant interior is reminiscent of fashion plates. The focus of fashion for Stevens is the shawl, an indispensable accessory during the Second Empire. *(Philadelphia Museum of Art, the W.P. Wilstach Collection)*

La Parisienne, painted by Pierre-Auguste Renoir, 1874.
The sitter was probably the young actress, Madame Henriot, through whom Renoir distils the essence of the modern *Parisienne*, turning her into a type. Her fashionable dress with its pleats and ruffles, her small hat tilted at an angle over one ear, and the toe of her boot, just visible, all lent themselves to a display of Renoir's talents as a fashion artist. The resultant image has the striking simplicity of the fashion plates of the *Directoire*. *(National Museum of Wales, Cardiff)*

engravings. Photographic records were undertaken by *couture* houses and these were very useful to fashion artists illustrating fashion magazines. According to an article written in 1894, Worth's premises included a studio where all his models were photographed.[45] The great stimulus to the photographic image was the *carte-de-visite*, a process that was patented by the French photographer, André Disderi, in 1854. A new camera

with a multi-lens could produce eight small images on one glass negative through the use of the wet-collodion process, whereby glass plates with silver salts could fix a negative image which in turn produced a positive image on albumen paper. This was a cheap method of reproduction which brought portraiture to a very wide social range. The images were trimmed to a size of $3\frac{1}{2}$ by $2\frac{1}{4}$ inches and mounted on cards of 4 inches by $2\frac{1}{2}$

The Ball on Shipboard, painted by James Tissot, c. 1874. Careful observance of the dress appropriate to the occasion and time of day was required. Here, the women wear dresses with tight jacket bodices with basques and apron-fronted overskirts puffed out at the back over a bustle. The lady coming up the staircase wears the new cuirasse bodice which is heavily whaleboned and extends over the hips, and ruffled, elbow-length sleeves. The fashionable hairstyle is a full-braided *chignon* worn with forward-tilting straw sailor hats or bonnets worn at a backward-tilted angle. Fans and parasols are appropriate accessories. *(Tate Gallery, London)*

A Sunday on La Grande Jatte, painted by Georges Seurat, 1884. The fashionable silhouette of the 1880s required a corset and a bustle. The bustle, or *tournure* as it was called in French, tied around the waist. It was a small pad or overlapping frills of horsehair cloth bound with braid and stiffened with steel bands or a frame of wires that supported the fullness of the large folds of the skirt and created a sharp, shelf-like projection. The bustle, the jacket with its cuirass bodice that extends over the waist and hips and the small, high hat shaped like an abbreviated cone show Seurat's flair for contemporary costume. Seurat used the imagery of fashion display and advertising for ready-to-wear clothing found in department stores where bustles were worn by ladies in profile and placed in the setting of a garden or park, venues where sartorial exhibition was important. *(Art Institute of Chicago, Helen Birch Bartlett Memorial Collection 1926.224)*

the Emperor Napoleon III and Queen Victoria was photographed and began collecting albums of pictures of her family, friends and the famous. Collecting became a robust pastime. Collectors were after *cartes-de-visite* of celebrities and also advertisements for them which were placed in fashion magazines such as *The Queen*, and farther afield, *Godey's Lady's Magazine*. M. Disderi was the most fashionable studio practitioner with royalty, politicians, and the military flocking to him in Paris. He made a copy of every portrait he took and all of them, totalling more than 50,000, have survived. His archive is an invaluable source for a study of the details of formal, fashionable dress.

Following the passionate interest in *cartes-de-visite*, large cabinet photographs were introduced in 1866. By 1880 they had replaced the smaller *cartes-de-visite* as the most popular portrait format. The life-size scale of these portraits and their spaceless backgrounds heightened their impact as images of fashion.[46]

Historical Revivals

The nineteenth century inherited a passion for historical revivals. In England, scholars continued to produce costume books which popularized English dress. The documentation of historical accuracy in dress was a necessity for history painting, a principal branch of nineteenth-century English art. Fashionable men and women, too, needed guidance for the sartorial recreation of the past. Nostalgia and historical dress were major themes of fashion journals such as *La Belle Assemblée* and *The Englishwoman's Domestic Magazine*.[47]

inches, the standard-size visiting card. *Cartes-de-visite* were introduced into England in the 1850s and cartomania developed in the 1860s when M. Disderi photographed

In nineteenth-century England it was the fruits of the historical-costume researches of J.R. Planché and F.W.

The Black Sash, painted by Giovanni Boldini, c. 1905. Fashions of the *Belle Époque* required an hourglass figure which was adorned with pale-tinted gowns made in luscious organza, silk or satin swagged with delicate laces and highlighted by a dramatic, elaborate effect such as a sash, billowing behind, a blaze of black velvet drawing all eyes. The intricate detail of this gown, designed by Worth, clearly inspired Boldini to bring out the opulence of this era. The sitter may be Mrs Law, a wealthy American socialite and a prominent member of high society who was also painted by Paul-César Helleu. *(Department of Nineteenth-Century Paintings, Christie's, New York)*

Portrait of Oscar Wilde. Photograph by N. Sarony, 1882. Oscar Wilde was photographed in New York in the costume he wore on his American lecture tour to promote "aesthetic values". Many artists and writers advocated dress reform from the 1850s onwards. Aesthetes and dress reformers of the late 1880s and 1890s favoured a costume based on the medieval past, or eighteenth-century styles. Wilde wears an informal double-breasted lounge or smoking jacket which is decoratively frogged and has a quilted silk collar and cuffs. Underneath he wears a shirt with a turned-down collar and a large silk tie. His eighteenth-century style breeches are worn with silk stockings and low-heeled shoes with ribbon ties. Wilde's long hair is in keeping with the aesthetic style. *(National Portrait Gallery, London)*

May 1842 at Buckingham Palace where she dressed up as Queen Philippa, Prince Albert was clad as Edward III and their retinue were garbed in fourteenth-century costume.[48] His *A Cylopaedia of Costume*, published in two volumes (1876, 1879), is still recommended for its black-and-white illustrations and clarity of text.

In 1846 F. W. Fairholt published his *Costume in England: a History of Dress from the Earliest Period till the Close of the Eighteenth Century*, which was based on articles that had appeared in the periodical, *Art-Union*. Dedicated to Strutt, Fairholt's costume book was of a larger format than Planché's, with the drawings consequently much clearer. It also had the advantage to contemporaries of containing a glossary of *recherché* terms. A second edition came out in 1860 with a preface even more robust than Planché's on the importance of historical accuracy in costume.

The periods most favoured by the nineteenth-century English appear to be the fourteenth and eighteenth centuries. As well as being emulated in high fashion and *bals costumés* these periods also appealed to dress reformers and aesthetes of the 1870s, 1880s, and 1890s. Such was her passion for dress reform that Mrs Mary Eliza Hawies, in her book *The Art of Beauty*, published in 1878, illustrated her work with historical costumes and expressed the wish for fashion to be based on the aesthetic lines of the flowing drapery of the past, especially medieval styles. Some contemporaries linked aesthetic dress to the Pre-Raphaelite Brotherhood whose paintings were first seen in 1849. One of the professed aims of the Pre-Raphaelite painters was to renew art by a meticulous study of nature and by a return to historical subjects. For correct medieval dress they made inexhaustible use of one of the nineteenth century's grandest costume books, Camille Bonnard's *Costume historique*, published in 1829-30, which illustrated the thirteenth, fourteenth, and fifteenth centuries.[49] Sir John Everett Millais, one of the founders of the Pre-Raphaelite Brotherhood, wore historical dress and in his genre pieces and portraits made detailed use of the dress of the seventeenth and eighteenth centuries.

From 1884, Liberty's, the fashionable London department store, had a costume department that sold dresses in the muted colours and flowing lines of

History of British Costume from the Earliest Period to the Close of the Eighteenth Century (1837) Planché states that '. . . the works of the indefatigable Strutt have . . . misled perhaps more than they have enlightened', because Strutt had not rigorously followed a chronological sequence. His aim was to correct Strutt's shortcomings, using as his basis, not only Strutt, but also Vecellio, Boissard and Jefferys. That Planché's illustrated costume book more than adequately fed the palate for information on historical details of dress was evident when it went into a third edition in 1874. Amongst those who had a love affair with the past was Queen Victoria who held many *tableaux vivants* and *bals costumés*. Planché's antiquarian authority was recognized when he provided the text of the commemorative volume of the Queen's *bal costumé* held in

Portrait of Mrs Bischoffsheim, painted by Sir John Everett Millais, 1873.

Mrs Bischoffsheim wears the Dolly Varden style of dress which was popular from c. 1870 and named after the heroine of Charles Dickens' novel *Barnaby Rudge*. This consisted of a *polonaise*-style robe, which was made of material with a floral pattern on a dark ground. Distinctive details included the tiered lace sleeve ruffles, a low-cut, square-necked tight bodice trimmed with lace, here bow-fronted, recalling the stomacher, and a skirt draped in *paniers*. Underneath is a flounced skirt in a plain colour and the whole ensemble is worn over a bustle. Eighteenth-century style accessories are the long pearl earrings, the pendant on a black-velvet ribbon worn around the neck, gloves and a fan. *(Tate Gallery, London)*

and illustrate their own costume books. He set the tone with his own publications including his vast cataloguing project of the objects in his *Musée* with a dissertation on the costume. His *Musée des Monuments français* was published from 1800 to 1806 (5 volumes).

One of the first artists to compile a costume book was Nicolas-Xaver Willemin. He spent a great deal of time studying in Lenoir's *Musée*. The culmination of this study was his *Monuments inédits pour servir l'histoire des arts*. It was begun in 1806 and finally published in two volumes in 1825, and was completely devoted to the dress of medieval and Renaissance France. Most of the costume plates were engraved by him although he enlisted the support of other artists. All of the text was written by Willemin and in his preface he stresses that his principal aim was to inspire artists. Willemin devoted a large number of costume plates to the statues of *chevaliers* in Lenoir's *Musée*. His attention was riveted on the belts that were a chief insignia of *chevaliers*, possibly because the fashionable ladies of the First Empire wore their belts in the style of *chevaliers* and also took to wearing their shawls draped in the manner of these belts. Exemplars of this fashion were Empress Josephine and her sister-in-law, Pauline Bonaparte (see p117).

One of the most renowned of the *troubadour* artists was Auguste Garneray. Josephine's *couturier*, M. Leroy, created her enchanting *toques* from the drawings made by his friend, Garneray, who had carefully observed the Renaissance *toques* in works on display in the galleries in the Louvre. Afterwards M. Leroy adapted these delightful little hats for his other elegant clients. France's past continued to appeal to Garneray and he went on to compile a costume book of lithograph drawings entitled *Costumes du siècle de Louis XIV*, published in Paris about 1820. Some of Garneray's drawings were after the engravings of Nicolas Arnoult of the celebrated family of seventeenth-century fashion engravers.

Under the restored Bourbons the number of paintings on French national history themes increased at an alarming rate.[51] Nothing demonstrates the scale of this increase better than the figures for works exhibited at the *Salon*. Under Louis XVI and Marie-Antoinette commissions from all sources, including the government, totalled

dresses in the muted colours and flowing lines of medieval dress that suited aesthetic tastes. Liberty's played a central role in the dissemination of aestheticism with artistic dress designs and the publication of a book in 1893 entitled *Evolution in Costume* which illustrated distinctive Liberty dresses *vis-à-vis* historical originals.

Informed and intelligent people in nineteenth-century France had a passionate interest in historical facts, and in particular those of their own country. According to contemporary art critics such as Charles-Paul Landon and Etienne-Jean Delécluze, Alexandre Lenoir's *Musée des Monuments français* cast a spell of enchantment over so many artists, especially the pupils of David.[50] Besides encouraging painting in *le style troubadour*, another great achievement of Lenoir was to encourage artists to write

'Aesthetic Dress'. Engraved caricature by George du Maurier. From *Punch*, 1880.
In artistic circles in England from the late 1870s, high fashion was rejected in favour of aesthetic dress. Although the gentleman's turned-down shirt collar, soft tie and lounge jacket, most probably made of velvet, were fashionable informal dress, velvet jackets were especially connected with

aesthetes. His long hair and clean-shaven face were also their trademarks, as was the long, frizzy hair of their female counterparts. Although du Maurier's cartoons in *Punch* criticised the Aesthetic Movement, he did admit that some women looked better in aesthetic dress than high fashion. (B.T. Batsford Ltd Archive)

by Ingres of 1856 (National Gallery, London) bears close comparison with portraits of Mme de Pompadour painted by Quentin de la Tour (Louvre) and Hubert Drouais (National Gallery, London). As late as 1890 Worth designed a dress for the comtesse Edmond Récoupé which she wore in her portrait by Debat-Ponsan (Musée de Petit Palais, Paris) that bears comparison with the dress of Mme Molé-Raymond painted by Mme Vigée-Le Brun in 1787. Worth considered himself above all to be an artist and was the *couturier* that ladies went to for sumptuously detailed costumes inspired by the dress and painters of the past.

A revival of Spanish art, costume, dance and music took place during the Second Empire encouraged by the Empress Eugénie's taste for her native country. Things Spanish held a particular fascination for Édouard Manet, and the dress in his *Young Woman Reclining in Spanish Costume* may have come from his collection of costumes.

The second half of the nineteenth century was inundated with costume books produced for the new mass market. Some were re-issues of earlier costume books discussed in previous chapters, such as Vecellio's *De gli Habiti antichi et moderni di Diverse Parti del Mondo*, originally published in Venice in 1590. The new crop were encyclopaedic in range, such as Paul Lacoix's ten volume *Les Costumes historiques de la France d'après les mouvements les plus authentiques, statues, bas reliefs . . .* This monumental study was published in 1852 and had very wide-ranging sources, including the celebrated *Le Recueil Gaignières*.

Fashion periodicals contributed to the interest in historicism in dress. In 1873 *La Mode artistique* offered a set of 96 plates of historical French costumes drawn and engraved by the Pauquet brothers, Hippolyte & Polidas, based on the best artists of the past and the most authentic documents.[52] Their costume book, *Modes et costumes historiques dessinés et gravés . . . d'après les meilleurs maîtres de chaque époque*, had been published in Paris in 1862 at the Bureaux des Modes et Costumes Historiques. It consisted of 96 hand-coloured engraved costume plates together with original watercolours of 21 of the plates, signed by either of the Pauquet brothers.

Jean-Etienne Quicherat's *Histoire du costume en France depuis les temps les plus réculés jusqu'à la fin du XVIII,*

approximately 36 paintings while at the *Salon* of 1817 alone, approximately 86 paintings were shown. These works in *le style troubadour* satisfied the propaganda requirements of the restored monarchy. The needs of the restored Bourbons were amply provided for by those everlasting stalwarts, the two *rois chevaliers*, François I and Henri IV. In the realm of fashion the successor to Marie-Antoinette and Josephine was Marie-Caroline, duchesse de Berry. She continued the tradition of court balls in historic dress; at her most celebrated in the Tuileries in 1829, all the guests wore dress based on the court of François II. She came dressed as his wife, Marie-Stuart.

The fashion for dressing in the style of the eighteenth century established itself during the Second Empire. The Empress Eugénie was devoted to the eighteenth century in general and to Queen Marie-Antoinette in particular. The adoration of Empress for Queen extended from the wearing of the simple Marie-Antoinette *fichu* to full-blown Marie-Antoinette style dress. After the Empress Eugénie's mania, interest in eighteenth-century fashionable dress never ceased. The floral patterned dress worn by Mme Moistessier in her portrait painted

published in 1845 with good black-and-white illustrations, is still invaluable today for the scope of its visual sources and for its erudite text. The first monumental costume book to take advantage of the nineteenth century's new reprographic techniques was Albert Racinet's *Le Costume historique*. This work originally came out in periodical or partwork form over a number of years. In 1888 it was published in six volumes in a large format, running to about 2,000 pages and containing 500 costume plates. Racinet's sources are wide-ranging as his work comprises the history and geography of dress not just in Europe but in the whole world. The most attractive feature of the book is its coloured costume plates. Racinet's main concern is the visual side of historical costume, and he ferreted out as many original colour illustrations as he could. They were often difficult to come by, especially for the early periods. He relied on black-and-white woodcuts and engravings of early costume books to which he often added his own colour which necessarily must be viewed with caution. Like any self-confident nineteenth-century scholar, Racinet had opinions which often make his text prejudicial and contentious. Notwithstanding these caveats, *Le Costume historique* remains one of the classic works of reference in the annals of the history of costume.

Young Woman Reclining in Spanish Costume, painted by Édouard Manet, 1862.
The Empress Eugénie, who was of Spanish origin, encouraged Spanish taste. The work of Velázquez and Goya had a profound effect on painters, especially Manet. In the world of the *demi-monde*, women dressed in men's clothes - as in this costume portrait - had a powerful sexual appeal for their clientele. Manet and Guys were the two artists who best evoked the languid atmosphere of the *demi-monde* in Paris of the Second Empire. *(Yale University Art Gallery, New Haven, Bequest of Stephen Wilton Clark)*

5: Fashion Illustration in the Twentieth Century

Fashion Photography

Photography's potential for illustrating fashion was not properly tapped until the beginning of the new century. The new, very chic, French fashion magazine *Les Modes* was an excellent vehicle for realizing its possibilities. Founded in 1901, *Les Modes* was published in Paris but sold as well in London, Berlin, and New York. It had a larger format than most of its competitors, measuring eleven by fourteen inches. Half-tone photographs and tipped-in pages of coloured photographs printed on high-quality glossy paper were available for the first time, featuring *haute couture* and the decorative and applied arts. Worth, John Redfern, Madame Paquin, Jacques Doucet, Doeuillet, and the Soeurs Callot were all eager to have their fashions photographed by the Paris studios of Mlle Reutlinger, Boyer, and Paul Nader.[1] The *beau monde* could see the latest fashions through a camera's lens which picked up every flowing flounce, layers of ruching, yards of lace, lavish beadwork and embroidery on the luxurious materials that made up the ostentatious dresses of the *Belle Époque* when the Art Nouveau style was at its zenith. The sinuous line of Art Nouveau was achieved in dress by using a new type of boned corset, invented in 1902, called the Gache Sarraute.[2] It produced an S-curved line, throwing the bust forward and the hips back, and hence the silhouette became known as the S-bend.

'Robe de diner en dentelle de Venise' designed by Jacques Doucet. Photograph from *Les Modes*, January 1903. Photographs were now beginning to replace the fashion plate in illustrating the latest styles in *haute couture*. In its surface ornamentation of lace with patterns and in its silhouette of softly undulating curves in the S-bend shape, the gown echoes Art Nouveau, then at its height. The train of the skirt has been carefully arranged towards the camera to show off the intricate detail and lustrous quality of the Venetian lace. The beautiful and elaborate bodice also displays the dazzling workmanship offered by *le grand couturier*. (Fashion Research Centre, Bath)

Madame Poiret photographed in the costume designed by Poiret for her to wear at his "1002nd Night" or "Persian Celebration", June 1911.
Poiret's attraction to fashions based on Orientalism extended to a series of much publicised *fêtes* and fancy dress balls which he gave. Madame Poiret wears harem pantaloons made of chiffon, her bodice made of the same material with the sleeves trimmed in fur. Her tunic is held in place by a cummerbund. It is made of gold cloth, wired at the bottom and edged with gold fringe, which the very next day after the *fête* entered the world of fashion as the lampshade tunic. A turban of gold cloth and chiffon with a large turquoise and aigrette completed her exotic outfit. Madame Poiret was her husband's muse and model, and the best interpreter of his fashion ideas. (Photo: B.T. Batsford Ltd Archive)

Into the flamboyant world of the *haute couture* of the *Belle Époque* burst a revolutionary *couturier* by the name of Paul Poiret. After serving an apprenticeship under Jacques Doucet and having worked at *La Maison Worth*, he opened his own fashion house in 1903 when he was just 24 years old. Poiret's first great 'revolution', as he called it, was to 'wage war' on the Gache Sarraute. Having jettisoned this constricting foundation, he went on to establish his *Directoire* Revival line of dress based on the Neo-classical fashions and the fabrics of the original *Directoire* of 1795-9. With a high waistline and long, straight lines, the effect was clearly to elongate the figure and make it more statuesque. Poiret achieved this by draping the fabric directly on to the model to see how it fell most naturally. Poiret's *Directoire* silhouette must have been considered revolutionary as Madame Paquin was still purveying the S-bend as late as 1914.[3] Poiret did not neglect his other great passion, Orientalia. Orientalism had been a craze in Paris since the turn of the century, reaching a peak with the arrival of the Ballets Russes in 1909. Poiret always insisted that his interpretation of Orientalism was a reaction to the over-elaboration of the *Belle Époque* which had drained fashion of its vitality. Poiret's *Directoire* Revival fashions were promoted in photographs in the periodical *Art et Décoration*, under the editorship of Lucien Vogel. The April 1911 issue featured a whole series of his designs photographed by Edward Steichen who used the new, soft-focus technique. The settings were the beautiful *Directoire* interiors of Poiret's *maison de couture*, a perfect union of fashion and art. Poiret supervised the backgrounds, the poses of the models and the lighting. These photographs were revolutionary not only for showing Poiret's new style of dress, but also for being the first collaborative project of *couturier*, photographer and magazine editor.

'Tailored costume'. Lithographed fashion plate from *Chic Parisien*, 1911.
The *Directoire* Revival suit shows the neat, tailored look of 1911. Poiret had taken the slim, straight *Directoire* style to its most incongruous extent. The long skirt was so narrow that it was aptly named the hobble skirt or the *jupe entravée* by the French. The original *élégante* of the *Directoire* period adopted masculine features in her attire, including a cutaway jacket with large, plain cloth buttons and wide lapels, derived from the riding coat, a large *fichu-cravate*, and large square-cut silver shoe buckles, all worn here by her twentieth-century counterpart. The headwear of the original *élégante* assumed a bewildering variety of forms, again reflected by the *Directoire* Revival *élégante*, including large, wide-brimmed picture hats, bedecked with ribbons and bows. *(Fashion Research Centre, Bath)*

'Robe Strozzi', designed by Paul Poiret. Photograph by Edward Steichen. From *Art et Décoration*, April 1911.
The theme of Neo-classical gown and tunic was a favourite with Poiret. Here the gown is overlaid with two tunics in differing lengths and colours and delicately edged with brilliants. The *Directoire* style of dress which he revived co-exists perfectly with Orientalism, just as in the eighteenth century. The model's turban with an aigrette enhances the elongation of her figure. The backdrop is a salon in Poiret's fashion house which was noted for its superb *Directoire* interiors. The costume and the interiors harmonize admirably and are well-served by the soft-focus photography worked out by Poiret and the photographer. *(Victoria and Albert Museum, London)*

Poiret's most notable collaboration was with the American painter and photographer, Man Ray. A Dadaist, Man Ray worked in New York until 1921 when he went, penurious, to Paris. His paintings were included in the first Surrealist exhibition held there in 1925. In his autobiography, Man Ray gives a vivid description of the assignment Poiret gave him for his Summer collection of 1922, which shows the inter-action of photography, sculpture and dress.

> The model came out wearing a close-fitting gown in gold-shot brocade gathered round the ankles in the hobble skirt style of today . . . The room upstairs was flooded with sunlight from the windows; I would not need any other light. I had her stand near the Brancusi sculpture, which threw off golden beams of light, blending with the colours of the dress. This was to be the picture I decided; I'd combine art and fashion.[4]

Everything that Poiret could possibly have wanted was captured by Man Ray: brilliant colour, economy of line, definition of textures, portraiture.

In making his prints for Poiret, Man Ray hit upon what he called his Rayograph process, or camera-less photography, which reproduced the effect of a photograph being sent by radio waves, making the camera an artist's tool as pliable as a paintbrush or drawing pencil. Poiret was the first to appreciate Man Ray's rayographs which quickly gained universal recognition.

Man Ray worked as a fashion photographer for various magazines including *Vanity Fair*, *Vogue* and *Harper's Bazar*. In 1901 *Harper's Bazar* changed from a weekly to a monthly. In 1913 it was bought by the Hearst publishing empire and in 1929 the second 'a' was added to 'Bazar'. Man Ray worked for *Harper's Bazaar* in the 1930s under its legendary editor, Carmel Snow, who was noted for her exciting editorial ideas and her ability to identify and promote artistic talent. Under the tenureship of Miss Snow and Alexey Brodovitch, the art director, Man Ray's

Poiret not only recorded fashions but also, through photography, suggests a life beyond the frame. Delphi's photograph of Denise Poiret, Poiret's wife and muse, wearing 'la robe mythe' which appeared in the December 1919 issue of *Les Modes* is in this category. She wears an ensemble which Poiret designed especially for her. It consists of a gold lamé bodice and a skirt made of monkey-fur fabric. Behind her is a crucial element, Constantin Brancusi's sculpture *Bird in Space*. Indeed, Mme Poiret's bird-like frame, her spiky hairstyle, the fine pleating on her gold lamé bodice and the feathery texture of her skirt all reflect the image of the bird behind her. The photograph illustrates the rapport between *couturier* and photographer as accomplices in style.

'La tunique Joséphine par Paul Poiret'. Fashion plate (*pochoir* process) from *Les Robes de Paul Poiret racontées par Paul Iribe*, 1908.
It is fitting that Poiret should have named one of his most purist *Directoire* creations 'la tunique Joséphine' after that noted patron of the Neo-classical taste. The 'Joséphine' model consists of a high-waisted dress in white satin with a black tulle tunic edged with gold braid. The *Directoire* commode, statue and portrait of Lady Emma Hamilton complement Poiret's interpretation of the Neo-classical style. (*Photo: B.T. Batsford Ltd Archive*)

A bronze figure of a woman, by G. Rigot, 1920s.
Sculpture is a useful source of information for the study of dress, the fully-dressed figures providing a realistic record of fashion in another medium. Rigot, along with Demetre Chiaparus and Frederick Preiss, made small, female figures clothed in the fashionable dress of the 1920s. This bronze figure with an ivory head wears a pyjamas suit, painted in olive green, black and gold. (*Sale Sotheby's London, 4 November 1994; Art Nouveau and Art Deco Department, Sotheby's, London*)

of the leading French designers. Louis's two sons, Jean and Albert, started working with the family in 1927 and 1930 respectively, and took over the business in 1939. During the Second World War, although working under great duress, they concentrated on studio fashion photography with professional models. Celestine Dars's book, *A Fashion Parade. The Seeberger Collection*, provides a superb cornucopia of Seeberger photographs from 1909 to 1950.

The Rejuvenation of the Fashion Plate

Harper's Bazar and *Vogue*, which was launched in 1892, were the forerunners of a new style of fashion journalism that used half-tone and line illustrations with 'word pictures' to convey the latest fashions.[5] Magazines continued to issue fashion plates but to many these seemed hackneyed promotional exercises and there was a distinct feeling for a new type of fashion plate for a new century. Paul Poiret was perceptive in sensing the need for a more elegant and expressive type of fashion plate that looked to the arts for inspiration.

Fashion illustration had attained a very high standard with the exquisitely hand-coloured fashion plates of Pierre de La Mésangère's *Le Journal des dames et des modes*. These clothes were sketched from life by artists who were outstanding draughtsmen and faithful social chroniclers. In the nineteenth century, the demand for large and ornate fashion plates with huge print runs produced by mechanical printing processes had brought about a decline in the artistic quality in the fashion plates of many fashion magazines. Poiret's originality lay in rejuvenating the fashion plate along the lines of La Mésangère's *Le Journal des dames et des modes*. Poiret commissioned artists for albums of fashion plates depicting his *Directoire* designs. In 1908, having been established in his own fashion house for a mere five years, Poiret commissioned Paul Iribe to produce *Les Robes de Paul Poiret racontées par Paul Iribe*. This album was so successful that it was followed in 1911 by *Les Choses de Paul Poiret vues par Georges Lepape*. The importance accorded to the artists is immediately recognizable in the titles of the works.

work had an enduring impact on the world of fashion drawing and fashion photography and continues to influence the visual look of fashion magazines today.

The collection of black-and-white photographs taken by the remarkable Seeberger family, housed in the Bibliothèque Nationale de France in Paris, are unique fashion records. Jules, Louis and Henri were artists who became fascinated by photography and turned professional. In 1909 *La Mode pratique* commissioned regular contributions from them and *Les Modes*, *Le Jardin des modes*, *L'Album du figaro*, *Fémina*, *L'Art et la mode*, *Vogue* and *Harper's Bazaar* followed suit. The Seebergers excelled at outdoor fashion photography. Their outstanding photographic quality is candour – they never interfered with their wealthy, sophisticated subjects and let the lens record them going about their leisure, from Paris to Deauville and Biarritz, wearing the *haute couture*

The Ranee of Pudukota wearing a Chanel cardigan suit. Photograph, 1926.
This three-piece cardigan suit consists of a straight, loose, checked jacket, a straight, slim, pleated skirt and a long sweater with a belt and a scarf to match. For Chanel details must be logical and practical – pockets placed exactly where you would expect to find them. Accessories to go with this casual, elegant suit were a strand of pearls, leather shoes with buckled straps over the instep and a cloche hat. Chanel dramatically shortened hemlines which has an effect on hairstyles, for only the very short, bobbed style complemented the cardigan suit. *(Fashion Research Centre, Bath)*

Tailor and Cutter Fashions.

COPYRIGHT.   1900

Les Robes de Paul Poiret came out in an edition of 250 copies priced at 40 francs each. It consisted of ten full-page fashion plates drawn by Paul Iribe, with no text, and was bound in cream-coloured boards. The cover had a narrow design in black of an oval plaque with thin garlands of roses – the same roses formed an irregular spiral line which became one of the most characteristic motifs of Art Deco. The exquisite ink drawings of Iribe were coloured by the *pochoir* process. *Pochoir*, which means stencil, was a method whereby a monochrome drawing was hand-coloured using a series of bronze or zinc stencils. The process, being manual rather than mechanical, was slow and painstaking as each area of colour was built up reproducing all the varying shades of the original, achieving a lustrous, brilliant effect. Iribe's treatment of Poiret's designs marked the beginning of a new era, not only in fashion but in its illustration too, 'heralding the birth of the style which is known today as Art Deco.'[6] It was the *Exposition Internationale des Arts Décoratifs et Industriels Modernes*, held in Paris in 1925, which gave Art Deco its name, for this exhibition was known simply as *Arts Déco*. *Arts Déco* was an eclectic style,

'Men's Fashions'. Engraved fashion plate from *The Tailor and Cutter*, 1900.
The three fashionable styles of day suits at the turn of the century are shown: morning suit (left), frock coat (centre) and lounge suit (right). The centre crease in the trousers became fashionable after the 1890s. The top hat is worn with the formal morning suit and frock coat, while the Homburg, a soft felt hat, is appropriate with the informal lounge suit. Gloves, walking stick, umbrella, flowers and handkerchief are the stylish accessories. Short, neat hairstyles and a moustache or clean-shaven faces are preferred to facial hair. *(Fashion Research Centre, Bath)*

drawing on the art of many cultures and periods; the exhibition drew the different strands together and helped to bring about some sort of fusion.[7] One of these strands, very discernable in the dresses of Poiret, was the Neo-classical line, reflected in the great simplicity and clarity of Iribe's work. Indeed, purity of line is one of the hallmarks of the Art Deco style. Another strand is

'Dioné-dessin de Bakst réalisé par Paquin', 1912. Engraved fashion plate (*pochoir* process) from *Le Journal des Dames et des Modes*, 1913.
The visits of the *Ballets Russes* to Paris in 1909 and to London in 1911 had a tremendous impact on fashion. The dazzling costumes of Léon Bakst inspired many fashion designers, including Madame Paquin. This fashion plate was based on the costume design of Bakst for the *Ballets Russes* production of *Dioné*. It shows Orientalism combined with the Neo-classical style. Lavish surface ornamentation reflects the taste for Orientalism while the Neo-classical line reflects the fashionable silhouette of the *Directoire* Revival. *(Fashion Research Centre, Bath)*

Pleated silk satin Delphos dresses and printed silk velvet evening coats, designed by Mariano Fortuny, 1915-35.
Mariano Fortuny (1871-1949) painter, stage designer, inventor, photographer, textile designer, and *haute couturier*, was of Spanish birth and settled in Venice in 1889. Fortuny's Delphos dresses were based on ancient Grecian robes and the evening wraps were inspired by the velvets of the Italian fifteenth and sixteenth centuries and tapestries from the East. Fortuny created a distinctive style of dress which revealed the female shape by caressing its surface with shimmering pleated silk satins. The Delphos gown was essentially a tube of three vertically-pleated silk satin panels sewn together at their selvedges and across the shoulders which undulated with rich colour, created by a special pleating process which Fortuny patented in 1909. The Venetian glass beads sewn into the side seams were more than decoration: their weight helped to hold the dress in place. No undergarment at that time could be worn under a Delphos dress as the supple fabric revealed the female form. *(Cincinnati Art Museum, Gifts of Patricia Cunningham and Mrs James Marjan Hutton)*

Orientalism, in the form of plain cloaks and coats, the severe, column-like line again so beautifully delineated by Iribe. Iribe was an artist, fashion designer and interior decorator. Noted for his subtle draughtsmanship, he created, illustrated and edited the witty, avant-garde magazine *Le Témoin*.

Les Choses de Paul Poiret was larger in format than *Les Robes de Paul Poiret* and was published in a far larger edition of 1,000 copies printed on *papier de luxe* of which the first 300 copies were numbered and initialled by Poiret. Also included were three fashion plates printed on paper from the Imperial Manufactory of Japan. These volumes sold at 50 francs apiece. The fashion plates were also coloured by the *pochoir* process and in some of them gold and silver metallic ink was used. The lack of printed text again concentrated the eye on the illustrations. Poiret continued to develop his themes of *Directoire* Revival and Orientalism. He revived the wearing of turbans after studying many examples in *Le Journal des dames et des modes* and the fine collection of Indian turbans in the Victoria and Albert Museum, London, which he visited in 1909. Building on the work of Iribe, Lepape provides a more complex demonstration of the relation of fashion with the arts. He stresses the integration of dress with setting, anchoring the models in their environment. Through his experience as a designer of posters and books, and his work as a painter, Lepape injected new life into the fashion plate.

> He followed Iribe's example of using bold areas of flat colouring but removed all vestiges of the traditional line-drawn background, leaving much of the page in some designs entirely white and empty, while his use of the dropped eye-level, to make the observer feel as if he were peering up at a raised stage, and his habit of drawing models with their backs to the viewer to give an air of mystery, became the stock-in trade for illustrators as well as fashion photographers right through to the 1930s.[8]

The enormous success of Poiret's designs and their visual documentation started the twentieth-century trend towards a more natural and relaxed shape of dress, dispelling the notion that the First World War 'liberated' women's fashions, and ignited a veritable renaissance in fashion illustration. In 1912 alone, *Modes et manières*

d'aujourd'hui, *Le Journal des dames et des modes*, and *La Gazette du bon ton* were launched, three titles reminiscent of their predecessors in the eighteenth and nineteenth centuries. *Modes et manières d'aujourd'hui* was published in Paris by Pierre Corrard and contained twelve illustrations in colour by Georges Lepape. This was the first of a series of seven special *de luxe* hand-printed albums of fashion designs which came out until 1923. As with the Poiret album, the method of printing was the hand-stencilled *pochoir* process in which each of the twelve illustrations went through 30 different hand-colouring processes using gouache paint which exactly matched the artist's original. The limited edition of 300 copies was printed on the finest Imperial Japon paper by Jean Saudé. Each copy was signed and numbered by the artist and the printer. In addition to the work of Georges Lepape, the *Modes et manières d'aujourd'hui* included that of Georges Barbier, Charles Martin and André Marty.

Film, so often associated with the 1930s, was already having an impact on fashion illustration. André Marty, in an illustration entitled 'Le Ciné' which he drew in 1919 and which appeared in the *Modes et manières d'aujourd'hui* for 1921, made clever use of lighting and silhouettes

'Les coussins'. Fashion plate (*pochoir* process) from *Les Choses de Paul Poiret racontées par Georges Lepape*, 1911.
The sharp, geometric outlines of the cushions and the window and the stylised floral motif serve perfectly to reinforce the Neo-classical line of the model's dress and anchor her in her environment. She wears one of Poiret's simple, white

Directoire gowns with delicate beads ornamenting and outlining the high waistline with as much geometrical precision as the interior itself. Poiret's Orientalism manifests itself in the close-fitting turban encircled with dark dots. (*Photo: B.T. Batsford Ltd Archive*)

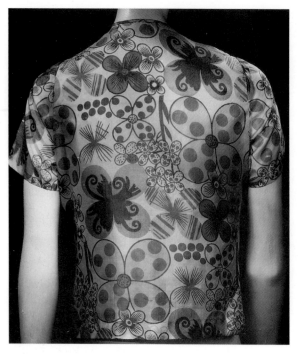

posed against a prominent image of Charlie Chaplin on a cinema screen.

Le Journal des dames et des modes followed the tradition of its illustrious predecessor not only in its title but also in its appearance, for the type, the paper and the format were the same. It was issued irregularly three times a month from 1 June 1912 until 1 August 1914 with a total of 79 issues published. The fashion plates, all printed by the *pochoir* process, were again the work of the leading artists of the day, including Georges Barbier, Léon Bakst,

Pierre Brissaud, Umberto Brunelleschi, Étienne Drian, Paul Iribe, Charles Martin and H. Robert Dammy. This magazine was imbued, like its forebear, with a refined artistic, cultural, and intellectual atmosphere, designed to appeal to an audience of connoisseurs and aesthetes.

Lady's printed silk blouse from the Wiener Werkstätte, c. 1918. At the turn of the century Vienna became the focal point for a remarkable burst of artistic activity. The Secessionist movement, led by Gustav Klimt and based at the Austrian Museum of Art and Industry and the School for Applied Arts, wanted to reform the concept of industrial design. This resulted in the foundation in 1903 of the Wiener Werkstätte (Vienna Workshop), an exciting enterprise that flourished until 1932. This *avant-garde* design group had a textile workshop and a fashion department established on the principle of the complete harmony of dress and interior. They show a constant dialogue with Paris fashion and Paul Poiret's designs in particular. The admiration was mutual. Poiret particularly liked the hand-painted silks and naturalistic style of design, called *Stylisierung*. Many of the workshop's floral patterns were reminiscent of folk art. (*The Metropolitan Museum of Art, New York, Gift of Mrs Federica Beer-Monti 1964*)

Evening coat, designed by Paul Poiret. Croquis No. VII by Raoul Dufy. From *La Gazette du bon ton*, No. 1, January/February 1920.
The first issue of this magazine to appear after the First World War was accompanied by a supplement containing a set of eight lithographs by Dufy. In all of them Dufy drew mannequins wearing Poiret garments made up in silks that Dufy himself had designed for the celebrated Lyon silk firm, Bianchini-Férier. This *croquis* shows Dufy's distinctive calligraphic draughtsmanship, the rapid hatching brilliantly evoking the Oriental quality of the silk velvet evening coat with its large brocade collar in a Persian-style design, as well as offering a contrast in fashion-illustration techniques to the (*pochoir*) illustrations featured in the fashion magazine. (*Victoria and Albert Museum, London*)

In November 1912, *La Gazette du bon ton*, the most celebrated of these limited edition, *de luxe* fashion publications, was published by the Librairie Centrale des Beaux-Arts in Paris with Lucien Vogel as *directeur*. Each issue contained between eight and ten *pochoir* fashion plates and 30 pages of text, all lavishly illustrated with detailed and stylish line drawings printed on hand-made paper. In all, 69 issues were published between November 1912 and December 1925, each one having the quality of a luxuriously compiled book, beautiful to touch and handle and a joy to read. That it was exclusive in its aim was apparent at the start for the editor said it was to be 'a showcase in which only the most luxurious examples of high fashion and the best of the decorative arts could be displayed, regardless of the cost involved'. Furthermore, each fashion plate was 'created as a beautiful picture of contemporary life with each design

shown in its contemporary setting.'[9] *La Gazette du bon ton* was sold, like the two other publications, in London, New York, Berlin, Geneva, Buenos Aires and St Petersburg.[10]

La Gazette du bon ton was *avant-garde* in many ways. Lucien Vogel devised a whole new style of fashion-magazine advertising by persuading several of the top *couturiers* to provide financial support for his enterprise. Worth, Chéruit, Doeuillet, Paquin, Doucet and Poiret all acquiesced. He also chose a brilliant team of artists to draw their fashions. These formed a sort of brotherhood, for most of them had trained at the École des Beaux-Arts. They included Georges Barbier, Paul Iribe, Georges Lepape, Charles Martin, André Marty, Bernard Boutet de Monvel and Pierre Brissaud.

The Hat Shop, painted by Henry Tonks, c. 1905.
This painting conveys the sense of space and leisure which were indispensable for the important art of selecting just the right hat, as this accessory was a status symbol. In the first decade of the new century the fashionable hat was small and was worn slightly tilted at an angle on the head. Feathers,

artificial flowers, ribbons and gossamer materials such as tulle were the most popular trimmings. There were many trade journals devoted to millinery and the rise of the big department stores provided much scope for milliners, as most of them had large millinery departments. *(The City of Birmingham Museum and Art Gallery)*

Vogel not only united *couturiers* to design clothes and artists to draw them in fashion plates, but also provided these artists with a forum for designing clothes 'invented by the artists themselves'.

When fashion becomes an art, a fashion magazine must itself become an arts magazine . . . It will offer, on the one hand, the most recent models to emerge from the ateliers of the rue de la Paix and, on the other hand, in the painters' watercolours, that fashion sense, that charming and bold interpretation that is their hallmark. Artists of today are in part creators of fashion: what does fashion not owe to Iribe, who introduced simplicity of line and the Oriental style, or to Drian, or to Bakst.[11]

'La Robe Rose', designed by Jacques Doucet. Drawn by H. Robert Dammy. Fashion plate (*pochoir* process) from *La Gazette du bon ton*, May 1913.
The artist's delicate, flower style evokes the movement and freedom of Art Nouveau. The soft, white muslin *fichu* and the two-tiered tunic create a floating effect due to the soft, fluid pleats. Ingenious use is made of three scarves. The enormous straw hat is secured by a black scarf that passes loosely beneath the chin. Around the model's neck and on top of the *fichu* is a second diminutive scarf in the form of a delightful pink bow-tie. The long, serpentine 'Empire' scarf in pink tones starts at the high waist and ends draped over the right arm. All the scarves play a vital role in describing the famous Art Nouveau curve, while echoing features of the dress itself. *(Private Collection)*

Paquin à cinq heures, painted by Henri Gervex, 1906. Photograph from *Les Modes*, January 1907.
Fashionable ladies would visit their favourite *maison de couture* in February or March to choose Spring and Summer garments and in August or September to select their Autumn and Winter clothes. The *vendeuses* were the *couturier's* saleswomen who showed them fabrics and helped them to choose their wardrobes. The social élite not only went for the latest fashions but also to be seen. Mr. Gervex conveys this sense of rendezvous in the luxurious *salon* of Madame Paquin. Renowned for her superb taste in clothes, accessories and décor, Madame Paquin was the first *couturière* to open fashion houses abroad, in the cities of London, Madrid and Buenos Aires in 1902. *(Fashion Research Centre, Bath)*

The new school of fashion artists, started by Poiret and reaching its apogee with Vogel, renewed fashion illustration by producing individually expressive, lively and cohesive fashion plates that embraced the other arts for inspiration. The artists were experienced in painting, book illustration and poster art. To them, the fashion pictorial was an important graphic medium and they raised the fashion plate to an art form.

Although fewer issues of *La Gazette du bon ton* came out during the First World War, the French government was determined that *haute couture* suffer as little as possible. It was adamant that *haute couture*, for which Paris was unique, would not go under and be taken over by London and New York. Poiret closed his fashion house and joined the army as a tailor, re-launching his fashion career in 1919. However, most of the *grands couturiers* continued as best they could. Americans thought this an opportune moment to seize the initiative and promote their own home fashion talent. The *Chambre Syndicale de la Couture Parisienne* was most displeased with *Vogue* for supporting a Fashion Fête in November 1914 that showed American fashions made by designers working for the New York stores Bergdorf-Goodman and Bendel in spite of proceeds going to the French for their war chest. To compensate Condé Nast sent a delegation to the *Chambre Syndicale*, offering a French Fashion Fête to be held in America to come to the aid of the beleaguered French *couturiers*. The ensuing Panama Pacific International Exposition held in San Francisco in 1915 exhibited the *haute couture* of Worth, Paquin, Premet, the Callot Soeurs, Chéruit, Beer, Doucet, Jenny, and Martial et Armand. A special souvenir edition of *La Gazette du bon ton*, in French and English editions, was published on 15 June 1915 in collaboration with Condé Nast.

The last great number of *La Gazette du bon ton*, the magazine by now under the directorship of Jean

'Volubilis' dress, designed by Madame Paquin. From an album of Paquin designs, no. 220, c. 1917.
The creation of a dress from *haute couture* required close collaboration between *couturière* and client. This design from a Paquin album has a swatch of material attached to the sketch and a detailed description of the dress written on paper of the fashion house. The album provides visual evidence of the appetite for the buying of *haute couture* among the very wealthy at this time. Madame Paquin, noted for her exceptional workmanship, provided dresses for glamorous socialites that blended drapery and good tailoring. *(Fashion Research Centre, Bath)*

Silk taffeta *robe de style*, designed by Jeanne Lanvin, 1927
The House of Lanvin was founded in 1890 when 23-year-old Jeanne Lanvin began to design and sell hats in a small apartment. It was, however, the clothing she made for her young daughter which first attracted attention and by 1909 formed the basis of her success. She established herself with a style popular among sophisticated young women noted for its romanticism, based on eighteenth-century designs. This silk taffeta *robe de style* was worn over an oval hoop petticoat. This dress has been associated so closely with the House of Lanvin that a 1922 sketch of a mother and young daughter both wearing a variation of the *robe de style* has been used on the Lanvin logo ever since. *(Cincinnati Art Museum, Gift of Mrs Raymond M. Lull)*

magazine by now under the directorship of Jean Labusquière, was its special Golden Issue to celebrate the 1925 *Paris Exposition Internationale des Arts Décoratifs et Industriels Modernes*. It focused on the Pavillon de l'Élégance where the fashions of the Callot Soeurs, Jenny, Lanvin and Worth were displayed, as well as the jewellery of Cartier and the furniture of Rateau. This was indeed a fitting finale to a fashion journal that had promoted fashion and the decorative arts in such a scintillating way. Shortly afterwards the magazine was bought by Condé Nast and merged with *Vogue*.

Other fashion magazines were founded in France during the First World War to promote *la mode féminine* abroad. One of the most successful was *Les Élégances parisiennes* which was published from 1916 to 1924. It was the official organ of Les Industriels Françaises de la Mode and organized the promotion of exports which not only the government but also the *couturieres* realized was essential for the survival of the fashion industry. By 1924 exports of women's clothing worldwide amounted to 500 million francs.[12] Attractive *pochoir* fashion plates illustrated *couture* clothes and accessories including the early designs of Coco Chanel.

A growing number of fashion magazines and fashion almanacs published in Paris with fashion plates *au pochoir* had *La Gazette du bon ton* as their prototype and engaged the services of many of that magazine's fashion artists. *Les Feuillets d'art* was an expensive, luxurious fashion magazine published from 1919 to 1922 under the direction of Lucien Vogel. Although it was envisaged as a twice-monthly publication, its appearance was irregular. Each issue consisted of a portfolio or wallet containing sections devoted to the arts and one or more fashion plates *hors-texte*. The influence of art on fashion, as in the *Gazette*, was discernible in most of them. *Les Feuillets d'art*'s contributors included Georges Barbier, Étienne Drian, André Marty and a newcomer, Benito. Benito's drawings appeared in *La Gazette du bon ton* regularly during the 1920s. His fashion plates, along with those of some of the other artists, were so highly thought of that they were bound together *sans texte* into two volumes of 100 plates under the title *Le Bon ton d'après guerre*, covering the period between 1920 and 1922. *La Guirlande des mois* was a fashion, art and literary review published monthly by Librairie Émile Jean-Fontaine et Jules Meynial from 1919

to 1920. It contained fashion plates by artists such as Barbier and Brunelleschi. *Le Goût du jour* was another of the interesting fashion and arts reviews, published by La Belle Éditions from 1920 to 1922 with, yet again, an illustrious rollcall of fashion artists, Benito and André Marty amongst them. *Sports et divertissements* published in 1920 under the aegis of Lucien Vogel, was a successful experimental series on sport and casual wear with the fashion plates drawn by Charles Martin. *Les élégances sportives* were being promoted by Coco Chanel and Jean Patou and Vogel's publication appealed to women who wanted to be lithesome, understated and modern. *Le Jardin des modes*, a monthly magazine with many supplements, came out in 1922. Yet another of Lucien Vogel's publications, it employed his favourite artists, Charles Martin, Georges Barbier, Georges Lepape, Pierre Brissaud, and André Marty, and also introduced a number of new artists, notably Marie Simon, Eric and Jacques Demachy. Vogel also pressed into service the photographic skills of the Seeberger brothers. It is considered one of the most distinguished French fashion journals. Georges Barbier was a prolific and sought after fashion artist from the years immediately prior to the First World War to the 1920s and was also responsible for the fashion plates of the *édition de luxe* almanac series, *Falbalas et Franfreluches*, which was published by Éditions Meynial from 1922 to 1926. He conveys all the decorative and graceful movement of figures in *haute couture* set in charming vignettes, fashion unfolding as if in a drama or story.

The last and longest-running of these modish French fashion magazines was *Art-Goût-Beauté*. It came out monthly from 1920 to 1933. On inception it was entitled *Les succès Art Goût Bon Ton* and the change of name took effect with the number for November 1921. In the annals of fashion literature it is abbreviated to *AGB*, which happened to be the initials of its founder and sponsor, Les Succrs (the Successors) d'Albert Goode, Bedin et Cie, a prominent textile firm. This partnership of *couture* and textiles meant that while its readership was mainly female high society, it was not exclusively so, since commercial buyers, who were mainly men, were interested in fabrics for a potential mass market.

The editor throughout most of the life of *AGB* was M. Goy. He maintained a high standard of fashion

English fashions during the First World War: Boy's sailor suit, c. 1914, lady's fashionable dress, c. 1916. Lieutenant's uniform (Bedfordshire regiment), 1914-18.
During the First World War a more utilitarian style of fashionable dress for ladies emerged. Once hostilities erupted and the services of women were mandatory for the war

effort, the shorter skirt swept in. The new length, which revealed the ankles was accepted because of the urgencies of the war. As the skirt shortened, its hem widened and by 1916 dresses with full skirts were very stylish. The high waistline gradually dropped and was nearing its normal length by 1920. (Museum of Costume, Bath)

rapportage by engaging the services of contributors such as Rosine and Lucie Neumeyer-Hirgoyen. Artistic coverage was provided by Henri Clouzot of the Musée Galliera in Paris and Eric Bagge, a well-known designer and architect who seems to have been given a substantial role in the organization of the Gallery of Modern Arts and Crafts which *AGB* opened towards the end of 1920s.[13] But the glory of *AGB* was its stunning visual appearance, no doubt due to having had only one art director, Henri Rouit, throughout its long run. The covers were made of grey or beige wove paper with black dentillated borders and with a fashion plate glued on the front. Inside there were six double sheets, which increased eventually to eight, on laid paper, loose-bound with cord. The general layout and the print of the text resembled *La Gazette du bon ton*, even though *AGB* was much larger in format, being quarto size, not changing to octavo size until October 1923. The working up of the drawings and the main layout were carried out at the Paris office, while the actual printing, involving the interaction of litho and *pochoir* hand-coloured work, an intricate process in itself, was undertaken at Lyon. The fashion plates were hand-coloured by the *pochoir* method, and were either printed or tipped-in. Their quality is of such a high standard that they have become collectors' items. It was rare for the fashion plates to be signed, an exception being those of R. Drivon. Contributors were listed at the end of each issue. However, fashion plates on the covers were quite often signed.

Rouit employed artists of the calibre of Georges Barbier, Georges Lepape and Paul Iribe. Colette, who had worked for *AGB* since its beginning, had a cover illustration in September 1925. Some of *AGB*'s artists, for example, Léon Bénigni, Zeulinger, and Regis Manset, also worked for other publications, while others, such as J. Dory, Froment, Marioton and Vittrotto deserve to be better-known. The art editor was especially proud of the quality of the colour of the fashion plates, a point that was stressed in the number of April 1921. It is thought that the self-congratulatory tone may possibly have been a way of showing its superiority to French *Vogue*, the first

issue of which was published in 1920, and which throughout the 1920s illustrated only black-and-white fashion plates, except for covers and some advertisements.[14] Throughout the 1920s *Vogue* made great strides in fashion photography. *AGB* did make use of photogravures and fashion *croquis*, quick pencil or chalk drawings on a tinted ground. Fashion *croquis* were also used for advertisements. All these types of fashion illustration appeared more frequently in the 1930s, for with the economic depression of the decade, the *pochoir* process was thought to be both expensive and *démodé*. *AGB* also began to use fashion photographs from agencies such as World Wide Studio while still including

'Ladies' automobile clothes by Burberry'. Engraved illustration from *Burberry's Proof Kit*, No. XIV, c. 1905.
The open motor car came into use in the early years of the twentieth century and special clothing was required for both men and women. This was provided by Burberry's, the quintessential British label, founded in Basingstoke in 1856, with a wholesale business established in London in 1891. The three coats are long and ample enough to provide protection against the elements and dust. Burberry's points out that the autocrat was one of their best motoring coats for rough and cold weather, while having an elegant design and appearance.

The car paletot was their only style of overcoat in which the art of the *corsetière* was allowed proper recognition, for the svelte figure is a picture of elegance in which the natural lines of the body are emphasized. The dust wrapper was an inexpensive, light garment for protecting a lady's apparel from dust on summer days, combining serviceability with chic. All the ladies wear large, flat-crowned headwear and one has added a long, enveloping veil, covering her hat, face and neck. Gauntlet gloves protected the hands of fashionable motoring ladies. (*B.T. Batsford Ltd Archive*)

but the credit for this revival goes to *Harper's Bazaar* and *Vogue*. These plates continued the Art Deco tradition of purity of line and were paralleled by black-and-white films, the work of artists like Fernand Léger who evolved a style based on machinery and clear, sober colours, and the Analytic phase of Cubism which enabled muted colours.

In the second half of the 1930s, when economic pressures caused by the Depression began to ease and political pressures began to mount, fashion and fashion illustration took on an escapist mood with the appearance of Surrealism. However, fashion plates were still the primary means of conveying information about fashions, even with rise of fashion photography. At *Vogue*, fashion plates on the cover were unbroken by photographs until the summer of 1932. It was *Vogue*'s 'underlying policy, unstated and unassumed as it was, that the graphic arts should have a useful and rightful place in the natural scheme of things.'[15]

Harper's Bazaar engaged the exclusive services of the brilliantly creative and entertaining Erté. In 1913, Erté worked in Poiret's fashion house, where he was much involved in the theatrical workshop there,[16] and he went on to enjoy a long association with *Harper's Bazaar* from 1915 to 1936. For the first 12 years Erté both designed fashions and illustrated them on colourful covers and black-and-white fashion plates. Many of Erté's Parisian fashions were made exclusively for the New York department stores, Altman and Bendel, thus making him a *couturier* for the all-important French export market to America during the war years. Erté designed gowns, coats, pyjamas, and sports costumes for each season that evoked a very feminine silhouette of what has been called the 'temptress type'. He must have learned from Poiret the draping of fabric in tandem with buttoning, knotting and lacing to give the necessary shape. Like Poiret, his aesthetic sensibilities expressed themselves in tassels, fringes, beads and ribbons which were in complete harmony with the times, and he had the intuition to realize when this fanciful side of fashion was at an end. During his last decade with *Harper's Bazaar* Erté designed only covers and story illustrations.

Another of *Harper's Bazaar*'s talented fashion illustrators was Marcel Vertès. Born in Hungary, he studied drawing

be remembered, had quite a long time span and the style of fashion illustration of each decade suited the fashion. The fashion plates of the 1920s were two dimensional, clear-edged and decorative which admirably reflected the Art Deco fashions, while during the 1930s, the figures were more economical and simplified.

AGB therefore shows the evolution of costume from the tubular styles of the 1920s to the complex bias-cut creations of the early 1930s, with full descriptions of their fabrics, all set against the social scene such as the world of sport, cars, nightclubs, and the theatre. In April 1933, *AGB* was sold to Éditions Édouard Boucherit and became *Voici la mode: art, goût, beauté,* and flourished in this form until 1936.

Brilliant stencil-coloured fashion plates continued to be produced in the late 1920s and early 1930s, yet this period is associated with a new emphasis on black-and-white fashion plates, except for covers and some advertisements. *Excelsior modes,* a quarterly published in Paris from 1929 to 1939, made a feature of such plates,

and painting at the Academy of Fine Arts in Budapest. Based in Paris from 1921, he drew fashion plates for *La Gazette du bon ton*, illustrated *Le Tableau de mode de G.-A. Masson*, made watercolour studies of high society, being especially fascinated by hairstyles, and designed costumes for the theatre and for films. In the 1930s Vertès was invited to draw black-and-white fashion plates for *Harper's Bazaar*. The most topical art movement and the one which dominated fashion and fashion illustration was Surrealism, and Vertès's light, graceful and witty style evokes the special relationship between the two.

For most of the twentieth century, *Harper's Bazaar* was in direct competition with American *Vogue*. At the beginning of the century *Vogue* was a small weekly paper and its transformation to the most influential fashion magazine of the century started in 1909 when it was purchased by Condé Nast. In 1910 he brought it out twice-monthly. British *Vogue* was inaugurated in 1916, followed by French, Australian, Spanish and German *Vogue*, even if Spanish *Vogue* only lasted from 1918 to 1920 and German *Vogue* survived only a few numbers in 1928.

He transformed it, and long before the First World War a magazine came into being that in its physical character and disposition, in its editorial scope, assumption of interests, was the Vogue we know today. This was a remarkable, even revolutionary coup, as imaginative as it was ambitious. The formula he devised, a potent mixture of high fashion, high society, the arts, social advice dressed up as satire, and gossip and snobbery unabashed, proved immediately and lastingly successful. The trick was simple: to appeal

both to society itself, whose self-importance it continued generously to indulge, and to that wider, newer public, the massed, aspiring middle classes upon whom, in an advertiser's age, its circulation and thus its life depended.[17]

Among the young *couturiers* who did not feature in the fashion plates of *La Gazette du bon ton* or *AGB* was Gabrielle (Coco) Chanel. That alone makes *Vogue* and *Harper's Bazaar* indispensable to fashion illustration for the 1920s and 1930s. Between the wars, in the fashion plates

and photographs of these fashion magazines she popularized clothes that were simple and elegant, contouring the natural shape of the body and she often borrowed ideas from workwear. The classic chic of tweed suits, cardigans and jerseys, the little black dress and costume jewellery all became her hallmarks. There is also, surprisingly, the flamboyant Chanel: her 1920s eveningwear and her exotic motifs of the 1930s inspired by Surrealism. The simplicity of her design and quality of

Ladies' suits, designed by Elsa Schiaparelli. Fashion plate from *Woman's Journal*, January 1938.
These fashions seem to anticipate the conditions of wartime, still a year away. The suits with their padded shoulders and short skirts are severely and economically tailored. Yet Schiaparelli, another of the star names in fashion design in the inter-war years, added her own distinctively amusing, stylish and very feminine touches such as the large, decorative buttons and floating scarf (centre) and the cupid clips on the lapels (left). Hairstyles are longer and looser and complement the high-crowned, military, and flat 'coolie' style hats. *(Fashion Research Centre, Bath)*

A black lace evening gown, designed by Coco Chanel, and a wine crêpe evening suit, designed by Elsa Schiaparelli, drawn by Edouard Benito. Fashion plate from American *Vogue*, 15 July 1938.
In Surrealist settings, unrelated objects, such as decapitated mannequins holding their own heads, masks, and broken columns strewn about a wasteland, are startlingly juxtaposed to create a sense, not so much of unreality, as of a fantastic and compelling reality outside the everyday world. Benito, one of the great graphic artists of Surrealism, saw the fashions of the two great rival *couturières*, Chanel and Schiaparelli, as perfect foils that could be used to advantage to evoke the mysterious world of Surrealism. *(Courtesy American Vogue © 1938, 1966 by The Condé Nast Publications Inc)*

her work foreshadow the major impact she would have on both the ready-to-wear and *haute couture* industry.

Throughout the 1920s American and British *Vogue* each produced two issues a month, occasionally extending to 26 issues a year. Their visual character was marked by distinctive black-and-white fashion plates: large, bold, with heavy borders and wide margins. They enjoyed a distinguished place as the focal point of fashion information. Condé Nast valued artists, especially those from *La Gazette du bon ton*, which he bought in 1925 and

Chemise dress, designed by Coco Chanel. Fashion plate from *Harper's Bazaar*, 1916.
The first Chanel dress featured in *Harper's Bazaar* shows her trim, pared-down look. The soft, simplified elegance is reflected in the details: masculine-style revers and waistcoat effect, wide sash, and delicate embroidery. This beautiful dress is set off to perfection by the sable muff and another of Chanel's large hats, one side of the high crown decorated with sable, considered a most unusual way to use fur as a trimming. *(B.T. Batsford Ltd Archive)*

'Le vrai et le faux chic'. Drawing by Sem. From *L'Illustration*, 28 March 1914.
The caricaturist Sem wrote and illustrated a series of albums entitled *Le vrai et le faux chic* with the first one, in 1914, devoted to fashion. At this early date Chanel was already designing the tailored, casual, mannish suits, that would become her hallmark. With the slightly raised hemline already apparent, elegant details, and with the line as smooth and sleek as the greyhound, Sem praised this suit as an example of "true chic". This drawing along with an article on *le vrai et le faux chic* appeared in the 28 March 1914 issue of *L'Illustration*, a leading French magazine. *(Victoria and Albert Museum, London)*

merged with *Vogue*. Those who came from the *Gazette* included Lepape, Marty, Brissaud and Benito. Benito, with his economy of line, especially conveyed the essence and elegance of Chanel's designs.

In 1929 Condé Nast appointed Dr Agha as artistic director. Dr Agha changed the visual style of *Vogue* through the introduction of *sans serif* typefaces and a more striking layout, although much of the preparatory work had been done by Benito.[18] Dr Agha was also influential in promoting the fashion work of photographers such as Horst, Hoyningen-Heune, and Cecil Beaton. In 1923 Edward Steichen had been appointed Chief Photographer for Condé Nast Publications, a position he held until 1938.

The 1930s saw *Vogue* enter its most exciting period, the introduction of colour fashion plates coinciding with a whole new generation of fashion artists. One of the most adventurous was Christian Bérard, whose work is often hailed as Expressionist romanticism. His free-spirited, cursory style of delineating shape and form and his brilliant use of colour were perfect for evoking Chanel's designs of the late 1930s, where she drew on eighteenth-century sources. Another artist whose fashion plates were in contrast to the flat, linear style of the 1920s was the American, Carl Erickson, known as Eric. He was noted for giving movement to the models in his fashion plates and also for concentrating on the importance of details. *Women's Wear Daily*, a non-glossy newspaper, existed side by side with the two glitzy fashion magazines. Founded in New York in 1910 exclusively for the garment industry, it developed into a fashion magazine catering for both the fashion trade and the fashionable public. *WWD*'s transforation was

Gabrielle Dorizat wearing a hat designed by Coco Chanel. Photograph from *Les Modes*, May 1912.
Coco Chanel began her career as a *modiste*. Her hats caught the attention of the fashionable public when the actress Gabrielle Dorizat wore them in a play in 1912 and modelled them in *Les Modes*. Shown here is a typical example of one of Chanel's large, perfectly shaped and proportioned hats, made of black straw, with a huge brim turned up to one side, the only trimming a large white feather. *(Victoria and Albert Museum, London)*

'Costumes de jersey', designed by Coco Chanel. Fashion plate from *Les Élégances parisiennes*, March 1917.
Although Coco (Gabrielle) Chanel said she woke up famous in 1919, the year she was officially registered as a *couturière*, she was already successful enough in 1917 to have a fashion plate of her jersey suits highlighted in a notable fashion magazine, even if the editor spelled her name Gabrielle Channel. She brought about a "jersey revolution", turning the humble material used for women's hosiery and male underwear into high fashion for female daywear. The hats, also designed by Chanel, are, as always, in perfect proportion to the ensembles. *(B.T. Batsford Ltd. Archive)*

due to the inspiration of its publisher, John Fairchild. It is noted for its diversity with its indepth reports on the rag trade, its incisive analyses of every collection in the major fashion capitals, as well as its gossipy coverage of fashion parties and charity functions. John Fairchild's innovations have included the promotion of the work of fashion artists and the founding of *W*, a

bi-weekly journal printed on heavy-quality paper, which makes possible the reproduction of photographs of technical excellence.

Cover from American *Vogue*, 1 July 1918.
In its "Hot Weather Fashions" number for 1 July 1918 American *Vogue* evoked a romantic nostalgia for the fashions of the late eighteenth century. The magazine advocated a return to soft, feminine garments and accessories such as *buffons* and *fichus*. The model on the cover wears a *fichu* made of white muslin. *(Private Collection)*

Cover from *American Vogue*, 1 June 1920.
Sports for women were crucial in dealing the death knell to the frills and furbelows of the *Belle Époque*. American women were always the most adventurous and *American Vogue* featured many of their favourite recreational pastimes. Tennis was a popular sport in the 1920s and this tennis player wears a comfortable Poiretesque Oriental coat over her costume. Tennis dresses generally had a boxy top with narrow straps and a pleated skirt with a hemline just above the knees. Her companion wears a casual checked dress with a small white

collar and a black scarf tied into a bow. Her hat is in the deep-crowned cloche style. *(Private Collection)*

Chanel dress and headdress, drawn by Christian Bérard. Fashion plate from American *Vogue*, 15 March 1938.
Called 'Chanel's eighteenth-century fantasy', the dress is made of light green tulle with red flowers and has a matching floating scarf. The headdress is made in the same fabric and has a large black velvet bow at the nape of the neck. Bérard linked Chanel's designs with one of the great Rococo artists of eighteenth-century France, François Boucher. Boucher's paintings are characterized by asymmetrical curves, prettiness, and capriciousness. Bérard has placed Chanel's model in the centre of a very Boucheresque frame surrounded by four angels whose costume echoes her own. The shape and form of the fashion plate evokes the elegant, free, light, vapoury style of Boucher. *(Courtesy American Vogue © 1938, 1966 by The Condé Nast Publications, Inc)*

Hollywood Image and Fashion

The inter-action of film and fashion has existed practically since the invention of the cinema by the Lumière brothers, the centenary of which was celebrated in 1995. As early as the 1910s fashion shows were filmed. While the relationship of film and fashion has been so close that it is sometimes difficult to determine which has influenced the other, it is clear that before the birth of the Hollywood film industry, fashion as a business in America hardly existed.

The roots of America's fashion industry initially lay in the early studios' use of locally copied *couture* to add

glamour to an emerging star system. But what was once a nickel-and-dime sideline for a Hollywood shirt-manufacturer would burgeon into one of the great success stories of twentieth-century capitalism. For, up to the 1920s, America was in deep recession. It may have been producing the goods, but its wage-poor workers could not afford to buy them. The country therefore needed to turn those workers into consumers. And Hollywood affected that change.[19]

By the 1930s the relationship of Hollywood with fashion was cemented with the establishment of the Modern Merchandising Bureau. The film, *Letty Lynton*, starring Joan Crawford, is a good example of how the merchandising game worked. In 1931 the Metro Goldwyn Mayer studio sent Macy's New York some stills

Gloria Swanson wearing a black satin, bias-cut gown, designed by Coco Chanel, in the film, *Tonight or Never*, 1931. Chanel's bias-cut gowns have an easy grace and suppleness. Like Poiret, Chanel worked on the live model. She enjoyed using satin for her designs on the bias-cut because it is a fabric that is unstructured, elastic and has great moulding ability, creating a soft, sleek look, beautifully exemplified by Miss Swanson. *(Department of Film, Museum of Modern Art, New York)*

of Miss Crawford wearing a wide-shouldered white organdy dress with ruffled sleeves and a narrow waist designed by Adrian, the studio's in-house designer, a whole year before the film was made. Macy's contracted out the manufacture of the 'Letty Lynton' dress so that it would be ready in time for the film's release. Metro Goldwyn Mayer then sent Macy's photographs of Miss Crawford wearing Adrian's creation together with details of all the cinemas where the film was to be shown. The result was that Macy's reportedly sold some 500,000 copies of Adrian's dress and Joan Crawford was given her visual emblem of the 1930s: wide, padded shoulders and a narrow waist that also made her hips look slender.

The 1930s also saw the establishment of Cinema Fashions, a chain of shops across America, where the prices of the garments started at $30, considered exorbitant at the time, but deliberately so, for

it was agreed with the studios that cheaper fashions, even though they would be eagerly received, would destroy the aura and exclusivity that surrounded a Norma Shearer or Loretta Young style.[20]

Another aspect of film-fashion fusion was the relationship of French fashion designers with Hollywood. In some cases, the *couturiers*, who were, in the main, female, did very well out of the studio system. Even when the great studio moguls were less than kind to them, they still

Gloria Swanson wearing a suit designed by Coco Chanel, in the film, *Tonight or Never*, 1931.
The disciplined, restrained and elegant Chanel suit of the 1930s, showing the alterations she made with regard to cut and fit. The jacket is cut shorter, and is shaped to the waist. As a guest on the Duke of Westminster's yacht where the crew wore uniforms with gold buttons, Chanel's basic idea for her suits was the concept of military uniform. The suit's simplicity, clarity and clear, contemporary edge is echoed in the crisp white blouse. (*Department of Film, Museum of Modern Art, New York*)

profited. However both camps were collaborators in exploiting women's voracious appetite for the exclusivity and extravagance of film fashions. Madeleine Vionnet went to Hollywood in the late 1920s where her newly-invented technique of bias-cutting was successfully

translated by Adrian who delighted in making bias-cut evening gowns in black crepe and in creating glitzy, form-fitting silk dresses cut on the bias for Jean Harlow, even if Madame Vionnet dismissed them as 'cinema satins'. Sam Goldwyn, the head of United Artists, thought the only

Coco Chanel with her model Muriel Maxwell wearing a black silk velvet Watteau suit. Photographed by Horst P. Horst. From American *Vogue*, 15 September 1939.

During the last years of the 1930s Coco Chanel drew upon art historical fashion sources of the eighteenth century. Here she recreates the lush, dark velvet jackets and skirts and frilly white ruffs and cuffs that were worn by women in the paintings of Watteau. With its full skirt and jacket with tight waist, Chanel's Watteau suit, designed at the beginning of the Second World War anticipated Christian Dior's post-war New Look. (*Courtesy American Vogue © 1939, 1967 by The Condé Nast Publications Inc*)

Silk velvet bias-cut evening dress, designed by Madeleine Vionnet, 1927.

Madame Vionnet was one of the most innovative *couturières* of the twentieth century whose inventive hand first incorporated the bias cut in modern fashion. This evening dress is a quintessential example of the bias cut which would characterize the fashion of the 1930s. To achieve her unique draping effect Madame Vionnet's fabrics had to be two yards wider than usual. She draped the fabric directly onto a large, jointed wooden mannequin of the kind used by artists so that her sensitivity to the material was never hampered. The silk velvet here flows into place, its supple lines uninterrupted by heavy seaming since all the joins are hand-sewn. The dress falls perfectly on the figure with a single piece of silk velvet forming the bodice front and its extension into a floor-length floating panel at the back. Only three large rectangular pieces of silk velvet comprise the skirt and its handkerchief hem. A particularly unusual detail is the high scarf neckline which is cut in one piece with the bodice and shoulder straps becoming a floating panel on the left shoulder. The back neckline is a deep V-shape. (*Cincinnati Art Museum, Gift of Dorette Kruse Fleischmann in memory of Julius Fleischmann*)

way to survive the economic crisis was to attract women, especially from 'the growing number of urban rich' to films. His game plan: these women would go to films 'one to see the pictures and stars, and two, to see the latest clothes.'[21] To this end he succeeded in luring Coco Chanel to Hollywood in 1931 with a lucrative contract of a million dollars a year to design fashions for actresses under contract to him both off and on the screen. However, the deal was short-lived. Chanel would not abandon her style nor the Hollywood goddesses theirs. The Chanel style was too simple and understated for the sensational stylizations favoured by the rebellious stars whom she described as overdressed. Goldwyn sided with the stars, dismissing Chanel's results as ranging from boring to calamitous. Yet Chanel made one good attempt at reconciliation with Gloria Swanson in *Tonight or Never*. The film was an adaptation of the Broadway play and won critical acclaim when it came out in December 1931. Miss Swanson's classic looks and svelte figure suited the Chanel style. Chanel created for her a stunning, bias-cut, black satin evening dress. She moulded the satin in the round, giving Miss Swanson's gown a fluid simplicity, indeed providing a twentieth-century Grecian silhouette. Chanel also dressed Miss Swanson in one of her classic suits. Not surprisingly, Chanel also had one that was exactly the same and she was often photographed in it. It epitomizes her style of the 1930s when she perfected much of the tailoring with regard to fit and cut. The jacket is now cut shorter and is shaped to the waist. Chanel emphasized this by wearing a very wide leather belt. The suit had revers and was given definition by an immaculate white blouse. Although her time in Hollywood was not an unqualified success and she was released from her contract by Goldwyn, Chanel's peregrinations in the New World were the way in which she observed the fashion scene in New York and met heads of department stores and fashion editors of magazines, all of which were invaluable for publicizing and marketing her fashions. She returned to Paris and gave a graceful kick-start to high fashion in European films by costuming in the late 1930s Jean Renoir's *La Marseillaise* and *La Règle du jeu* and Jean Cocteau's *La Beauté et la bête*, providing her little black dress for Renoir and her brocaded collars and cuffs for Cocteau. The mantle of Chanel's frisson of film glamour fell upon Hubert de Givenchy, who dressed the elfin Audrey Hepburn in some of her best Hollywood films, from her pedal pushers, Capri pants and polo-neck sweaters in

Funny Face (1957) to her elegant little black dresses and evening gowns in *Breakfast at Tiffany's* (1961), providing, just like Chanel did in the 1930s, a visual document of fashion in the late 1950s and early 1960s.

Fashion during the Second World War, *Le Théâtre de la Mode* and the New Look

Cut off from France when Paris fell to the Germans in June 1940, British fashion had to make do as best it could in the face of government regulations. Styles were set down by the Board of Trade's Utility Scheme (1941-52). In June 1941 clothes rationing was introduced, limiting, with the use of coupons, the procurement of

'Stand up to It'. Nicolls advertisement, 1940.
War-time styles in Britain were influenced by the large number of women in military uniform. Shoulders were padded, skirts touched the knee, and waists were belted which gave a square, boxy silhouette. A tailored suit, day dress and overcoat were the essentials in a British lady's wardrobe. One new item was the all-in-one shelter suit or siren suit. Shoes were heavy and hard-wearing. The masculine air of women's fashions was offset by feminine hats and hairstyles. (*Fashion Research Centre, Bath*)

Fashion Illustration in the Twentieth Century

garments by civilian women and men. This was followed up in 1942 by a series of Making of Clothes (Restrictions) Orders by the Government. All clothes, hats and shoes made under the Utility Scheme were labelled or printed CC41, the abbreviation for Civilian Clothing 1941, the year the scheme was started. These labels are difficult to detect, as they were sewn unobtrusively on the side seams, but Utility clothing is distinctive and can be recognized by the simplicity of its cut and fabric. The Board of Trade completely oversaw the production of the Utility Scheme, specifying the manufacturers, the cloth, and the styles. For women's fashion, the Utility Scheme designated the number of pleats, seams, buttons and buttonholes, and materials. Elastic, for example, could only be used for underwear, though this was relaxed towards the end of the war. The one bright note was that leading London fashion designers formed themselves into the Incorporated Society of London Fashion Designers in 1942 and they worked in tandem with the Board of Trade Utility restrictions to produce some stylish clothes for the ready-to-wear market. The hallmarks of the 1940s' look are wide shoulders, narrow waists, and short skirts on the knee, producing a boxy silhouette. *Weldon's Ladies Journal* flourished, supplying paper dress patterns that were highly recommended for their abstemious use of clothing coupons. British *Vogue* continued to publish throughout the war years, and shows that despite the adversities, evening dress did not entirely disappear.

Vogue called its issue for June 1945 its Victory Number but the clothes featured still looked like those of the war years. The leading women's fashion magazines such as *Woman's Own*, *Woman's Journal*, and *The Lady* gave women ideas on how to re-fashion their garments with the minimum of material to add a few details such as yokes and ruching. For *Vogue* the newest and most handsome illustrated item was a Jacqmar victory scarf. The final design, in a series of five that had been made throughout the war, was called 'Lauriers de la Victoire' and was priced at a hefty 55/10d plus two coupons, and could be had 'at many high class stores throughout the country or direct from Jacqmar'.

The outbreak of war had put an end to any advances in fashion for men. Utility regulations governed the number of pockets and buttons on their suits. Trousers could not be wider than 19 inches and had no turn-ups. In order to save on fabric (good fabric in any case was difficult to find) pockets and waistcoats were often omitted from the suit. Wartime restrictions even extended to braces which were made of carpet webbing. At the end of the war the de-mobilized forces were issued with 'de-mob' suits that were mass produced on Utility lines and cut in the style of the late 1930s with a wide-shoulder line and rather shapeless appearance. These suits became to be considered as old-fashioned and, by the late 1940s elegantly tailored suits cut on narrower lines were designed which bear comparison with the exquisite tailoring of the suits cut on trim lines in the early years of the twentieth century. Fashion-conscious men who wore these suits were called the 'neo-Edwardians'.

Years of austerity and crisis were also experienced on the French fashion front. Unrestricted *haute couture* ceased with the German occupation of Paris in June 1940 and did not re-emerge intact until France was liberated in 1944. Some *couturiers*, for example Molyneux and Mainbocher, went to America, while Chanel, who stayed in the Ritz, closed her fashion house, leaving open only her boutique of accessories and perfumes. The *couturier* Lucien Lelong, as President of the Chambre Syndicale de la Haute-Couture from 1937 to 1947, persuaded the occupying Germans to permit *maisons de couture* to remain in Paris and not transfer them to Berlin.[22] However, no aspect of the fashion business escaped the eyes of the Nazis, including fashion illustration. The office of *Vogue*, which continued to appear in France into the late Spring of 1940, was raided, and the editor, Michel de Brunhoff, decided to close the magazine down rather than succumb to censorship.[23]

Another prominent fashion magazine that voluntarily ceased publication for the same reason was *Fémina*. However, many fashion journals continued to publish throughout the war years, including *Marie Claire*, *Mode du jour*, *Modes et travaux*, *La Femme chic* and *Silhouette*. On only one occasion did descriptions and reports of *haute couture* extend beyond France

in 1943 when a copy of Michel de Brunhoff's luxury magazine *Album de Mode de Figaro* reached New York and Paris. It was a clandestine edition, produced with great risk in Monte Carlo. This fact, however, was not

---

Utility suit, designed by the Incorporated Society of London Fashion Designers for the Board of Trade. Photograph, 1942. This suit made in woollen tweed has a hip-length waisted jacket with high, wide lapels, patch pockets, and large buttons. The slightly flared skirt is panelled and skims the knee. Touches of femininity are the blouse, made of rayon crêpe, the felt hat, the gloves and the earrings. Fashion magazines promoted good grooming and make-up which on this model reflects the influence of Hollywood movie stars such as Joan Crawford. *(The Trustees of The Imperial War Museum, London)*

known abroad. Above all the sketches of the flamboyantly vulgar hats caused a scandal. *Picture Post* got hold of some sketches and published a shocked and hostile article. Elsa Schiaparelli, touring the United States to raise funds for French charities, found herself in deep and stormy waters. She tried to explain to the US press and public that these styles represented to the French women who wore them a slap in the face for the Nazis. They were, she said, a symbol of the indomitable, free and creative spirit of Paris. No matter how much the Nazis made them suffer, the jaunty hats remained a constant irritant to the Germans or so she argued. She found few who accepted this view, either amongst her friends or in the US press. [24]

Apart from this episode, *haute couture* remained a closed world within the Franco-German axis during the Occupation.

When Paris was liberated in August 1944 the first fashion reporters to arrive were the American Lee Miller and the British Alison Settle.

The discovery by Alison Settle that at least one hundred fashion houses had kept running more or less intact through the Occupation caused even more profound surprise. When news leaked out about the extraordinary extravagance of designs there was an international scandal. There were whispers of collaboration, and the fate of the huge French fashion industry was held in the balance. [25]

The *maisons de couture* escaped any charges by the committees concerned with seeking out collaborators. [26] *Haute couture* had survived, but how was it to revive its great fashion trade, especially exports which the newly-installed French government was ardently anxious to get going again, and to re-assert its international fashion

Fashion dolls dressed by Jean Dessès and Jacques Fath, for *Le Théâtre de la Mode*, 1945.
The *poupées mondaines* of *Le Théâtre de la Mode* were made of wire and were dressed most elegantly in the designs of 40 leading *couturiers*. On the left is an example of the work of .

Jean Dessès, who specialized in dresses with tight jackets and flowing, boldly patterned evening skirts. On the right is a creation by Jacques Fath, who had a flair for soft, curving lines and embroidery applied to costume. *(Maryhill Museum of Art, Goldendale, Washington)*

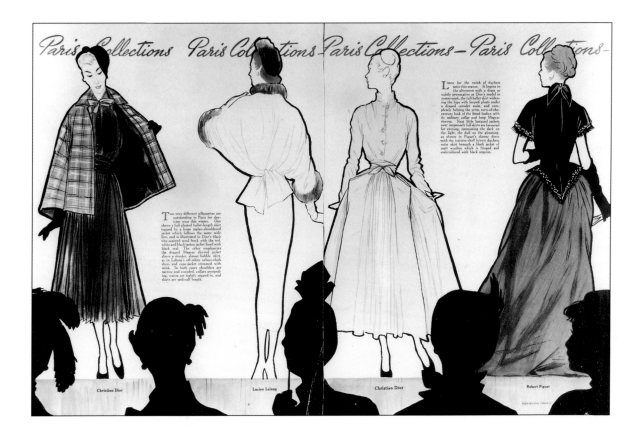

Two very different silhouettes are outstanding in Paris for day-time wear this winter. One shows a full-pleated ballet-length skirt topped by a loose raglan-shouldered jacket which follows the same wide line, and is illustrated in Dior's black tiny-waisted wool frock with the red, white and black tartan jacket lined with black seal. The other emphasizes the draped Magyar sleeved jacket above a slender, almost bubble skirt, as in Lelong's off-white velour-cloth dress and cape-jacket trimmed with mink. In both cases shoulders are narrow and rounded, collars outstanding, waists are tightly nipped-in, and skirts are mid-calf length.

Listen for the swish of duchess satin this season. It begins in the afternoon with a dress as subtly provocative as Dior's model in oyster-pink, the full ballet skirt widening the hips with looped pleats under a draped corselet waist, and completely belying the prim, turn-of-the-century look of the fitted bodice with its military collar and long Magyar sleeves. Neat little basqued jackets over immensely full-skirts are favoured for evening, contrasting the dark on the light, the dull on the gleaming, as shown in Piguet's dinner dress with the tortoise-shell brown duchess satin skirt beneath a black jacket of matt woollen which is fringed and embroidered with black sequins.

Christian Dior   Lucien Lelong   Christian Dior   Robert Piguet

leadership? Although *Vogue* did not enjoy anything like a regular sequence of issues until 1947, it was re-launched in January 1945 with *Vogue Libération*, a special number which, Michel de Brunhoff hoped, would be 'worthy of our magazine of the past . . . the first demonstration of our recovered freedom.'[27] According to British *Vogue*, French *Vogue* was 'the first magazine of this nature for which the French Ministry of Information has given a special paper allowance.'[28] While only a small run of French *Vogue* was produced, it was the fact that it was re-launched which was the salient point, for it was a big boost to both the *couturiers* and fashionable women.

The Chambre Syndicale de la Haute Couture organized an exhibition of 228 fashion dolls called *Le Théâtre de la Mode* at the Pavillon de Marsan in March 1945. Forty *couturiers* designed *haute couture* for these little mannequins which stood 70 cm high and were made of wire, the creations of Elaine Bonabel. They were placed in sets depicting scenes of Parisian life designed by artists involved in fashion such as Jean Cocteau and Christian Bérard. In the Spring of 1946 *Le Théâtre de la Mode* went to America and toured New York and San Francisco.

The *couturier* who re-established Paris's role as the international fashion leader was Christian Dior. It is very rare that a precise date can be assigned to a change in fashion, but Dior's first collection was a benchmark. In 1947, Dior, who had been an art dealer running a gallery, and, after that, a designer at Robert Piquet's and Lucien Lelong's, was established in his own fashion house by the renowned textile firm of Marcel Boussac. Dior presented his first collection, called *Corolle*, in February 1947. The word 'Corolle' derives from Corolla, a botanical term

Paris Collections. Fashion plate from *Woman's Journal*, London, November 1947.
Post-war designs by Christian Dior, Lucien Lelong and Robert Piguet. Dior presented his first collection in the Spring of 1947 which he called "Corolle", derived from *Corolla*, a botanical term meaning the delicate ring of petals opening in the centre of a flower and it was aptly dubbed the "New Look". Although other *couturiers* such as Coco Chanel and Jacques Fath had been working toward this shape by 1939, it is generally attributed to Dior. Lelong offered an alternative post-war look, a blouson top and pencil-slim skirt. *(Fashion Research Centre, Bath)*

meaning the delicate rings of petals opening in the centre of a flower. In his books Dior explained his *Corolle* collection which was nicknamed the 'New Look'.

> We were emerging from a period of war, of uniforms, of women – soldiers built like boxers. I drew women-flowers, soft shoulders, flowering busts, fine waists like liana and wide-skirts like corolla. No one person can change fashion – a big fashion change imposes itself. It was because women wanted to look like women again that they adopted the New Look.[29]

The new feminine ideal which Dior presented, which in reality harked back to France's Golden Ages of elegance (the eighteenth century, the Second Empire and the *Belle Époque*), consisted of a corseted waist, rounded bust and hips, and a long full skirt. Dior tightened the waist by means of intricate cutting, and by a mini-corset called a *guêpiere*. He padded out the front hip bones and set the sleeves into a rounded shoulder-line, in complete contrast to the dour, masculine, square-shouldered, severely tailored clothes that marked the war and end-of-war period. This was a silhouette that was applied to all garments. To this ultra-feminine costume equally feminine accessories were added: small, flowered hats with veils, high-heeled shoes, coloured gloves to match a buttonhole or handkerchief, long slim umbrellas to tone with the shoes and handbag and two or four strings of pearls. The New Look, lavishly illustrated in all the fashion magazines, revived the art of *haute couture*.

Kaleidoscope

Since the end of the Second World War fashion has been conveyed in a myriad of ways. The artists at *Vogue* resumed their distinctive role as descriptive and interpretative fashion illustrators. Of the three main editions, French *Vogue* seemed to have recaptured that special pizzazz of the fashion plates of the early years of the century. At American *Vogue* Alexander Liberman was appointed art director in succession to Dr Agha in 1943. In 1962 he was promoted to editorial director of Condé Nast Publications, and, as he did not retire until 1994, his influence on the world of fashion illustration has been considerable. An artist himself, he encouraged all types of

art forms. That celebrated triumvirate of fashion artists, Eric, René Bouché, and René de Boutet-Willaumez continued to produce superb fashion plates, but Eric's death in 1958, followed by Bouché's in 1963, dealt a blow to fashion drawing, although photographers, under the benefice of Liberman, were already making their mark. British *Vogue* was markedly different from its two sisters. In the austere postwar years it seemed to have been hit the hardest, and consequently took the longest to recover. All three editions of *Vogue* had a common denominator: the 1950s' image they depicted expressed what was probably the last period in the history of costume when fashion had absolute certainties. The visual fashion statement that prevailed was of women in beautifully extravagant lady-like styles worn with stiletto-heeled shoes.

The fashion photographer who most consistently captured the world of *haute couture* in the 1950s was Henry Clarke. His rather arch style of photography was nevertheless imbued with wit and the speed of photojournalism. Clarke's great attribute was his precision in defining the fashionable image, showing how a high-fashion dress was cut and how it hung. It was his meticulous attention to detail which won him the admiration of both *couturiers* and fashion editors, most famously, Diana Vreeland, editor-in-chief of American *Vogue*. Clarke signed up with Condé Nast in 1951 and negotiated a unique contract whereby his photographs were submitted to American, French and British *Vogue*. This meant he cornered the market with *Vogue*, as he covered the *haute couture* collections more frequently than any of its other fashion photographers.

Yet even before women broke free from the way fashion controlled them, fashion photographers and fashion artists were starting to embrace new stylistic techniques to convey costume. Irving Penn's post war work for *Vogue*, whilst still a blueprint for sartorial correctness and selling a dream of elegance and glamour, nonetheless revolutionized fashion photography by eschewing the elaborate, cluttered, theatrical settings of contemporaries like Cecil Beaton in favour of plain white studios or outside sets. In the mid-1950s the bold work of William Klein brought street photography to fashion. The culture of youth and of street fashion had its parallels in rock 'n'

Lady's suit, designed by Christian Dior, 1947, and man's suit, 1948.
Christian Dior shot to instant fame in 1947 with his 'New Look', so-called because it threw over the plain, wide-shoulder, boxy-lines of wartime styles and introduced a softer, more feminine shape with long, full skirts, tiny waists, fitted bodices, and softly-rounded shoulders. Near the end of the 1940s men's suits were dark and elegant, cut with an emphasis on narrowness and slimness. The jacket tapered to fit neatly at the hips, with the lapels wide and long, dropping to double-breasted fastenings. Trousers corresponded in shape with turn-ups at the hems. Knitted waistcoats, sleeveless pullovers and seaters were popular for informal wear. *(Museum of Costume, Bath)*

roll music, juke boxes, coffee bars, films, television and advertising. This accelerated in the 1960s with Pop Art, Opt Art, the hippy movement and flower power. The fashion model Twiggy was photographed on the street, her skinny legs clad in Opt-Art hose. A whole new generation of fashion designers sprung up who brought a modern look to fashion which both appealed to youth and also answered the call for what was felt was a need for smart, youthful clothes.

The name which will always be linked with the 1960s is Mary Quant. In 1955 she opened her first shop, Bazaar,

in the King's Road, Chelsea, London. Her young, inexpensive fashions were spotted by *Harper's & Queen*. She popularizd mini skirts, coloured tights, sleeveless crochet tops, skinny-rib sweaters, low-slung hipster belts, and a 'wet' collection of PVC garments. She was given exposure and spreads in British *Vogue* along with two other rising British fashion designers, Ossie Clark and Zandra Rhodes.

Woollen suit, 1962, and bonded jersey dress, 1966, designed by Mary Quant.
Mary Quant's outfits represented a simpler, sharper, sassier line developed with the slimmer, A-line skirts which were worn with shoes with pointed toes and stiletto heels. The hemline rose to the knee in 1962 and the mini-skirt rose to its shortest length around 1966. (Museum of Costume, Bath)

Silk faille and velvet evening dress, designed by Charles James, 1956.
Charles James ignored the idea of traditional twice yearly collections, and re-worked an original idea year in, year out, so that it could be reproduced again and again over many years in a variety of fabrics and colours. He is most celebrated for his sculpted "tulip" ball gowns, the first one created in 1949.

This version, from 1956, is typical of James's exacting, artistic technique. The bodice and torso which tightly conform to the body are rigidly boned to maintain their shape. At knee-level, a huge flounce bursts out to an amazing width. The under-structure is so stiffly boned that it, too, holds its complex shape even when removed from the body. (Cincinnati Art Museum, Gift of Mr and Mrs J.G. Schmidlapp, by exchange)

Outfit for the office in pure new wool Prince of Wales check from Next womenswear, Spring/Summer 1996.
Next, the British chain store, here presents its 'business class' fashions. Tailored pieces mix and match, so creating a confident and contemporary image. Through such advertisements, retailing giants communicate – and illlustrate – high fashion to the masses. (Next Press Office, London)

who was to have a formative influence on him. He became the foremost artist on both sides of the Atlantic, elevating the nearly forgotten art of fashions drawing to a new eminence.

An original idea for the illustration of fashion is the scheme conceived by Mrs Doris Langley Moore, who founded the Museum of Costume in Bath, England, in 1963. Mrs Moore displayed her own collection in chronological order to illustrate how fashion undergoes changes in the process of its development. Since 1963 the Museum has been adding to the evolving history of fashion through its 'Dress of the Year', where a leading fashion journalist is invited to choose a dress or set of clothes which in his or her view illustrates a new influential idea in contemporary fashion. As *haute couture* represents such a small portion of the fashion market, and, in any case all the leading international fashion designers work in the ready-to-wear sector, the 'Dress of the Year' always comes from their ready-to-wear collections. It was fitting that Mary Quant, the British originator of 'Mod Fashions', should be the first recipient in 1963.

In France the tradition of *haute couture* continued. In 1954, at the age of 71, Coco Chanel made an astonishing comeback, increasing the momentum of the Chanel name which now flourishes under Karl Lagerfeld. By the 1960s couture was beginning to become less exclusive, as the *prêt-à-porter* or ready-to-wear collections assumed greater importance, Coco Chanel catering to it assiduously. She had been active in the 1930s designing a sweater collection for Harvey Nichols, the stylish department store and also selling a dress and jacket to Jaeger's to launch their fashion department. In the late 1930s, another financially perceptive *couturier*, Lucien Lelong, was already making *prêt-à-porter* collections and Paris designs were increasingly being sold for direct copying to ready-to-wear manufacturers.[30] These egalitarian convictions were matched by Christian Dior, who in 1949 opened a wholesale house in New York which sold

After 1963, *Vogue* magazines commissioned only one artist with any regularity. This was Antonio, born in Puerto Rico and raised in New York. He studied at the Fashion Institute of Technology in New York and worked in the early 1960s as an artist drawing fashions on Seventh Avenue, the garment district of New York, until he met the American fashion designer, Charles James,

Stretch-denim skirt, Lurex-threaded tweed jacket and white T-shirt, designed by Karl Lagerfeld for Chanel, chosen as Dress of the Year 1991, Museum of Costume, Bath.
In 1991 one needed to look no further than the popular street style of gilt-buttoned and braided mock Chanel jacket, with a stretchy short skirt, for an endorsement of Lagerfeld and his vibrant up-date of the Chanel style. This look had everything in fashion that year and several before: the stretch in the denim, the sparkle of Lurex in the tweed and a T-shirt with ropes of jewellery underneath. Lagerfeld is noted for moving fashion forward and pushing ideas one step further. *(Museum of Costume, Bath)*

Men's clothes designed by Nino Cerruti, chosen as Dress of the Year, 1978, Museum of Costume Bath, and outfit by Jeff Sayre, 1979.
Jeff Sayre's outfit shows the trend for more informal wear associated with the 1970s. For more conventional men of fashion in the later 1970s, suits were classically tailored and made in subtly-coloured quality fabrics. Cerruti was the acknowledged leader of this style. *(Museum of Costume, Bath)*

off-the-peg Dior models to department stores throughout America. All these ventures were important in the development of direct selling by the *maisons de couture* to department stores worldwide. They began to make contracts with department stores giving them exclusive rights to sell their fashions. By the 1960s boutiques had become a wonderful means of illustrating high fashion to the public. They had been popular since the 1920s as shops within *maisons de couture*, selling accessories, for example, jewellery and handbags at Chanel. Lucien Lelong opened a boutique to sell his 'éditions', less expensive ranges of his couture clothes. After the Second World War boutiques opened worldwide selling designer clothes and accessories and they came into their own in the 1960s as sales venues ideally suited to the young.

As in Britain, another generation of *couturiers* emerged in France in the 1960s with their own revolutionary fashion ideas aimed at the young but not just for the young. Yves Saint Laurent, who took over the House of Dior when the master died in 1957, presented a collection in 1960 composed of items such as black leather jackets, turtleneck sweaters and fur-trimmed hats. The audience watched 'modern, street fashion redesigned in the hands of a *couturier*.'[31] When he presented his first collection under his own name in January 1962 *Life* magazine called his designs 'the best suits since Chanel.'[32] His Autumn/Winter collection for 1962 focused on pea jackets and Norman smocks in jersey, satin and silk.

Subsequent collections were equally innovative: in 1963 his thigh-high boots filtered to the street; in 1965 his Mondrian-inspired cocktail dress was a supreme example of the influence of art on fashion, which again was widely copied; and in 1966 his 'le smoking' or 'tuxedo' suit was the highlight, whose sartorial repercussions still resonate today. Saint Laurent launched his Rive Gauche chain of boutiques in 1966 and in 1996 is still looked upon as a *couturier* who initiated a whole new way of dressing.

Evening dress and coat made of black and white ostrich feathers, designed by Yves Saint Laurent, 1964.
Ostrich feathers were used extensively in the late nineteenth and early twentieth centuries for the making of boas, adorning hats and trimming garments. The master *couturier* has devised a whole new concept in fashion design with the feathers of the flightless bird. This ensemble shows that Saint Laurent does not conform to tradition but is on a plane all his own. (Museum of Costume, Bath)

Trouser suit, designed by André Courrèges. Pen and ink sketch on paper. From *The Sunday Times*, London, 1964.
With the unisex vogue of the 1960s, trousers became fashionable for day and evening wear. Space Age was the name given by Courrèges to his collection in 1964, noted for its sleek, functional lines and geometric shapes in plain colours. Courrèges subjected his trouser suit, made in a stiffly-textured white cloth with top-stitched seams, to a highly disciplined design, a very straight, angular jacket worn over narrow, straight-legged trousers with slits at the front hem. Typical Courrèges accessories are his 'baby bonnet' in the shape of a spaceman's helmet, white gloves and white leather boots. (*The Sunday Times Fashion Archive, Fashion Research Centre, Bath*)

experimented with a variety of fabrics and his hallmarks are his rich, vivid printed materials. Ungaro produced his first *prêt-à-porter* collection in 1968.

Another European trend of the 1950s and 1960s was the paring down of the male silhouette under the aegis of the Italian fashion designers. The 'Italian suit' had a narrow cut and tight fit with a natural shoulder line and was made in a lightweight material. In the realm of *haute couture*, Pierre Cardin designed unfussy, modish clothes for men. An important contribution to youthful and stylish clothes for men was made by Yves Saint Laurent, who, in the 1970s, started his ready-to-wear collections for them. Another fashion variation was unisex dressing. This included trousers, jackets, waistcoats and shirts worn by either sex. Although men enjoyed wearing floral patterned shirts, women's fashions were drawing closer to men's rather than the reverse. With the movement to greater informality in dress, even the venerable House of Dior extended the wearing of trousers into evening dress, albeit by matching them with brilliantly coloured silk tunics.

Christian Dior's New Look had deflected attention away from important post-war fashion developments: the naturalism of the American look and the growth of the American ready-to-wear market, which was an unknown quantity to Europe.

Two disciples of Balenciaga, André Courrèges and Emanuel Ungaro contributed to the youth craze in France. Courrèges opened his own fashion house in 1961 and in the early 1960s created a sensation with short skirts, mini dresses with trousers, trouser suits, all imbued with perfect tailoring and severity of design. He is most celebrated for his Space Age Collection of 1964, a novel approach to fashion, but still betraying his uncluttered, crisply tailored silhouette. Typical outfits were hipster trousers worn with sleeveless or short-sleeved jackets and dresses and trouser suits. In 1961 Ungaro moved to Courrèges and in 1965 opened his own fashion house. He followed the Courrèges line but

During the First World War, rather than rely on Paris, Edna Woolman Chase, the editor of American *Vogue*, had exhorted American manufacturers to encourage American designers and to champion them by providing home fashion shows. American fashion went from strength to strength, with designing and manufacturing skills honed during the Second World War, when French fashions were again unavailable. A whole group of American fashion designers emerged, including Traina-Norell, Hattie Carnegie, Adrian and, most influential of all, Claire McCardell, who created casual clothes, separates and co-ordinates, the sportswear style, that were in tandem with the lifestyle then prevailing and which also looked to the future.

Claire McCardell, a graduate of Parsons, laid the blueprint for the American concept of easy, simple dressing that was soft and fluid. She promoted humble materials – denim, gingham and jersey – and designed neat, practical clothing, often using detail as the focus of her fashion, ornamenting her fabrics with top-stitching, patch pockets, and bows that actually worked as fastenings. Among her big successes was her monk dress of 1938, loose, free and flowing, cut on the bias and made of wool jersey, which she developed into a tent dress, which could be worn belted or unbelted and became a basic garment of contemporary fashion. Her 'popover' of 1942, an unstructured wrap-around dress, and her shirt dress with a pleated bodice and small tie at the neck became classics. Her great feat was that to make comfort and wearability modish. Donna Karan, Calvin Klein and Ralph Lauren remain faithful to the pioneering tradition of Claire McCardell. Her style has colonized global fashion, ever present in the designs of the mainstream British, Italian and French fashion designers.

A major influence on fashion and its illustration, especially in regard to textiles, was the coming to prominence in the 1970s and 1980s of several Japanese fashion designers who questioned the cut and shape of Western women's clothes and introduced a whole new way of dressing based on Japanese taste. Foremost amongst them was Issey Miyake, an admirer of Claire McCardell, who worked with Givenchy in Paris and Geoffrey Beene in New York in the 1960s.[33] By the late 1970s and early 1980s he had developed his unique style, adapting the traditional clothing of his native country for modern women of fashion in the West. This was characterized by roomy oversized shapes, layering, asymmetry and complex draping along with subtle colours, unexpected combinations of materials, and a new approach to cutting, all combined to produce the most important new fashion of the 1980s.[34]

One of the great phenomena of the 1980s was power dressing. Sartorial authority and assertiveness were the most important characteristics of the 'Yuppie' (Young Urban Professional) wardrobe, exemplified in the power suit. Wide shoulders, emphasized by shoulder pads, were the key details of the power suit. His jacket was double-breasted worn with front-pleated trousers, whilst her jacket was clearly appropriated from the male wardrobe. The shoulders were so grotesquely padded that American fashion journalists invented the phrase 'power shoulders'. The jacket was worn with a short, sharply cut, tight-fitting suit. Image-conscious Yuppies required a designer label. In America, Calvin Klein and Ralph Lauren, and in Europe, Giorgio Armani, cornered the Yuppie market. The means of fashion illustration to disseminate the philosophy of power dressing was television and film: Joan Collins, as the archetypal business woman in the American television soap opera series, *Dynasty*, brilliantly defined this female image.

There was bound to be a reaction in the 1990s against the philosophy of the 1980s. The whole shape and cut of fashion in the 1990s was marked by the return of the dress and its accompaniment, the jacket. In the 1950s and 1960s this combination was the outfit of the well-bred fashionable woman. In the 1990s, this classic formula, while retaining its gentility, became the executive suit of the reformed high-class business woman: a shift or cap-sleeved or sleeveless dress, beautifully seamed and darted to fit with a softly tailored, single-breasted jacket. The jacket was designed in

Trouser suit, designed by Ralph Lauren, chosen as Dress of the Year 1992, Museum of Costume, Bath.
This pin-striped, double-breasted woollen trouser suit, worn with a white shirt and dark tie, illustrated a return to dependable classics of quality. Lauren developed the idea of selling his clothes against carefully chosen props in his flagship store on Madison Avenue in New York, and his shop on Bond Street in London, as well as through advertising campaigns, thereby imparting a lifestyle. (*Museum of Costume, Bath*)

several flattering ways: a short, spencer-style, or a long-line, three-quarter length cut. These styles were altogether less rigid and structured than those of the 1980s, the line following the female form rather than forcing it to conform to the masculine shape. Versatility, another key component of 1990s dressing, meant that the dress and jacket could be worn together or as separates. Betty Jackson, Caroline Charles and Nicole Farhi in the United Kingdom, Donna Karan and Liz Claiborne in America and Jil Sander in Germany, all have a reputation for clothes that do not restrict femininity and for designing a cohesive wardrobe for the career woman in soft materials and natural tones. Amongst the male fashion designers, Giorgio Armani, Calvin Klein and Ralph Lauren produced clean, uncluttered lines in quality materials. Klein has acknowledged the

influence of Claire McCardell, who laid the foundations of American sportswear. The visual message from the menswear shows held in Milan and Paris as early as 1991 was than the male wardrobe, too, favoured jettisoning power dressing. Armani summed it up with the word, *normalità*. The male silhouette, like its female counterpart, can be characterized by a return to softness, with the jacket following the natural line of the shoulder and the trousers slimly and narrowly cut. Sampling sartorial film images from throughout the century became the height of fashion in the 1990s. Trouser suits for women, though not popular until the 1960s, first appeared in the films of Marlene

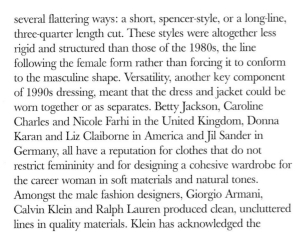

Shirt dress, designed by Issey Miyake, 1985.
Miyake's aesthetic comprises many elements of traditional Japanese taste, including a fascination for fabrics with unusual textures and patterns. The textiles that make up this jaunty shirt dress illustrate his exacting technique in which he introduced a whole new way of looking at fashion. The black, brown and white blend of silk, cotton and linen used for this striped double weave has a warm, rough texture like old homespun cloth. Humble black mylon plain weave is highlighted in the collar and sleeves. (*Cincinnati Art Museum, Gift of Arlene C. Cooper*)

'Rebecca', by Aquascutum, London, Spring 1989.
This double-breasted suit in navy chalk striped-wool, with its shoulder-line clearly emphasized by padding, and with its sharply-cut white pique collar, conveys the aura of the successful business executive of the 1980s, and exudes glamour mixed with authority. (*Aquascutum, London*)

Dietrich and Katharine Hepburn in the 1930s and 1940s. In the 1990s the trouser suit for women is a staple item in the collections of Ralph Lauren and Giorgio Armani. The tuxedo worn by Miss Dietrich in the 1930s was reincarnated as high fashion by Yves Saint Laurent in 1966 in *le smoking*. Saint Laurent teamed the tux with a sheer blouse and mannish trousers. Its progress from the *maison de couture* to the street occurred on 28 May 1996 when the Autumn/Winter catalogue of *La Redoute*, France's biggest mail order company, offered an Yves Saint Laurent four-piece suit, consisting of jacket, waistcoat, trousers and skirt. Humphrey Bogart's trenchcoat worn in *Casablanca* was reinvented for women in the Winter 1995 collection of Gianni Versace, cut short and sharp, and made in bright vinyl or PVC. Another 1940s classic, *Queen Christina*, starring Greta Garbo, showed the film goddess in a nineteenth-century style military coat with double yoke at the shoulders, a style which was recreated for fashion in Winter 1995.

The art of fashion drawing and painting of the quality seen earlier in the century staged a comeback in the late 1980s and early 1990s. When American *Glamour* magazine was launched in a French edition in 1988 the artist Jean-Philippe Delhomme was chosen to write a fashion column and to accompany it with colourful gouache paintings and captions. When Barney's launched two flagship stores in New York and Los Angeles in 1994, Delhomme was again called upon to help in the publicity, illustrating a new range of *haute couture* designs of fashion designers such as Givenchy and Armani, with drawings that had an economy of line and a freshness of the fashion plates of the 1920s. One of the artistic and literary growth industries in the UK has been the number of magazines aimed at men. The work of the fashion designer Paul Smith provided much momentum, for his clothes had the same liberating effect on men as Armani had a decade earlier.

Fashion magazines, fashion designers, department stores and chain stores have collaborated in the visual dissemination of fashion in the 1990s. A novel idea has been 'Fashion Theatre'. Department stores such as Selfridge's in London have had their windows sparkling in Springtime with advertisements of daily fashion shows featuring men's and women's clothes presented in association with leading fashion magazines such as *Vogue* and *Woman's Journal*. Even ready-to-wear designer labels are beyond the ken of most women, and top fashion designers started as early as the 1980s to produce diffusion lines as the answer to the wardrobe problems of fashionable women. The fact that diffusion lines have accelerated in the 1990s show that women want clothes designed for their basic wardrobe and not the built-in obsolescence of high fashion. High street also met high fashion magazines. The special issue of British *Vogue* for April 1995 was called 'High Street Fashion'. The clothes of chain stores, especially Marks and Spencer, were prominently featured. Marks and Spencer, in turn, had the windows of its two flagship stores on Oxford Street, London, bedecked with their latest garments and posters variously proclaiming, 'as styled by *Vogue*', 'as seen in *Vogue*', 'as chosen by *Vogue*'.

During the last two decades of the twentieth century, fashion designers have become much more aware of visual means at their disposal to disseminate their personal commitment to causes, political, social and ecological. A notable example is the British fashion designer, Katharine Hamnett. A supporter of the peace movement, she produced in the mid-1980s outsize T-shirts with anti-war slogans illustrated on them. For this she entered the Dress of the Year collection in 1984 at the Museum of Costume, Bath, where a male model displayed a thin, silk, loose-fitting jacket and trousers, and a cotton T-shirt printed with a political slogan. It was seen as reflecting the influence of street fashion on contemporary design.

Film has also continued in the 1980s and 1990s to be a potent means of conveying the quest of fashion designers for perfection in their craft. Martin Scorsese's *Made in Milan* reverentially depicted Giorgio Armani's search for perfect tailoring. Armani's extensive wardrobe for Richard Gere in *American Gigolo*, is regarded as a definitive early 1980s male fashion statement. *Unzipped*, which came out as a feature film in 1996, starred the American fashion designer, Isaac Mizrahi, a natural performer, and provided a documentary record of his Autumn 1994 collection from inception to presentation. It was Elsa Schiaparelli who commented that 'the film fashions of today are your fashions of tomorrow'. A hundred years of film have proved the truth of her remark.

Natalia Bashkatova, star of the Grigorovich Ballet of the Bolshoi Theatre, wearing garments designed by Nicole Farhi, for a 'Tactel' cinema commercial, September 1991.
The 1980s and the 1990s have been marked by the discovery of high-performance textiles, which have taken the lead in what may well be the start of a new era in fashion. One of these is Tactel, a high-quality polyamide that can take on the texture of a wide variety of different materials, from silk to wool. Tactel also has the property to impart colour and light. Its aesthetic versatility, durability and underlying elements of comfort make it perfectly suited to the large range of activities and roles of the modern fashion consumer. *(Heather Tilbury Associates, London)*

The symbiosis of the cinema with costume design was one of the themes of a series of exhibitions linking fashion with the arts, held in Florence in 1996. The exhibitions involved international artists such as Damien Hirst, Julian Schnabel and Roy Lichtenstein, and fashion designers from Giorgio Armani to Vivienne Westwood.

Fashion designers continue to project a mirror image of the twentieth-century world of clothing. They enjoy exploration, a dip into the past, borrowing and recycling from different periods and styles. The exhibition, *Streetstyle: From Sidewalk to Catwalk*, held at the Victoria and Albert Museum, London in 1994-5, showed that fashion, once set by the designers, is now often absorbed by them from the street, the 'trickle-down, bubble-up' philosophy explained by Ted Polhemus in his comprehensive book to accompany the exhibition.[35] Streetstyle itself is a general term for the special forms of dress worn by groups of young people, bonded together by the common denominators of ideology, lifestyle and music. These groups have their own territory such as retail outlets, bars and clubs and are part of a community of 'tribes'.

As street fashion is about tribalism a whole new breed of magazine was launched in the United Kingdom in the 1980s. Mixing together dress and music, and catering for both sexes, *The Face*, *i-D* and a host of other small 'style magazines' confounded the previous divisions of primarily female-oriented 'fashion magazines' and the more male-oriented 'music press'. *The Face*, created by ex-*New Musical Express* editor, Nick Logan, underlined the increasingly crucial relationship between music and appearance. It features series of articles about specific sub-cultures ranging from the Teddy Boys to Mods, Rockabilies to Raggamuffins, and also, most notably via the work of Neville Brody, forged new graphic styles. *i-D*, the brainchild of ex-*Vogue* Art Director, Terry Jones, put streetstyle at the top of its agenda. This was especially evident in its emphasis on 'straight-up' photography in which interestingly dressed 'real people' were displayed in all their glory. While fashion magazines had traditionally shown professional models wearing someone else's clothing, *i-D*'s approach spot-lit the creativity of the not, or not yet, famous. This reflected and pushed forward the growing importance of streetstyle in the 1980s. The 'street-up' tradition was picked up by *Dazed and Confused* which had documented an ever wide-range of styles in its 'Blow Up' project. Make-shift photo studies were set up in various club settings and the more interestingly dressed clubbers were invited to pose. In Japan 'straight-up' style images of 'ordinary' kids displaying their own choice of clothing and hair-styles has always been a principal feature of *Cutie* magazine. *Cutie* has demonstrated the extraordinary extent to which a wide-range of streetstyles first seen in the West have been re-interpreted in Japan. While such style magazines have provided a general

overview of developments in contemporary street/club looks, another breed of small, sub-cultural magazines, each typically focused on particular 'tribes' like Indie, Grunge, Riot Girls, Pervs, Mods, Country and Western, Techno, Acid Jazz, Rave, and Rap, have provided a voice for the values and beliefs which underline and energize each of these streetstyle looks. High fashion and the streetstyle of the tribes have always forged an on-going relationship. We saw the process illustrated earlier by the young Yves Saint Laurent when he showed biker jackets and thigh-high lace-up boots for Christian Dior in 1960. The result shocked society, the designer was ousted by Dior's management and Paris fashion changed direction. By 1983 Karl Lagerfeld was encouraging the street to storm the fashion salon donned in jackboots. He has dabbled in street fashions ever since: biker jackets and boots, short stretch-denim skirts, bum-bags, and visible underwear. For his Autumn/Winter 1993 collection, Jean-Paul Gaultier went Cyberpunk. In the United Kingdom Zandra Rhodes presented in 1977 her Punk-motivated 'Conceptual Chic' collection with its jewelled, safety-pinned, slashed silk-jersey dresses. Gianni Versace was still riding the fashion waves of the 1990s 'Punk Revival' with his similarly-derivative styles. In the 1990s Paul Smith re-interpreted the suits of the Teddy Boys and the Mods. In the United States Ralph Lauren drew upon Beatnik/Existentialist influences for his Spring/Summer 1993 collection, while Donna Karan has been influenced by Grunge, perhaps a practical antithesis to power dressing.

In her biography of Coco Chanel, Mme Charles-Roux said that Mademoiselle was 'a creator of original designs who was only happy when being plagiarised by others.'[36] Advances in the illustration of fashion, at the height of Chanel's fame, consisted of a proliferation of fashion magazines and developments in the cinema. As the twentieth century draws to a close, with the growth of computer technology and computer graphics, one wonders if she might now feel a victim of the fashion information super highway. Wireless communications, digital cameras, and the Internet mean that fashions can be copied while the fashion show is taking place and flashed around the globe within minutes. With the collections often shown months before they reach their sales outlets, counterfeiters have ample time to produce their own versions. By 1996 leading French *couturiers* wanted rules to curb computer illustration of fashion that they felt made it easy for pirates. The Chambre Syndicale, France's ruling body which controls press accreditation to French fashion shows, was examining

a ban on digital cameras, severe cuts in photographer accreditation and even the imposition of a five-week embargo on publication of show pictures.[37]

The most menacing means of illustration to them is the

digital camera, since it captures images directly with no need to process and can also transmit the images while the fashion show is in progress.

'It's all to do with timing', says Clive Howes, a photographer who specialises in digital cameras. 'If you're at a fashion show you can have a picture in the Far East in five minutes after a model steps off the catwalk.'[38]

One of the top *couturiers* fighting back against the high-tech illustration of his collections is Karl Lagerfeld at Chanel.

At his Chanel show, models appeared at lightning speed from five or six separate entrances and marched at breakneck pace across the room at all angles, making it impossible for any one photographer to get much more than a sampling of the clothes.[39]

More generally, at the fashion shows held in Paris in 1996, magazines and newspapers had to give a strict undertaking on the use of images for illustration and television stations were limited to three minutes coverage. There is, however, one exception to this rule, which was reported in the issue of the International Herald Tribune for 3 July 1996:

Yves Saint Laurent is venturing where no other *couturier* has dared before: cyber on opening day. On July 10 when he unveils his 1996-7 fall/winter *haute couture* collection in Paris, YSL is going online in 'real' time. 'We're not afraid of the Internet,' says YSL President Pierre Bergé. 'You can't turn your back on your time, just as you can't continue to believe that *haute couture* will have the same life as it had in the 1930s'. To tap into YSL website, type http://fashionlive worldmedia.fr/YSL/.[40]

It is the global community of computers that offers much scope for the future design and illustration of fashion. Vermilion plc, Europe's largest supplier of company clothing, asked Jeff Banks, the fashion designer and presenter of BBC TV's *The Clothes Show*, to design a twenty-first century uniform that was stylish, functional and that also speculated upon the

movement towards 'telecommuting', whereby the traditional office is rendered redundant. On 25 April 1996 the fashion guru unveiled his vision for the working wardrobe of the next millennium. Models clad in Bond-girl-style space-age silver bodysuits, Day-Glo thermo-minis and hooded cyber-jackets with built-in computers, security laser microphones, solar panels, and telephone, paraded at the Commonwealth Institute, London. These are the kinds of costumes that, while they may seem *outré*, threaten to oust the fashionable office suit in the twenty-first century.

Little black dress, designed by Coco Chanel. Fashion plate from American *Vogue*, 1 October 1926.
With her little black dress, Coco Chanel institutionalised the *garçonne* look. The name itself came from the novel, *La Garçonne*, written by Victor Margueritte in 1922. Key ingredients of the *garçonne* look, or the flapper, as it was called in America were the same as the Chanel look: a youthful, slender, boyish figure, short hair, comfortable clothes and short hemlines. *(Courtesy American Vogue © 1926, 1954 by the Condé Nast Publications Inc.)*

Notes

Chapter 1

1.
F. Boucher, *A History of Costume in the West*, new enlarged ed., London, 1988, p.191

2.
J. Laver, *Early Tudor 1485-1558*, Costume of the Western World Series, ed. J. Laver, London, 1957, pp.5-6

3.
B. Castiglione, *The Book of the Courtier*, trans. G. Bull, Harmondsworth, 1986, p.134

4.
J. Morley, *Regency Design 1790-1840*, London 1922, p.15

5.
F. Schevill, *A History of Europe from the Reformation to the Present Day*, New York, 1941, p.66, quoted in J.A. Olian, 'Sixteenth-Century Costume Books', *Dress*, Journal of the Costume Society of America, New York, 1977, p.21

6.
J.L. Nevinson, 'The Origin and Early History of the Fashion Plate', U.S. National Museum Bulletin 250, Contribution from the Museum of History and Technology Paper 60, Washington, D.C., 1967, p.70

7.
V. Holland, *Hand-Coloured Fashion Plates 1770-1899*, London, 1988, pp.21-2

8.
C. Vecellio, *Habiti antichi et moderni di tutto il mondo*, 2nd ed., Venice, 1598, p.119

9.
J.L. Nevinson, 'The Origin of the Fashion Plate', *Congrès International d'Histoire du Costume*, Venice, 1952, p.2

10.
Olian, *op. cit.*, p.31

11.
Vecellio's Renaissance Costume Book, New York, 1977, unpaginated

12.
B.B. Baines, *Fashion Revivals from the Elizabethan Age to the Present Day*, London, 1981, pp.33, 111, 149

13.
E. Ewing, *History of Children's Clothes*, London, 1982, pp.24, 29, 41

Chapter 2

1.
M. Contini, *Fashion from Ancient Egypt to the Present Day*, New York, 1965, p.145

2.
J. Evelyn, *Tyrannus, or The Mode*, London, 1661, p.87

3.
P. and A. MacTaggart, 'The Rich Wearing Apparel of Richard, 3rd Earl of Dorset', *Costume*, No.14, 1980, p.47

4.
A. Mackrell, *Dress in le style troubadour, 1774-1814*, unpublished Ph.D. thesis, Courtauld Institute of Art, London, 1987, p.194

5.
R. Gaudriault, *Répertoire de la gravure de mode française des origines à 1815*, Nantes, 1988, pp.29-30

6.
Charles I Clothing Account, Victoria and Albert Museum, London, Ms.86,GG.2: R. Strong,

'Charles I's clothes for the years 1633 to 1635', *Costume*, No.14, 1980, pp.73-89, for a discussion of The Account of George Kirke, Gentleman of the Robes for the years 1633 to 1635, A.O.3/910, Public Record Office, London

7.
London, Victoria and Albert Museum, *Hollar to Heideloff: an Exhibition of Fashion Prints drawn from the Collections of Members of the Costume Society*, 1979, p.11

8.
J.L. Nevinson, ed., *The Four Seasons by Wenceslaus Hollar*, Costume Society Extra Series No.6, 1979, p.7

9.
J.L. Nevinson, 'Fashion Plates and Fashion, 1625-1635', *Apollo*, Vol. LI, 1950, p.140

10.
A. Mackrell, *Shawls, Stoles and Scarves*, London, 1986, p.12

11.
Pepys, *The Diary*, edited by R. Latham and W. Matthews, London, 1970, entry for 8 October 1666

12.
Baines, *op. cit.*, pp.158-9

13.
ibid., p.36

14.
London, Tate Gallery, *The Swagger Portrait: Grand Manner Portraiture from Van Dyke to Augustus John 1630-1930*, 1992, p.86, catalogue no.12

15.
Baines, *op. cit.*, p.36

16.
Quoted in Waugh, *The Cut of Women's Clothes, op. cit.*, p.65. The British Museum contains many volumes of Holme's manuscript. See Harley MS 2014, an illustrated source for the history of dress

17.
Paris, Musée de la Mode et du Costume, *La Mode et ses métiers du XVIIIe. siècle à nos jours*, 1981, p.13

18.
J.L. Nevinson, The 'Mercury Gallant' or European Fashions in the 1670s', *Apollo*, Vol.CXXXVI, 1955, p.87

19
Gaudriault, *op. cit.*, p.88

20.
Nevinson, 'The "Mercury Gallant" or European Fashions in the 1670s', *op. cit.*, p.89

Chapter 3

1.
Gaudriault, *op. cit.*, p.95

2.
duchesse d'Orléans, *Letters from Liselette, Elizabeth, Charlotte, Duchess of Orléans, 'Madame', 1652-1722*, edited and translated by M.Kroll, London, 1970, p.235

3.
Gaudriault, *op. cit.*, pp.112-17

4.
Christie's, London, *Old Master Drawings*, 15 December 1992, p.89

5.
The Spectator, 28 July 1712, quoted in J.L. Nevinson, *The Exact Dress of the Head by Bernard Lens 1725*,

Costume Society Extra Series No.2, 1970, p.4

6.
Victoria and Albert Museum, London, *Hollar to Heideloff, op. cit.*, p.21

7.
J.L.H. Campan, *Mémoires sur la vie privée de Marie-Antoinette, Reine de France*, 3 vols., Paris, 1822, Vol.I, p.290, P. Huisman and M. Jallut, *Marie-Antoinette*, London, 1971, p.124; Madame la Comtesse d'Ossun, *Garde Robes de la Reine, Gazette pour l'année 1782*, Archives de France, No.Ae 16, no.2

8.
For a good summary of the re-cycling of eighteenth-century fashions see R.H. Kemper, *Costume*, New York, 1979, p.105

9.
Walpole, *Letters*, edited by W.S. Lewis, et. Al., 48 vols., New Haven and London, 1937-83, Vol.XVI, p.27, on Montfaucon; Scottish National Portrait Gallery, Edinburgh, Visions of the Ottoman Empire, 1994, p.11, on van Mour; Sotheby's London, *Printed Books and Maps including a Section on Greece, Cyprus, Turkey and the Levant*, 29 June and 5-6 July 1993, catalogue no.403, p.59

10.
Museum of London, *Masquerades*, 1983, p.8

11.
Mackrell, *Dress in le style troubadour, op. cit.*, pp.194-5

12.
M. Tosca, *Dolls*. Trans. by W. Dallas, London, 1989, p.15

13.
The Lady's Magazine, London, 1773, p.199

14.
A. Mackrell, *The Dress of the Parisian Élégantes with Special Reference to the Journal des dames et des modes* from June 1797 until December 1799, unpublished M.A.

thesis, Courtauld Institute of Art, London, 1977, p.9

15.
C. White, *Women's Magazines 1693-1968*, London, 1971, p.31

16.
Victoria and Albert Museum, London, *Hollar to Heideloff, op. cit.*, p.30; White, *op. cit.*, pp.29-31

17.
Victoria and Albert Museum, London, *Hollar to Heideloff, op. cit.*, p.30

18.
Waugh, *op.cit.*, p.124

19
Gaudriault, op.cit., pp.194-5; for Jefferson and French fashion see H.C. Rise Jr., *Thomas Jefferson in Paris*, Princeton, 1976, p.22; for fashion in Colonial America see Metropolitan Museum of Art, New York, *John Singleton Copley in America*, 1995

20.
Mackrell, *The Dress of the Parisian Élégantes, op. cit.*, pp.10-11.

21.
Gaudriault, *op. cit.*, p.213

22.
E. Bénézit, *Dictionnaire critique et documentaire des Peintres, Sculpteurs, Dessinateurs et Graveurs . . .*, nouvelle édition, 10 vols, Paris, 1976, vol.4, p.4

23.
Mackrell, *The Dress of the Parisian Élégantes, op. cit.*, pp.48-54

24.
Le Journal de la Mmode et du goût, No.6, 15 April 1791, pp.1-2

25.
Mackrell, *The Dress of the Parisian Élégantes, op. cit.*, p.55

26.
A.C. Morris, ed., *The Diary and Letters of Gouverneur Morris*, 2 vols., London, 1889, Vol.I, p.252

27.
Le Journal de la mode et du goût, No VIII, 5 May 1790, pp.3-4

28.
Gaudriault, *op. cit.*, p.235; Mackrell, *The Dress of the Parisian Élégantes*, *op. cit.*, pp.17-21

29.
Mackrell, *The Dress of the Parisian Élégantes*, *op. cit.*, pp.14-15

30.
Le Journal des dames et des modes, No.XXXVIII, 25 pluv. An VII; 13 February 1799, p.453; Mackrell, *The Dress of the Parisian Élégantes*, p.15

31.
For the term Neo-classical and its use *see* London, The Royal Academy of Arts and the Victoria and Albert Museum, *The Age of Neo-classicism*, 1972, p.xxii: 'The word "Neo-classical" was first applied to works of art of the late eighteenth and early nineteenth centuries at a time when they were generally out of favour and when the very notion of a classical revival was suspect - in the 1880s. The more obviously opprobious adjective "pseudo-classical" was also used, especially for the paintings of David and his contemporaries. Such terms were never used by the artists and critics of the late eighteenth century. It is important to remember that what we now call Neo-classicism was described by them as quite simply the "true" or "correct" style.'

32.
Le Journal des dames et des modes, No.I, June 1797, p.1; Mackrell, *The Dress of the Parisian Élégantes*, *op. cit.*, p.23

33.
For a discussion of cashmere shawls *see* Mackrell, *Shawls, Stoles and Scarves*, *op. cit.*, pp.31-47

34.
For a complete list of fashion plates in the fashion magazines for this period *see* Gaudriault, *op. cit.*, pp.129-225

35.
E. Vigée-Le Brun, *The Memoirs of Elisabeth Vigée-Le Brun*, trans. by S. Evans, London, 1989, pp.27-8 and pp.43-4

36.
ibid., p.241

37.
For a discussion of Spanish dress and *le style troubadour* see Mackrell, *Dress in le style troubadour*, *op. cit.*, pp.155-61

38.
Los Angeles County Museum of Art, *Women Artists 1550-1950*, 1979, p.200

39.
Mackrell, *The Dress of the Parisian Élégantes*, *op. cit.*, pp.45-6

40.
Mackrell, *The Dress of the Parisian Élégantes*, *op. cit.*, p.21

41.
D. Langley Moore, *Fashion through Fashion Plates, 1771-1970*, London, 1971, p.15

42.
ibid., p.14

43.
Holland, *op. cit.*, pp.42-3; S. Sitwell, *Gallery of Fashion*, London, 1949, p.3

44.
The Hague, Nederlands Kostuum-museum, *Mode in Prent, 1550-1914*, 1988-89, pp.38ff

45.
Boucher, *op. cit.*, p.326

46.
H. Morley-Fletcher, *Meissen Porcelain in Colour*, London, 1971, p.46

47.
Le Magasin des modes nouvelles, françaises et anglaises, No.24, 10 July 1787, p.188

Chapter 4

1.
A. Adburgham, *Women in Print. Writing Women and Women's Magazines from the Restoration to the Accession of Victoria*, London, 1972, p.220

2.
Moore, *op. cit.*, p.22; Adburgham, *op. cit.*, p.227

3.
Mackrell, *Dress in le style troubadour, op. cit.*, pp.15-16, 22, 202. For the origins of *le style troubadour*, see ch. 1

4.
ibid., ill.58; *Le Journal des dames et des modes, op. cit.*, No.10, 28 February 1807, p.96

5.
S. Grandjean, *Inventaire après l'décès de l'Impératice Joséphine*, Paris, 1964, p.50, no.10

6.
Le Journal des dames et des modes, op. cit., No.53, 15 June 1806, pl.730; No.59, 15 July 1806, pl.737; No.23, 25 April 1807, p.184; No.21, 15 April 1808, p.168; No.22, 20 April 1808, p.176

7.
Gaudriault, *op. cit.*, p.260; G. Vicaire, *Manuel de l'amateur du livres du dix-neuvième siècle, 1801-1893*, 8 vols., Paris, 1894-1910, Vol.IV, 1106

8.
Paris, Musée de la Mode et du Costume, *La Mode et ses métiers, op. cit.*, p.59

9.
F. Tétart-Vittu, 'The French-English Go-Between', *Costume*, No.26, 1992, p.40

10.
Holland, *op. cit.*, pp.51, 146

11.
Tétart-Vittu, *op. cit.*, p.44

12.
Paris, Mairie du VIe. Arrondisement, *Dessins de Mode. Jules David 1808-1892 et son temps*, 1987, pp.8-9

13.
ibid., p.13

14.
ibid., p.27

15.
ibid., p.11

16.
Holland, *op.cit.*, pp.102, 105

17.
Paris, Musée de la Mode et du Costume, *La Mode et ses métiers, op. cit.*, p.61; J. Olian, *Authentic Fashions of the Twenties. 413 Costume Designs from 'L'Art et la Mode'*, New York, 1990, unpaginated

18.
Paris, Musée de la Mode et du Costume, *La Mode et ses métiers, op. cit.*, p.34

19.
R. Waissenberger, *Vienna in the Biedermeier Era 1815-1848*, London, 1986, p.217

20.
ibid., p.218

21.
ibid., p.218

22.
ibid., p.220

23.
ibid., p.221

24.
M. Braun-Ronsdorf, *The Wheel of Fashion. Costume Since the French Revolution 1789-1929*, trans. by O. Coburn, London, 1964, p.42

25.
Waissenberger, *op. cit.*, p.224

26.
ibid., p.226

27.
Braun-Ronsdorf, *op. cit.*, p.139

28.
Cincinnati, Ohio, Cincinnati Art Museum, *Grace & Favor*, 1993, p.vii

29.
S. Blum, ed., *Fashions and Costumes from Godey's Lady's Book*, New York, 1985, unpaginated

30.
Cincinnati, Ohio, Cincinnati Art Museum, *Grace & Favour*, *op. cit.*, p.vii

31.
S. Blum, *Fashions and Costumes from Godey's Lady's Book*, *op. cit.*, unpaginated

32.
S. Blum, ed., *Victorian Fashions and Costumes from Harper's Bazar: 1867-1898*, New York, 1974, p.vi

33.
For an interesting article on nineteenth-century European genre paintings see 'Sentimental Reeducation' by S. Gardiner, *Art and Auction*, November 1995, pp.126-31, 168

34.
L.B. Hyslop, ed., *Baudelaire as Love Poet and Other Essays*, University Park and London, 1969, p.89

35.
J.-H. Champfleury, 'Du réalisme, lettre à Madame Sand', *L'Artiste*, 2 September 1855

36.
J.-H. Champfleury, *Souvenirs et portraits de jeunesse*, Paris, 1872, p.134

37.
C. Baudelaire, 'De l'héroïsme de la vie moderne', *Salon de 1846*, p.496

38.
T. Gautier, *De la mode*, Paris, 1858, pp.11-12

39.
C. Baudelaire, *The Painter of Modern Life and other Essays*, ed. and trans. by J. Mayne, London, 1964, p.12

40.
ibid., p.29

41.
J. Rewald, *History of Impressionism*, 4th rev. ed., New York, 1973, p.208

42.
M. Roskill, 'Early Impressionism and the Fashion Print', *Burlington Magazine*, June 1970, pp.391-4

43.
Sotheby's New York, *19th Century European Paintings and Sculpture*, 17 February 1993, catalogue no.70

44.
ibid., catalogue no.52

45.
P. Byrde, *Nineteenth-Century Fashion*, London, 1992, p.139

46.
Sotheby's London, *Impressionist and Modern Paintings, Drawings and Sculpture, Part I*, 29 November 1994, catalogue no.24, pp.18-19

47.
Baines, *op. cit.*, p.123

48.
Edinburgh, Scottish National Portrait Gallery, *Van Dyck in Check Trousers*, 1978, p.67

49.
R. Smith, 'Bonnard's Costume Historique - a Pre-Raphaelite Sourcebook', *Costume*, No.7, 1973, pp.28-37

50.
Mackrell, *Dress in le style troubadour, op.cit.* For a full discussion of Lenoir's *Musée* see Chapter I, part 4, 'Lenoir's Medieval Shrine' and Chapter II, Part 3, 'The Troubadour Painters of the Consulate and Empire'.

51.
ibid., p.257

52.
M. Simon, *Fashion in Art*, London, 1995, pp.89-90

Chapter 5

1.
J. Robinson, *The Golden Age of Style*, London, 1985, p.34

2.
A. Mackrell, *Paul Poiret*, London, 1990, p.19

3.
ibid., pp.20-21

4.
M. Ray, *Self-Portrait*, new ed., London, 1988, p.102

5.
Robinson, *op. cit.*, p.118

6.
ibid., pp.38, 43

7.
Mackrell, *Paul Poiret, op. cit.*, p.14

8.
Robinson, *op. cit.*, pp.43-4

9.
M. Battersby, *Art Deco Fashion: French Fashion Designers 1908-1925*, London, 1984, p.72

10.
Robinson, *op. cit.*, p.57

11.
C. Lepape and T. Defert, *From the Ballets Russes to Vogue: The Art of Georges Lepape*, New York, 1971, pp.72-3

12.
Olian, *Authentic French Fashions of the Twenties, op. cit.*

13.
M. Ginsburg, *Paris Fashions. The Art Deco Style of the 1920s*, London, 1989, p.177

14.
ibid., pp.172-3

15.
W. Packer, *Fashion Drawing in Vogue*, London, 1989, p.10

16.
Mackrell, *Paul Poiret, op. cit.*, pp.28-9

17.
Packer, *op. cit.*, p.34

18.
ibid., p.42.

19.
T. Dewe Matthews, 'Wow! Where can I get a straight-jacket like that?', *The Independent*, London, 24 February 1996, p.6

20.
L. Francke, 'Cutting Edge', *The Guardian 2*, London, 21 February 1996, p.9

21.
Mackrell, *Coco Chanel*, London, 1992, p.66

22.
De Holden Stone, 'French Fashion Survives the Nazis', *Art and Industry*, New York, July 1945, p.4

23.
ibid., pp.8-9

24.
J. Ash and E. Wilson, eds., *Chic Thrills*, London, 1992, pp.133-4

25.
ibid., p.135

26.
ibid., p.136

27.
Packer, *op. cit.*, p.108

28.
T. Glenville and M. Hume, 'We'll meet again on the design front', *The Independent*, London, 28 April 1995, p.23

29.
C. Dior, *Christian Dior and I*, New York, 1957, p.35; C. Dior, *Talking About Fashion*, New York, 1954, p.23

30.
Mackrell, *Coco Chanel*, *op. cit.*, p.37; Ash and Wilson, *op. cit.*, p.127

31.
G. O'Hara, *The Encyclopaedia of Fashion*, London, 1989, p.218

32.
New York, Metropolitan Museum of Art, *Yves Saint Laurent*, 1983, p.37

33.
B. Morris, 'Reality in Clothing: Ode to Claire McCardell', *International Herald Tribune*, Paris, 30 October 1995, p.6

34.
Cincinnati, Ohio, Cincinnati Museum of Art, *Simply Stunning*, 1988, p.101

35.
T. Polhemus, *Streetstyle*, London, 1994, p.10

36.
Mackrell, *Coco Chanel*, *op. cit.*, p.12

37.
H. Alexander, 'Fashion Victims', *The Daily Telegraph*, London, 23 April 1996, p.3

38.
ibid., p.3

39
ibid., p.3

40
International Herald Tribune, Paris, 3 July 1996, p.24

Bibliography

Primary reference

Alcega, J. de, *Libro de Geometria, Practica y Traca*, Madrid, 1589

Almanach Dauphin, ou tablettes royales du vrai mérite des artistes célèbres du royaume, Paris, 1777

Amman, J., *Kunst und Lehrbüchlein*, Frankfurt, 1578, *Pictorial Archive of Decorative Renaissance Woodcuts (Kunstbüchlin)* by J. Amman, New York, 1985

Andúxar, M. de, *Geometria, y Trazas Pertenecientes al oficio de Sastres*, Madrid, 1640

Ashmole, E., *The Institution, Laws and Ceremonies of the Most Noble Order of the Garter*, London, 1672

Balzac, H. de, *Traité de la vie élégante*, originally published in *La Mode*, 1830

Baudelaire, C., *The Painter of Modern Life and other Essays*, ed. and trans. by J. Mayne, London, 1964

Boullay, B., *Le Tailleur Sincère*, Paris, 1671

Caroso, F., *Il Ballarino*, Venice, 1581

Castiglione, B., *The Book of the Courtier*, trans. by G. Bull, Harmondsworth, 1986

Depain, M., *Les Coiffures de Depain*, Paris, c. 1770-90

Diderot, D., *Encyclopédie, ou dictionnaire raisonné des sciences, des arts et des métiers par une société, de gens de lettres*, 17 vols., Paris, Neufchastel, 1761-65, Vol. IX: Tailleur d'Habits

Dunton, J., *The Ladies Dictionary*, London, 1694

Eloffe, Mme, *Livre-Journal de Madame de Eloffe, marchande de modes, couturière lingère de la Reine et des dames de sa Cour*, ed. Le comte de Reiset, Paris, 1885

Evelyn, J., *Tyrannus, or The Mode*, London, 1661

Garsault, F.A. de, *L'Art du Tailleur*, in Académie Royale des Sciences, *Descriptions des Arts et Métiers*, Paris, 1769

Garsault, F.A. de, *L'Art de la Lingerie*, in Académie Royale des Sciences, *Descriptions des Arts et Métiers*, Paris, 1771

Garsault, F.A. de, *L'Art du Perruquier*, in Académie Royale des Sciences, *Description des Arts et Métiers*, Paris, 1767

Gautier, T., *De la mode*, Paris, 1858

Genlis, S.-F., Mme la comtesse de, *Dictionnaire critique et raisonné des Etiquettes de la Cour et des Usages du Monde*, 2 vols., Paris, 1818

Goncourt, E. and J. de, *French Eighteenth-Century Painters*, 2nd edition, Oxford, 1981

Holme, R., *An Academy of Armory*, Chester, 1688

Jaubert, P., *Dictionnaire raisonné universel des Arts et Métiers*, Paris, 1773

Le Gros, A., *L'Art de la coëffure des dames Françoises* Paris, 1768

Nivelon, F., *The Rudiments of Genteel Behaviour*, London, 1737

Pluvinel, A. de, *L'Instruction du Roi en l'exercise de monter à cheval*, Paris, 1629

Reynolds, Sir J., *Discourses on Art*, Introduction by R.R. Wark, 1966

Rocha Burguen, F. de la, *Geometria, y Traça Perteneciente al Oficio de Sastres*, Valencia, 1618

Saint-Aubin, *L'Art du Brodeur*, Paris, 1770

Stewart, J., *Plocacosmos; or the Whole Art & Hairdressing*, London, 1782

Stubbes, P., *The Anatomie of Abuses, 1583*, Part II: *The Display of corruptions requiring reformation*, ed. F.J. Furnivall, London, 1882

The Taylor's Complete Guide, or A Comprehensive Analysis of Beauty and Elegance of Dress, London, 1796

Chronicles, Letters, Diaries and Memoirs

Abrantès, L., Mme la duchesse d', *Mémoires*, 18 vols., Paris, 1831-35

Avillon, Mlle, *Mémoires*, Paris, 1969

Barbier, E.-J.-F., *Chronique de la Régence et du Regne de Louis Xv, ou Journal de Barbier*, 8 vols., Paris, 1857

Baretti, J., *An Account of the Manners and Customs of Italy*, 2 vols., London, 1769

Campan, J.-L.-H., *Mémoires*, 3 vols., Paris, 1822

Carr, J., *The Stranger in France*, London, 1803

Champfleury, J.-H., *Souvenirs et portraits de jeunesse*, Paris, 1872

Evelyn, J., *The Diary*, edited by E.S. de Beer, Oxford, 1959

Mercier, L.-S., *Le Nouveau Paris*, 6 vols., Paris, 1798

Mercier, L.-S., *Tableau de Paris*, 8 vols., Amsterdam, 1782-88

Montagu, E., *Elizabeth Montagu: Correspondence, 1720-61*, ed. by E.J. Climenson, 2 vols., London, 1906

Morris, A., ed., *The Diary and Letters of Gouvener Morris*, 2 vols., London, 1889

Moryson, F., *An Itinerary. . .*, London, 1617

Orléans, la duchesse d', *Letters from Liselotte, Elizabeth Charlotte, Princess Palatine and Duchess d'Orléans, 'Madame' 1652-1722*, edited and trans. by M. Kroll, London, 1970

Pepys, S., *The Diary*, edited by R. Lathan and W. Matthews, London, 1970

Reiset, le vicomte de, *Marie-Caroline, duchesse de Berry 1816-1830*, Paris, 1906

Rémusat, C.-E., la comtesse de, *Mémoires, 1802-8*, ed. By P. de Rémusat, and trans. by C. Hoey and J. Lillie, 2 vols., London, 1880

Vigée-Le Brun, E., *The Memoirs of Elisabeth Vigée-Le Brun*, trans. by S. Evans, London, 1989

Walpole, H., *Letters*, ed. by W.S. Lewis, et. al., 48 vols., New Haven and London, 1937-83

Costume books and books of costume engravings

Amman, J., *Fronspergers Kriegsbuch*, Frankfurt, 1577

Amman, J., *Gynaeceum Sine theatrum Mulierum, (Frauenzimmer Trachtenbüch)*, (German edition), Frankfurt, 1586

Amman, J., *Habitus Precipuonum Populorum . . . Trachtenbüch*, Nuremberg, 1577

Baxter, T., *An Illustration of Egyptian, Grecian and Roman Costume*, London, 1814

Beaunier, M.-M.-F. and Rathier, L., *Recueil des costumes français . . . depuis Clovis jusqu'à Napoléon Ier inclusivement*, 2 vols., Paris, 1810

Bertelli, D., *Le Vere Imagini et Descritioni delle più nobili città del mondo*, Venice, 1569

Bertelli, F., *Omnium Fere Gentium Nostrae Aetatis Habitus, Nunquam Ante Hac Aediti*, Venice, 1563, 2nd edition, 1569

Bertelli, P., *Diverarum Nationum Habitus . . .*, Padua, 1589, 2nd edition, 1591

Boissard, J.-J., *Habitus Variarum Orbis Gentium*, Malines (Mechlin), 1581

Bonnard, C., *Costume historique. Costumes des XIIIe., XIVe., et Xve.*, 2 vols., Paris, 1829-30

Bosse, A., *Le Jardin de la Noblesse Françoise dans lequel ce peut ceuillir leur mannierre de Vettemens*, Paris, 1629

Bosse, A., *Pièces concernant la mode et les édits*, Paris, 1634

Brummell, G., *Male and Female Costume . . .*, edited and introduction by E. Parker, New York, 1932

Bruyn, A. de, *Diversarum Gentium Armatura Equestris*, Cologne, 1577

Bruyn, A. de, *Omnium Poene Europae, Asiae, Aphicae Atque Americae Gentium Habitus*, Antwerp, 1581

Callot, J., *La Noblesse de Lorraine*, Paris, 1624

Challamel, A., *Histoire de la mode en France*, Paris, 1881

Chalon, J.-J., *Twenty-Four subjects exhibiting the Costume of Paris (Types parisiens 1820-21-22 par J.-J. Chalon)*, London, 1820-22

Dandré Bardon, M.-F., *Costume des anciens peuples*, Paris, 1772

Desprez, F., *Recueil de la diversité des habits qui sont de présent un usage*, Paris, 1562, 2nd edition, 1564, 3rd edition, 1567

Dupin, N., *Les Costumes François . . .*, Paris, 1776

Fabri, A. de, *Diversarum Nationum Habitus*, Padua, 1593

Fairholt, F.W., *Costume in England . . .*, London, 1846

Ferriol, C. de, *Recueil de cent estampes représentant différentes nations du Levant . . .*, Paris, 1714

Franco, G., *Habiti d'Huomini et Donne venetiane*, Venice, 1610

La Gallerie des Modes et Costumes français . . ., Paris, 1778-87 (P. Cornu, *Préface à la réimpression de la Galerie des Modes et Costumes français, 1778-1787*, Paris, c. 1912

Garneray, A., *Costumes du siècle de Louis XIV*, Paris, c. 1820

Glen, J. de, *Des Habits, moeurs, cérémonies, façons de faire anciennes et modernes du monde*, Liège, 1601

Hérisset, A., *Recueil des différentes modes du temps*, Paris, 1729

Hollar, W., *The Four Seasons*, London, 1641 (³⁄₄ length figures) (1643-44, full-length figures)

Hollar, W., *Ornatus Muliebris Anglicanus: the Severall Habits of English Women from the Nobilite to the Country Woman as they are in these times*, London, 1640

Hollar, W., *Theatrum Mulierum*, London, 1643 (enlarged and entitled *Aula Veneris*, London, 1646)

Hooghe, R. de, *Figures à la mode . . .*, Amsterdam, c. 1670

Hope, T., *Costume of the Ancients*, London, 1809

Hope, T., *Designs of Modern Costume.* Illustrated by H. Moses, London, 1812

Iribe, P., *Les Robes de Paul Poiret racontées par Paul Iribe*, Paris, 1908

Jefferys, T., *A Collection of the Dresses of Different Nations*, 4 vols., London, 1757, 1772

Lacroix, P., *Les Costumes historiques de la France . . .*, Paris, 1852

Le Clerc, S., *Divers costumes français du Règne du Louis XIV*, Paris, c. 1680

Lenoir, A., *Musée des Monuments français*, 5 vols., Paris, 1800-6

Lens, A., *Le Costume des peuples de l'antiquité*, Paris, 1776, nouvelle édition, Dresden, 1785

Lens, B., *The Exact Dress of the Head, drawn from Life at Court, Opera, Theatre, Park & c. By Bernard Lens in the years 1725 & 1726 from the quality & Gentry of ye British Nation*

Lepape, G., *Les Choses de Paul Poiret vues par Georges Lepape*, Paris, 1911

Le Vacher de Charnois, J.-C., *Costumes et annales des grands théâtres de Paris*, 4 vols., Paris, 1786-89

Le Vacher de Charnois, J.-C., *Recherches sur les costumes et sur les théâtres de toutes les nations tant anciennes que modernes*, Paris, 1790

Liberty, *Evolution in Costume*, London, 1884

Molé, G.-F.-R., *Histoire des modes françaises*, Amsterdam, 1777

Montfaucon, B. de, *Les Monumens de la Monarchie française*, 5 vols., Paris, 1729-33

Nicolay, N. de, *Quatres premiers livres des navigations et pérégrinations Orientales*, Lyon, 1567

Octavien, F., *Figures Françoises nouvellement . . .*, Paris, 1725

Pauguet, H. and P., *Mode et Costumes historiques . . .*, Paris, 1864

Picart, B., *Diverses modes dessinées d'après nature*, Amsterdam, 1728

Planché, J.R., *A Cyclopaedia of Costume . . .*, 2 vols., 1876, 1879

Planché, J.R., *History of British Costume from the Earliest Period to the Close of the Eighteenth Century*, London, 1837

Quicherat, J.-E., *Histoire du costume en France depuis les temps le plus reculés jusqu'à la fin du XVIIIe. siècle*, Paris, 1875

Racinet, A., *Le Costume historique*, 6 vols., Paris, 1888

Sergent-Marceau, A.-L.-F., *Les Costumes des peuples anciens et modernes*, Venice, 1799

Spallart, Robert von, *Tableau historique des costumes . . .*, 8 vols., Paris, 1804

Strutt, J., *A Compleat View of the Manners, Customs, Arms, Habits, etc. of the inhabitants of England . . .*, London, 3 vols., 1774-76

Strutt, J., *A Complete View of the Dress and Habits of the people of England . . .*, London, 2 vols., 1796-99

Suite d'Estampes pour servir à l'Histoire des Moeurs et du Costume des Français dans le dix-huitième siècle, année 1775, Paris, 1775, *Seconde suite d'estampes . . . année 1776*, Paris, 1777, *Troisième Suite d'Estampes . . . année 1783*, Paris, 1784. Published as *Le Monument du Costume physique et moral de la f in du XVIIIe. siècle*, Paris, 1789 (text by restif de la Bretonne and engravings from drawings by Freudeberg and Moreau le Jeune)

Vecellio, C., *Corona delle nobili et virtuose donne*, Venice, 1591

Vecellio, C., *De gli Habiti antichi et moderni di Diverse parti del Mondo . . .*, Venice, 1590, 2nd enlarged edition, 1598. *Vecellio's Renaissance Costume Book*, New York, 1977

Vernet, H., *Le Bon Genre*, Paris, 1817, 2nd edition, 1822, 3rd edition, 1827

Vernet, H., *Incroyable et merveilleuses*, Paris, 1810-18

Vico, E., *Diversarum Gentium Aetatis Habitus*, Venice, 1558

Viero, T., *Raccolta Di 126 Stampe rappresantano Figure ed Abiti di vaire Nazione*, Venice, 1783

Watteau, J.-A., *Figures le différentes Caractères*, 2 vols., Paris, 1726, 1728

Weiditz, C., *Trachtenbüch von seinen Reisen nach Spanien, 1529, und der Niederlanden, 1531-32*, edited by T. Hampe, Nuremberg, 1927

Willemin, N.-X., *Choix de costumes civils et militaires des peuples de l'antiquité*, Paris, 1798-1806

Willemin, N.-X., *Monumens français inédits pour servir à l'histoire des arts, des costumes viviles et militaires . . .*, 2 vols., Paris, 1806-25

Secondary reference

Bénézit, E., *Dictionnaire critique et documentaire des Peintres, Sculpteurs, Dessinateurs et Graveurs . . .*, nouvelle édition, 10 vols., Paris, 1976

Black, J.A., et al., *A History of Fashion*, London, 1983

Boehn, M. von, *Modes and Manners in the Nineteenth Century*, trans. by G. Rhys, 3 vols., London and New York, 1909

Boucher, F., *A History of Costume in the West*, new enlarged edition, London, 1988

Bouchot, H., *Toilette à la cour de Napoléon*, Paris, 1895

Brunet, C.J., *Manuel du libraire et de l'amateur de livres*, 6 vols., Paris, 1860-65

Byrde, P., *Nineteenth-Century Fashion*, London, 1992

Byrde, P., *A Visual History of Costume: The Twentieth Century*, London, 1986

Cohen, H., *Guide de l'amateur de livres à gravure de XVIIIe. siècle*, 6th edition, revised by S. de Ricci, Paris, 1912

Colas , R., *Bibliographie générale du costume et de la mode*, 2 vols., Paris, 1933

Coleman, D. and E., *Collector's Book of Dolls*, London, 1976

Cunnington, C.W. and P., *Handbook of English Costume in the Sixteenth Century*, London, 1962

Cunnington, c.W. and P., *Handbook of English Costume in the Seventeenth Century*, London, 1966

Cunnington, C.W. and P., *Handbook of Costume in the Eighteenth Century*, London, 1972

Cunnington, C.W. and P., *Handbook of Costume in the Nineteenth Century*, London, 1970

Cunnington, C.W. and P., *Handbook of Costume in the Twentieth Century*, London, 1976

Davenport, *The Book of Costume*, 2 vols., New York, 1968

Earnshaw, P., *A Dictionary of Lace*, Aylesbury, 1982

Ewing, E., *Hisory of Twentieth Century Fashion*, revised and updated by A. Mackrell, London, 1992

Franklin, A., *Dictionnaire des arts, métiers et professions*, Paris, 1906

Garner, P., ed., *The Encyclopedia of the Decorative Arts 1890-1940*, New York, 1978

Gaudriault, R., *La Gravure de mode féminine en France*, Paris, 1983

Gaudriault, R., *Répertoire de la gravure de mode française des origines à 1815*, Nantes, 1988

Grandjean, S., *Inventaire d'après décès de l'Impératrice Joséphine*, Paris, 1964

Lacroix, P., *Directoire, Consultat et Empire: moeurs et usages, lettres, sciences, et arts, France, 1795-1815*, Paris, 1884

Lambourne, L., *An Introduction to Caricature*, London, 1983

Leloir, M., *Dictionnaire du costume et ses accessoires, des armes et des étoffes des origines a nos jours*, Paris, 1951

Lipperheide. *Der Katalog der Freiherlich von Lipperheidischen Kostümbibliotek*, 2 vols., new edition edited by E. Nienholdt and G. Wagner-Neumann, Berlin, 1965

McDowell, C., *McDowell's Dictionary of Twentieth-Century Fashion*, new revised edition, London, 1987

Mackrell, A., 'Fashion Plate and Costume Book', *The Macmillan Dictionary of Art*, London, 1996

O'Hara, G., *The Encyclopedia of Fashion from 1840 to the 1980s*, London, 1989

Tosca, M., *Dolls*, trans. by W. Dallas, London, 1989

Vicaire, G., *Manuel de l'Amateur de livres du XIXe. siècle*, 8 vols., Paris, 1894-1920

Waugh, N., *Corsets and Crinolines*, New York, 1993

Waugh, N., *The Cut of Men's Clothes 1600-1900*, London, 1964

Waugh, N., *The Cut of Women's Clothes 1600-1900*, London, 1968

Accessories

Alexander, H., *Fans*, London, 1984

Buck, A., *Victorian Costume and Costume Accessories*, Bedford, 1984

Clark, F., *Hats*, London, 1982

Kennett, F., *The Collector's Book of Twentieth-Century Fashion*, London, 1983

Mackrell, A., *Shawls, Stoles and Scarves*, London, 1986

Art and fashion

Mackrell, A., *Dress in le style troubadour, 1774-1814*, unpublished Ph.D. thesis, Courtauld Institute of Art, London, 1987

Moreno, E., *Sonia Delauney, Art into Fashion*, New York, 1986

Newton, S.M., *Health, Art and Reason: Dress Reformers of the Nineteenth Century*, London, 1974

Simon, M., *Fashion in Art. The Second Empire and Impressionism*, London, 1995

Vertès, M., *Art and Fashion*, New York, 1944

Art history

Bryson, N., *Tradition and Desire. From David to Delacroix,*. Cambridge, 1984

Bryson, N., *Word and Image*, Cambridge, 1981

Brookner, A., *Jacques-Louis David*, London, 1980

Chaudonneret, M.-C., *Fleury Richard et Pierre Révoil. La peinture troubadour*, Paris, 1980

Dayot, A., *Les Vernets: Joseph, Carle, Horace*, Paris, 1898

Descargues, P., *Goya*, London, 1979

Green, C., *Léger and the Avant-Garde*, New Haven, 1976

Herbert, R.L., *Impressionism: Art, Leisure and Parisian Society*, New Haven and London, 1988

Hyslop, L.B., ed., *Baudelaire as a Love Poet and*

Other Essays, Univesity Park and London, 1969

Konody, P.G., *The Painter of Victorian Life. A Study of ConstantinGuys*. With an Introduction and a translation of *Peinture de la Vie Moderne*, London, 1930

Kosinski, D., *Douglas Cooper and the Masters of Cubism*, Basel, 1987

Laver, J., *Vulgar Society: The Romantic Career of James Tissot*, London, 1936

Pupil, F., *Le Style troubadour, ou nostalgie du bon vieux temps*, Paris, 1985

Reff, T., *Manet and Modern Paris*, Chicago and London, 1982

Rewald, J., *History of Impressionism*, 4th edition, New York, 1973

Rosenblum, R., *Ingres*, New York, 1985

Schefer, G., *Moreau le Jeune*, Paris, 1915

Shawe-Taylor, D., *The Georgians. Eighteenth-Century Portraiture and Society*, London, 1990

Shayo, A., *Chiparus, Master of Art Deco*, New York, 1993

Silverman, D.L., *Art Nouveau. Fin-de-siècle France*, Berkeley, 1989

Spencer, M., *The Art Criticism of Théophile Gautier*, Generva, 1969

Strong, R., *And when did you last see your father? The Victorian Painter and British History*, London, 1978

Warner, M., *Tissot*, London, 1982

Wentworth, M., *Tissot*, Oxford, 1984

Wood, C., *Victorian Panorama*, London, 1976

Zimmerman, M.F., *Seurat and the Art Theory of his Time*, Antwerp, 1991

Articles

Adler, K., 'Objets de luxe or propaganda? Camille Pissarro's fans', *Apollo*, November 1992

Boyce, M.S., 'Barbier Manuscripts', *Textile History*, Vol. 12, 1981

Buck, A. and Matthews, H., 'Pocket Guides to Fashion. Ladies' Pocket Books Published in England 1760-1839', *Costume*, No. 18, 1984

Clark, K., 'Ingres: Peintre de la vie moderne', *Apollo*, Vol. XCIII, No. 111 (New Series), May 1971

Coleman, D., 'Fashion Dolls/Fashionable Dolls', *Dress*, Vol. 3, 1977

Delpierre, M., 'Marie Antoinette, reine de la mode', *Versailles*, 1975

Deslandres, Y., 'Josephine and La Mode', *Apollo*, Vol. CVI, No. 185, July 1977

Gardiner, S., 'Sentimental Re-education', *Art and Auction*, November 1995

Gerstein, M., 'Degas's Fans', *The Art Bulletin*, New York, No. LXIV, 1 march 1982, pp. 110, 117

Ghering van-Ierlant, M.J., 'Anglo-French Fashion, 1786. The *Fashionable Magazine* and *Le Cabinet des Modes Nouvelles françaises et anglaises*, 1785-86, later *Le magazin des Modes Nouvelles françaises et anglaises*, 1786-89', *Costume*, No. 17, 1983

Ginsburg, M., 'The Tailoring and Dressmaking Trades, 1700-1850', *Costume*, No. 6, 1972

Hart, A., 'Court Dress for a French fashion doll, 1765-1775'. *Haute Couture* in Miniature. *Annual Review of the National Arts Collection Fund*, 1993

Horton, A., 'Fashion Plates', *Art and Auction*, February 1994

Mackrell, A., 'French Fashion', *Print Quarterly*, Vol. V, No. 3, 1988

Mac Taggart, P. and A., 'The Rich Wearing Apparel of Richard, 3rd Earl of Dorset'. *Costume*, No. 14, 1980

Mayor, A.H., 'Two Renaissance Costume Books', *Bulletin of the Metropolitan Museum of Art*, Vol. XXXVII, June 1942

Mortier, Bianca du, 'Fashion in Prints', *Print Quarterly*, Vol. VII, No. 3, 1990

Nevinson, J.L., 'Fashion Plates and Fashion, 1625-1635', *Apollo*, Vol. LI, 1950

Nevinson, J.L., 'Illustrations of Costume in the *Alba Amicorum*', *Archaeologia*, Vol. CVI, 1979

Nevinson, J.L., 'The Mercury Gallant' or

'European fashions in the 1670s', *Connoisseur*, Vol. CXXVI, No. 136, 1955

Nevinson, J.L., 'The Origin and Early History of the Fashion Plate', U.S. National Museum Bulletin 250, Contribution from the Museum of History and Technology, Paper 60, Washington, D.C., 1967

Nevinson, J.L., 'The Origin of the Fashion Plate', *Congrès International d'Histoire du Costume*, Venice, 1952

Olian, J.A., 'Sixteenth-Century Costume Books', *Dress*, Vol. 3, 1977

Ormond, L., 'Female Costume in the Aesthetic Movement of the 1879 and 1880s', *Costume*, No. 1, 1967

Petrascheck-Heim, I., 'Tailors' Masterpiece-Books'. *Costume*, No. 3, 1969

Roskill, M., 'Early Impressionism and the Fashion Print', *Burlington Magazine*, Vol. CXII, No. 807, June 1970

Rothstein, N., 'The Leman Album', *National Art Collections Fund Review*, 1992

Smith, R., 'Bonnard's *Costume Historique*—a Pre-Raphaelite Source Book', *Costume*, No. 7, 1973

Stone, De Holden, 'French Fashion Survives the Nazis'. *Art and Industry*, July 1945

Strong, R., 'Charles I's clothes for the years 1633-1635', *Costume*, No. 14, 1980

Tétart-Vittu, F., 'The French-English Go-Between'. '*Le Modèle de Paris*' or the 'Beginning of the Designer, 1820-1880', *Costume*, No. 26, 1992

Tétart -Vittu, F., 'La Gallerie des modes et costumes français', *Nouvelles de l'estampe*, Vol. 91, March 1987

Ward-Jackson, P., 'Some rare Drawings by Melchior Lorichs in the collection of Mr. John Evelyn of Wotton, and now at Stonor Park, Oxfordshire', *The Connoisseur*, Vol. CXXXV, No. 135, 1955

Weisberg, G., 'Women of Fashion', *Sotheby's Preview*, January 1993

Costume Society Extras

Nevinson, J.L., *Alexander Piccolomini, 'A Dialogue of the Fair Perfectioning of Ladies', 1538*, No. 1, 1968

Nevinson, J.L., *Designs of Modern Costume engraved for Thomas Hope of Deepdene by Henry Moses 1812*, No. 4, 1973

Nevinson, J.L., *The Exact Dress of the Head by Bernard Lens, 1725*, No. 2, 1970

Nevinson, J.L., *The Four Seasons by Wenceslas Hollar*, No. 6, 1979

Nevinson, J.L., *Mundus Muliebris or The Ladies Dressing-Room Unlock'd by Mary Evelyn. Prepared for the Press by her Father John Evelyn, 1690. (Together with the Fop-dictionary, compiled for the Use of the Fair Sex)*, No. 5, 1977

Fashion and costume designers

Battersby, M., *Art Deco Fashion: French Fashion Designers 1908-1925*, London, 1984

Dior, C., *Christian Dior and I*, trans. by A. Fraser, New York, 1957

Dior, C., *Talking About Fashion*, New York, 1954

Erté, *Things I Remember: An Autobiography*, London, 1975

Godfrey, R.T., *Wenceslaus Hollar*, London, 1995

Kennett, F., *Secrets of the Couturiers*, London, 1984

Langlade, E., *La Marchande de modes de Marie Antoinette, Rose Bertin*, Paris, 1911

Mackrell, A., *Coco Chanel*, London, 1992

Mackrell, A., *Paul Poiret*, London, 1990

Osma, G. de, *Mariano Fortuny*, New York, 1980

Vreeland, D., *Inventive Paris Clothes 1900-1939*, London, 1977

White, P., *Elsa Schiaparelli. Empress of Paris Fashion*, London, 1986

Fashion plates, fashion magazines, fashion illustrators

Adburgham, A., *A Punch History of Manners and Modes 1841-1940*, London, 1961

Adburgham, A., *Women in Print, Writing Women and Women's Magazines from the Restoration to the Accession of Victoria*, London, 1972

Antonio, 60, 70, 80. *Three Decades of Fashion Illustration*, London, 1995

Ballard, B., *In My Fashion,* London, 1960

Barnes, C., *Fashion Illustration*, London, 1994

Battersby, M., *The Decorative Twenties*, London, 1969

Blum, S., ed., *Ackermann's Costume Plates: Women's Fashions in England 1818-1828*, New York, 1978

Blum, S., ed., *Eighteenth-Century French Fashion Plates*, New York, 1982

Blum, S., ed., *Fashions and Costumes from Godey's Lady Book*, New York, 1985

Blum, S., ed., *Paris Fashions of the 1890s*, New York, 1984

Blum, S., ed., *Victorian Fashions and Costumes from Harper's Bazar: 188867-1898*, New York, 1974

Chase, E.W. and I., *Always in Vogue*, Garden City, 1954

Designs by Erté. Fashion Drawings and Illustrations from "Harper's Bazar", New York, 1976

Drake, N., *Fashion Illustration Today*, revised ed., London, 1994

Fashion in Paris from the 'Journal des Dames et des Modes' 1912-1913, Introduction by C. Nuzzi, trans. by J. Shepley, London, 1980

French Fashion Plates in Full Color from the Gazette du Bon ton (1912-1925), New York, 1979

Ferguson, M., *Forever Feminine: Women's Magazines and the Cult of Femininity*, London, 1983

Gibbs-Smith, C.H., *The Fashionable Lady in the Nineteenth Century*, London, 1960

Ginsburg, M., *An Introduction to Fashion Illustration*, London, 1980

Ginsburg, M., *Paris Fashions. The Art Deco Style of the 1920s*, London, 1989

Holland, V., *Hand-Coloured Fashion Plates 1770 to 1899*, London, 1988

Johnson, J.M., ed., *French Fashion Plates of the Romantic Era*, New York, 1991

Laver, J., *Costume Illustration: The Seventeenth and Eighteenth Centuries*, London, 1951

Laver, J., *Costume Illustration: The Nineteenth Century*, London, 1947

Laver, J., *Fashion and Fashion Plates 1800-1900*, London, 1943

Lepape, C. and Defert, T., *From the Ballets Russes to Vogue: The Art of Georges Lepape*, New York, 1971

Mackrell, A., *The Dress of the Parisian Élégantes with Special Reference to the Journal des Dames et des Modes from June 1797 until December 1799*, unpublished M.A. thesis, Courtauld Institute of Art, London, 1977

Men's Fashion Illustrations from the Turn of the Century, New York, 1990

Moore, D.L., *Fashion Through Fashion Plates 1771-1970*, London, 1971

Olian, J., *Authentic French Fashions of the Twenties: 413 designs from "L'Art et la Mode"*, New York, 1990

Olian, J., *Children's Fashions 1860-1912, 1065 Costume designs from La Mode Illustrée*, New York, 1994

Packer, W., *The Art of Vogue Covers 1909-1940*, Twickenham, Middlesex, 1987

Packer, W., *Fashion Drawing in Vogue*, London, 1989

Polhemus, T., *Streetstyle from sidewalk to catwalk*, London, 1994

Robinson, J., *Fashion in the 30s*, London, 1978

Robinson, J., *The Fine Art of Fashion: An Illustrated History*, New York, n.d.

Robinson, J., *The Golden Age of Style*, London, 1976

Seebohm, C., *The Man Who Was Vogue: the Life and Times of Condé Nast*, New York, 1982

Sitwell, S., *Gallery of Fashion, 1790-1822*, London, 1949

Snow, C., *The World of Carmel Snow*, New York, 1962

Umberto Brunelleschi. Fashion-stylist, illustrator, stage and costume designer, New York, 1979

Weigert, R.-A., *Incroyables et Merveilleuses, Paris, 1810-18. Par H. Vernet*, Paris, 1955

White, C., *Women's Magazines 1693-1968*, London, 1971

Period history and fashion

Ash, J. and Wilson, E., eds., *Chic Thrills. A Fashion Reader*, London, 1992

Baines, B., *Fashion Revivals from the Elizabethan Age to the Present Day*, London, 1981

Blum, A., *Early Bourbon 1590-1643*, London, 1951

Blum, A., *The Last Valois 1515-90*, London, 1951

Braun-Ronsdorf, *The Wheel of Fashion: Costume since the French Revelotuion 1789-1929*, trans. by O. Coburn, London, 1964

Cobban, A., *The Eighteenth Century. Europe in the Age of the Enlightenment*, London, 1969

Dorsey, H., *The Belle Époque in the Paris Herald*, London, 1986

Garland, M., *The Indecisive Decade. The World of Fashion and Entertainment in the 1930s*, London, 1968

Friedrich, O., *Olympia. Paris in the Age of Manet*, New York, 1992

Hughes, P., *Eighteenth-Century France and the East*, London, 1981

Huisman, P. and Jallut, M., *Marie Antoinette*, London, 1971

Laver, J., *Dandies*, London, 1968

Laver, J., *Early Tudor 1485-1558*, London, 1951

Laver, J., *Taste and Fashion from the French Revolution until Today*, London, 1937

Moeurs, E., *The Dandy: Brumell to Beerbohm*, London, 1960

Morley, J., *Regency Design 1790-1840*, London, 1992

Perrot, P., *Fashioning the Bourgeoisie: A History of Clothing in the 19th Century*, trans. by R. Bienvenu, Princeton, 1994

Pilon, E. and Saisset, F., *Les Fêtes en Europe au XVIIIe. Siècle*, Saint-Gratien, 1943

Reade, B., *The Dominance of Spain 1550-1660*, London, 1951

Reynolds, G., *Elizabeth and Jacobean 1558-1625*, London, 1951

Roche, D., *Culture of clothing: dress and fashion in the Ancien Régime*, trans. by J. Birrell, Cambridge, 1994

Sladen, C., *The Conscription of Fashion: Utility Cloth, Clothing and Footwear 1941-1952*, London, 1995

Thienen, F. van, *The Great Age of Holland 1600-60*, London, 1951

Waissenberger, R., ed., *Vienna in the Biedermeier Era 1815-1848*, London, 1986

Waller, J. and Vaughan-Rees, M., *Women in Wartime*, London, 1990

Index

Note: Numbers in italics refer to pages on which illustrations appear.